Using the art of storytelling, Dr. James Lewis explains the ingredients for a successful project: determine a strategy, be flexible, identify and manage risks, and plan for contingencies. His key ingredient is how to work creatively with people. The book is a must-read for all project managers who want to learn how to be effective project leaders.

—Marcus Udokang
Project Manager, Aivaz Consulting, Inc.

There are thousands of project management books out there, but if you are looking for a book that teaches you how to successfully deliver projects on time and on budget, and within the scope, this is the book. The sixth edition contains the most recent advancements in the project management world without losing the fundamentals that have made this book a go-to to acquire project management knowledge. I highly recommend this book. It is a must-have for all project management professionals.

—Tony Prensa, PhD, PMP
President and CEO,
TP Global Business Consulting LLC

Good project management is difficult. Lewis fills in the practical gaps where most project management texts fall short. This work empowers the reader by making project management real, fun, and accessible. If you are serious about project management, be prepared to dog-ear more than half of this book.

—Chris Pappas
CEO, Forthea

PROJECT PLANNING, SCHEDULING & CONTROL

PROJECT PLANNING, SCHEDULING & CONTROL

SIXTH EDITION

THE ULTIMATE HANDS-ON GUIDE TO BRINGING PROJECTS IN ON TIME AND ON BUDGET

JAMES P. LEWIS, PhD

New York   Chicago   San Francisco   Athens   London   Madrid
Mexico City   Milan   New Delhi   Singapore   Sydney   Toronto

1 2 3 4 5 6 7 8 9   LCR   27 26 25 24 23 22

ISBN   978-1-264-28627-0
MHID   1-264-28627-9

e-ISBN   978-1-264-28628-7
e-MHID   1-264-28628-7

Library of Congress Cataloging-in-Publication Data

Names: Lewis, James P., author.
Title: Project planning, scheduling, and control : the ultimate hands-on guide to bringing
     projects in on time and on budget / James Lewis.
Other titles: Project planning, scheduling, & control
Description: Sixth Edition. | New York : McGraw Hill, [2023] | Revised edition of the
     author's Project planning, scheduling & control, c2011. | Includes bibliographical
     references and index.
Identifiers: LCCN 2022028456 (print) | LCCN 2022028457 (ebook) |
     ISBN 9781264286270 (hardback) | ISBN 9781264286287 (ebook)
Subjects: LCSH: Project management. | Scheduling.
Classification: LCC HD69.P75 L493 2023 (print) | LCC HD69.P75 (ebook) |
     DDC 658.4/04—dc23/eng/20220729
LC record available at https://lccn.loc.gov/2022028456
LC ebook record available at https://lccn.loc.gov/2022028457

High Performance Project Management and Full-Spectrum Project Management are trademarks of The Lewis Institute, Inc. The Lewis Method and Projects are People are registered trademarks of The Lewis Institute, Inc. PMI, PMBOK, and PMP are registered trademarks of the Project Management Institute. Microsoft Project, SharePoint, PowerPoint, Outlook, and Word are registered trademarks of Microsoft Corporation. Mind Map is a registered trademark of Tony Buzan. Whole Brain is a registered trademark of Herrmann International. HBDI is a trademark of Herrmann International. The grid containing a thinking profile is also copyright by Herrmann International, and all such figures in this book are used by permission. MindManager is a trademark of MindJet. Kerzner Approach is a registered trademark of International Institute for Learning, Inc. Adobe PhotoShop is a registered trademark of Adobe Systems Incorporated. Expert Choice is a registered trademark of Decision Support Software, Inc. Post-it is a registered trademark of 3M Company. Skype is a registered trademark of Skype Technologies. Bluetooth is a registered trademark of Bluetooth Sig, Inc. The Neuro-Linguistic Programming is a trademark of The Society of Neuro-Linguistic Programming. Stategate is a registered trademark of Dr. Robert G. Cooper.

Dedicated to the memory of my parents,
without whom I would never have become an engineer,
a PhD psychologist, and an author.

Hazel Inez McDaniel (1919–1999)
Moffett Palmer Lewis (1920–1998)

And with gratitude to Frances Ann Scherl
for marrying me in 2013 and bringing with her four daughters
and nine grandchildren, who are our future.

CONTENTS

SECTION FOUR
EXECUTION AND CONTROL

SECTION FIVE
OTHER ISSUES IN PROJECT MANAGEMENT

This came to me fully written in a meditation a few years ago. I present it as a message to all of you who think you need to struggle to make a living in this world. Think Again.

You Are Already There
We are now,
And always have been,
Perfect in our true spiritual being.
The struggle
To perfect this human sense of self
Simply obscures
The perfection of the "I"
That we already are.
There is no path,
No destination.
Open your eyes.
You are already there,
Where you imagine
You need to be.

PREFACE

Sometime in 1991 a student in one of my project management seminars asked, "Have you ever thought about writing a book on this topic?" I had, but since 1981 I had been traveling around the world teaching the subject and related topics such as leadership skills, and writing a book just hadn't been on my radar.

The idea did appeal to me, however, so I wrote short letters to three publishers that I found in *Writer's Digest* and waited. In less than a week I received a call from Pamela van Geissen, who was an acquisitions editor at Probus Publishing in Chicago. She was interested in the book and wondered if I ever made it to Chicago.

If you believe in synchronicity—and perhaps if you don't—this will rock your boat. "I'll be up there next week," I said.

It was definitely a sign. I seldom worked in Chicago, but the next week I was in Pamela's office and within an hour had signed an agreement to write the book. It was only about an inch thick in the first edition, with a purple cover, which I told Pamela was often the favorite color of mental patients, so I was uncertain if that was a negative sign. As it turns out, it was anything *but* negative.

The little purple book did remarkably well in the market. Project management was just coming into its own, and for a while it was recommended by PMI as a study guide for the PMP® exam. Then Pamela asked if I could do some more books, and *The Project Manager's Desk Reference* and *Mastering Project Management* were to follow. I also proposed a book on project teams, but Pamela felt that Probus may not be able to sell it, so she referred me to an editor at AMACOM, who agreed to publish it—and *Team-Based Project Management* joined the lineup.

As is true of small companies, Probus caught the eye of someone at Irwin Professional Publishing, and they bought the company. I was now working with a much larger company, but the ride didn't slow down. Irwin was later bought by McGraw Hill, and now I was with a behemoth of a company. They had my second or third edition translated into Chinese, Portuguese, Spanish, and Lithuanian. My book *Project Leadership* was also translated into Russian. I'm not sure if Vladimir Putin read it, and I hope not, as he didn't learn much from me if he did.

So now I am getting ready to send the manuscript of the sixth edition to my editor, Judith Newlin, at McGraw Hill. Thirty years ago, I wouldn't have dreamed the little purple book would stand the test of time, surviving several recessions, a global pandemic, and an abundance of other books on project management.

I am grateful to all of my readers and students. I posted a copy of the fifth edition cover on LinkedIn last year and had over 6,000 views of it—more than any other post I've made.

And I'm grateful to the folks at McGraw Hill for supporting me all these years. I was in New York the day before 9/11 and flew out making a big circle around the city. It was a beautiful view of the city and the Twin Towers, and the next day my wife called me at my office and told me to turn on the TV. I watched in horror as the plane hit the second tower and immediately thought of everyone I knew at McGraw Hill and some in the Twin Towers as well. Sadly, I never learned the fate of those in the World Trade Center, but happily the folks at MH were fine.

I've dedicated this edition to the memory of my parents. My father had only an eighth-grade education and was ambitious enough to climb out of the cotton mills and learn to drive an 18-wheeler. My mom finished high school and worked as a seamstress her entire adult life. I hardly ever saw her without a crochet needle in one hand and a book in the other.

And since I'm on memory lane, I should mention that a fellow named Kenneth Suther, who had learned electronics in the navy, gave me a start into ham radio, which led to the career in electrical engineering. I will be forever grateful to him for the encouragement he gave me. For 15 years I fulfilled a dream of designing the equipment that I couldn't afford to buy at age 16 when I became K4SAM.

All that childhood experience led to two careers—engineering and teaching—and a life I never dreamed of. I have taught in 30 countries, with more than 60,000 people attending my classes. I got to circle the globe twice, visiting my exchange student "daughters" and their families, and I have friends all over the world. As they say, who knew?

Fairview, North Carolina (near Asheville)
March 22, 2022

James Palmer Lewis
Jim to my friends

SECTION ONE

INTRODUCTION TO PROJECT MANAGEMENT

CHAPTER 1

An Introduction to Project Management

I became a project manager (PM) in 1966. I never chose to be a PM, but later I learned it came with the job, even though it was not contained in my job description. Today I would be called an accidental project manager, but in 1966 I wasn't even recognized as a manager—just an engineer, and like a scientist told me about 40 years later, "nobody told me when I was working on my doctorate that I was going to have to manage people. I have no idea how to do that."

He was right. Yet companies (meaning the people who comprise the company) do this again and again, assuming that if you are any good at your work, you know how to be a manager. It's the greatest way to make an ass-out-of-u-and-me (assume) and wreaks havoc with individuals, teams, and organizations. It lives on, however, and perhaps it has lived for as long as organized work has existed.

PROJECT MANAGEMENT:
THE BEGINNING

Projects have been going on for thousands of years of recorded history and there is evidence that they were being conducted many years before that. The building of the great pyramids, the sites in India carved out of the rock, the Mayan, Incan, and Aztec buildings, and the stone circles that exist throughout the world are all examples of projects.

Did they have official managers? Surely someone had to conceive them and someone had to lead them. Whether the conceiver and the manager were the same individual is unknown. Furthermore, I once wrote an expert on Egypt at the British Museum and asked if there was any evidence of plans on skins or papyrus, and he said there were none that he knew of. Yet it is hard to imagine the Great Pyramid of Giza being built without detailed plans—and the current unofficial dating of that structure is 12,500 years ago. And while Stonehenge is not nearly as complex as the pyramids, it did require a lot of ingenuity to move the stones to the site, align them with astronomical sources, raise them vertically, and (in the case of lintels) place them on top of the vertical supports.

In thinking about this, I imagine Hrog chiseling away at a big slab of stone that would soon become one of the lintels. The clan chief sees him at work and observes that he is an impeccable chiseler. "You're really good at chiseling, Hrog," he says. "I want you to turn the chisel over to Arg and start supervising the work. Make a plan so we can ensure that the circle is oriented according to the Seer's instructions." (The Seer was the high priest, who knew how to orient the circle to catch the rays of the sun exactly right on the summer solstice.)

Hrog bit his lip. He could hardly tell the chief that he knew less than nothing about planning, and even less about supervising other workers. His dad had only taught him how to chisel, not supervise other workers. They would likely feed him to the pack of wild dogs that hungrily watched the camp hoping to find a morsel of food—or better yet, a tasty supervisor who had been stabbed in the back by the workers who were pissed at him for thinking he knew more about building a Henge than they did.

"You have to wear a uniform too," said the chief, "so the workers can recognize you wherever you are on the site."

Now Hrog groaned audibly. He was dead meat for sure.

"What's that?" asked the chief.

"Just clearing my throat, sir," Hrog replied.

Sure enough, they dressed Hrog in a fine leopard skin that had been imported from far-away Ungafa (now called Africa) and told everyone to do whatever he told them to do. Fortunately for Hrog, the workers weren't inclined to kill him, because none of them wanted his job, so for a year, he prospered. And besides, if they did what he told them, and it didn't work out, it wouldn't be their fault. They could point at him and the chief would kick his behind, not theirs.

As it turned out, the first phase of the Henge was completed about two months before the next solstice and the sun shone directly through the appointed opening and onto the target, and Hrog was awarded the designation of project manager of the year. Thus, Hrog may have been one of the first accidental project managers. (The experts believe that Stonehenge was built in six phases that spanned 1,500 years, so my imagination is just fantasy, as no one knows how long any of the phases actually required.)

In fact, the chief told Hrog that a new association had been formed on the mainland south of the island. It was called SOP-CAM, for Society of Professional Chiselers and Managers, and they were certifying individuals as PUMPs (Project United Management Professionals. (Apologies to PMPs everywhere.)

The chief wanted Hrog to take the certification exam. After all, he had proven his ability to manage projects, and the exam only required that he answer a few questions and he would be a PUMP. The chief would even pay the 400 clams that the association charged as a certification fee.

PUMP Certification Erupts

Soon the PUMP certification developed into a huge success. Clans throughout Europe insisted that their projects be led by a PUMP, and SOPCAM found itself swamped with applicants for the exam. The profession grew exponentially. However, with the success of the program came an unexpected issue. Many of the newly minted PUMPs were found to be incompetent. They knew the answers to the exam questions, but many of them had only shared a tent with a real project manager and had no personal skills, so they wrecked the jobs they tried to manage. Or they had been members of a team led by a true manager but had no skills themselves for leading people, so they also failed.

The World Today

I have framed this little story as a parable for what has happened to the project management profession since it began to be recognized in the 1960s. The intent behind certification of project managers as PMPs (Project Management Professionals) was good, but the unintended consequence has been exactly what I have suggested in my fantasy tale. Although PMI® (Project Management Institute) requires 2,000 hours or more of experience *leading projects*, there are large numbers of individuals who do not meet that requirement. They have passed the written test only and their supervisors have fraudulently signed off that they met the work requirement. The reason they have done this is that some government contracts require that a PMP lead them, and in order to get those contracts, supervisors need to ensure that their people get certified. And they can't wait two years for them to gain the required experience, so they lie. (I make no apology if I am stepping on your toes. Not only is it fraud, but it is going to destroy the reputation of the PMP, which honest people have worked hard to earn.)

In fact, I am beginning this edition of my book in this way in hope of drawing attention to this sad situation. I have spent 60 years of my life in project management, first as a working manager and since 1981 as a teacher and author of books on the subject. I hate to see the dishonest people undermine what the people like myself have worked so hard to establish.

Now with that off my chest, let us turn our attention to detailing the management of projects.

WHAT IS A PROJECT?

The Project Management Institute is the professional association for project managers (more about them later). In the latest edition of the *Project Management Body of Knowledge,* or *PMBOK®* *GUIDE,* PMI defines a project as "a temporary endeavor undertaken to produce a unique product, service, or result." *Temporary* means that every project has a definite beginning and end. *Unique* means that this product, service, or result is different from others that may have preceded it.

Unfortunately, textbook definitions often don't reflect the real world. There is no doubt that Stonehenge was a project, but it is doubtful that a fixed finish date could be established, and given that six phases spanning 1,500 years were required to achieve the result we see today, there was no temporary nature to it, nor was the scope well defined. It was unique, so far as we know, and perhaps the Seer anticipated a specific completion time. We can only guess.

> A project is "a temporary endeavor under-taken to produce a unique product, service, or result" [*PMBOK® GUIDE* (2021)].

The thing is, not only was Stonehenge no textbook project, but many contemporary jobs don't fit the textbook definition either, yet no one would deny that they are projects. What we can say is that we would *like* for a job to fit the definition, and it is the job of a project manager to make this happen to the best of her ability.

In reality, the only part of the definition that fits all projects is that all of them are jobs that produce something unique. A repetitive job is not a project. Neither is performing a single task. Nevertheless, a substantial number of jobs do qualify as projects, and there are many people managing them (or at least trying to).

I also feel it is important to point out that if you are on a single-person job, you can be said to be managing a project but are not a project manager in the real sense of the term, because there should be a team involved for it to be called project management. This is my opinion and not everyone will agree, which is fine with me.

Now what I do want to emphasize is the importance of project management for every organization. You should know first off that we did not invent the methods or tools of project management. They were invented to control manufacturing work. The work breakdown structure allows for eating an elephant in small bites, rather than a single large one. Earned value is a standard cost system to assess manufacturing efficiency, and scheduling was a way of staging work to get the most output in the least time. That means that the methods of project management are the only ones designed to manage work in general, which leads me to say that all management should be thought of as a derivative of project management. This includes the activities of the CEO right on down the typical hierarchy to the lowest levels of the pyramid.

As for projects themselves, Tom Peters (1999) has argued that as much as 50 percent of the work done in organizations can be thought of as projects. I believe that in many organizations, this number is far greater. This means that, even though not everyone who is running these operations is called a project manager, these people are *de facto* managing projects anyway. And, while they may not need the formality of critical path schedules and earned value analysis, they do need some skills in project planning and control.

Dr. J. M. Juran, who was a quality expert, has said that a project is a problem that is scheduled for solution. I like this definition because it makes us realize that a project is conducted to solve a problem for the organization. However, the word *problem* almost always conveys something negative. When someone says, "We have a problem," that is usually bad news. Environmental cleanup projects might be thought of as solving the "bad" kind of problem. But developing a new product or software program is also a problem—a positive problem. So *problem* is being used here in a very broad sense, and projects deal with both kinds of problems, positive and negative.

WHAT IS PROJECT MANAGEMENT?

The *PMBOK® GUIDE* defines project management as "application of knowledge, skills, tools and techniques to project activities to meet project requirements. Project management is accomplished through the application and integration of the project management processes of initiating, planning, executing, monitoring-and-controlling, and closing." These processes are further defined in the *PMBOK® GUIDE*, and the objective of this book is to explain how all of these are accomplished in practice.

I think it is important to mention that these processes do not fully capture the essence of project management. Much of project management consists of dealing with political issues, trying to get team members to perform at the required level, and negotiating for scarce resources. These activities are not really captured by the *PMBOK® GUIDE* processes, and no single document can do justice to the true complexity of project management. At best, the guide captures the tools and systems aspects of project management but not the *leadership* component.

In fact, this raises an important issue. We need to think more about project leadership, because in almost all situations project managers do not "own" their resources. That is, the team members do not report directly to the PM. They generally report to a manager in a functional department and are assigned to the PM on a dotted-line basis. For that reason, the PM must use leadership skills to get the best performance from team members, and I will discuss this more fully in a later section of the book.

"INSTANT-PUDDING" PROJECT MANAGEMENT

In December 1999, I had a meeting with a project manager in Germany, in which we discussed whether project management in Germany was the same as it is in the United States. I showed him my model of project management, which I call The Lewis

Method®, and compared it to his process. We found that his method and mine were very similar.

"I have been trying to explain project management to senior management here, but I'm afraid with very little success," he said sadly. "In one meeting, one of our vice presidents got very frustrated and said, 'I don't understand why we don't just buy Microsoft Project® and do it!'" He added, "Meaning, of course, why don't we do project management."

I almost laughed. "It's the same in the United States," I assured him. "Senior managers there also assume that project management is just scheduling and that if they buy a scheduling tool for everyone, they will have instant project managers."

He looked a bit relieved.

"I think we should put the scheduling software in a box and rename it 'Instant Project Manager,'" I said. "On the side of the box, the instructions would say, 'Just add water, stir, shake, bake, and you will have instant project managers'—sort of an 'instant-pudding' approach to project management."

He thought for a moment. "That's what we are doing now, isn't it? Practicing instant-pudding project management!"

"Yes," I agreed. "And I can tell you that this approach is followed throughout much of the world."

TOOLS, PEOPLE, AND SYSTEMS

Project management is not just scheduling.

It is not just tools.

It is not a job position or a job title.

It is not even the sum total of these. But my experience shows that few people understand this. They believe that project management is scheduling and that if a person can do some technical job (using the word *technical* in a very broad sense), then that individual can manage a project (as I pointed out in my parable of Hrog.)

This is a pervasive problem. We forget that there are two aspects to all work, including projects—the *what* and the *how*. The *what* is the task to be performed. The *how* is the process by which it is performed. But process also applies to how the team functions overall—how its members communicate, interact, solve problems, deal with conflict, make decisions, assign work, run meetings, and every other aspect of team performance. The tools they use—such as scheduling software, team meeting software like Teams and Zoom, computers, project notebooks, tablets like the iPad, and personal digital assistants (PDAs) now in the form of cellphones—help with both the *what* and the *how*. But the tools do not make an instant project manager of a person who has not been trained in the *how*. Rather, good project management is the joint optimization of three components, as shown in Figure 1.1.

Figure 1.1   Project Management Is Tools, People, and Systems

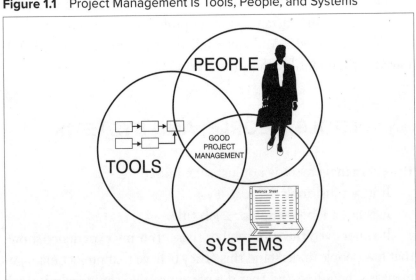

Organizations and project teams are *people*. I think we forget this. An organization has capital equipment, buildings, inventory, and other paraphernalia for the sole purpose of enabling human beings to do work that will result in desired organizational outcomes.

Yet managers often focus on everything but people. I have been told of many managers who are brilliant with computers but horrible at dealing with people. They are rude, condescending, and dictatorial. You wonder how such individuals survive in their jobs, but they do.

In any case, the message should be understood—organizations are people, and people engage in processes to get results. If the people do not function well, neither will the processes; and if the processes don't work, task outcomes will suffer. The sad thing is that we know more about how to get performance from capital equipment than about how to get it from people.

As I have already said, project management deals with tools, people, and systems. The tools are work breakdown structures, PERT scheduling, earned value analysis, risk analysis, and scheduling software (to name a few). And tools are the primary focus of most organizations that want to implement project management.

Tools are a necessary but not a sufficient condition for success in managing projects. The processes or techniques are far more important, because if you do not employ the correct processes for managing, the tools will only help you document your failures with great precision.

A simple example is that you give a person an automobile so that he can get around, but you give him no training in how to drive the car. He must learn by trial and error. By the time he has become a competent driver (if he ever does), he will have battered up the car badly, and in the process done quite a bit of damage to others. This is what happens when you give people scheduling software with no training in how to use it properly.

On the other hand, training someone who has no car how to drive is a waste. Absent the car, the training is irrelevant.

In short, the PMI definition of project management is not bad, as long as you understand that you must include dealing with politics, exercising leadership, and, for good measure, having a small dose of public relations expertise.

THE FOUR PROJECT CONSTRAINTS

It has been common to talk about the triple constraints in project management—performance, time, and cost. Colloquially, they are often referred to as good, fast, and cheap, and as the saying goes, "Good, fast, or cheap—pick two." The point is that you can dictate only two of them, and the third will have to vary.

> **SCOPE: the magnitude or size of the project.**

When I wrote the first edition of this book, I realized that there was a fourth constraint—scope. The magnitude or size of the job is also related to the other three constraints, and I started pointing out that you could assign values to any three of them, but the fourth must be allowed to vary. In fact, scope changes probably cause more missed project deadlines and cost overruns than any other factor short of defining the project requirements incorrectly to begin with. These scope changes occur in small increments, which we refer to as *scope creep*. Sometimes these are caused by feature creep, but more often it is because something is forgotten that must be added for the project to be functional. In any case, the changes can be nickel in size and add up to many dollars of total impact.

Many people are confused by the term *performance*, so I want to clarify it here. A project is intended to produce a result of some kind. Construction projects produce buildings for people to occupy, roads for them to travel on, or dams that provide water to communities. Product development projects provide products for people to use; software projects do the same.

There are two kinds of performance requirements, which together are called *specifications*. One is *functional requirements*. These describe what the deliverable is supposed to do. The other is *technical requirements*, which describe the features of the deliverable. They may specify dimensions, weight, color, speed, horsepower, thrust, or any of a million other specifications that can apply to a deliverable. As a former engineer, I used to ask if a change would affect the form, fit, or function of a product. You can see how this relates to what has just been said.

Defining project requirements is a major aspect of project definition, and doing so incorrectly or inadequately is, I believe, the single most common cause of project failures. I was once told a story by a fellow that illustrates this beautifully. He had a friend over at his house one day, and they were doing some yard work. He said to his friend, "You see this small tree in front of my house? How about trimming the limbs off this tree to a height about like this?" He indicated what he meant by holding his hand a certain distance above the ground.

He then left his friend to trim the tree and went to the back of the house to do some work. When he returned to the front of the house, his friend had just finished the job. It was nicely done, except for one significant detail. His friend had cut all the limbs off the top of the tree, down to the proper height, when what the fellow wanted was to have the limbs trimmed off the trunk of the tree from the *ground up* to the height he had indicated!

What happened here is all too common. "Trim the tree" meant something different to each of them. We call this a communication problem. And because communication problems happen so frequently, we had better take care to achieve a *shared understanding* of what is supposed to be done in the project. We will talk about how this is done in Chapter 5.

P = performance requirements, technical and functional

C = labor cost to do the job. (Note that capital equipment and material costs are accounted for separately from labor.)

T = time required for the project

S = scope or magnitude of the work

Elsewhere, I have said that project management is the application of knowledge, skills, tools, and techniques to project activities to meet project requirements. These requirements are defined by the PCTS targets and are the constraints on every project, no matter how large or how small. Because you can never escape them, you must understand how they interact.

The relationship between them is given by the following expression:

$$C = f(P, T, S)$$

In other words, cost is a function of performance, time, and scope. Ideally, this could be written as an exact mathematical expression. For example,

$$C = 2P + 3T + 4S$$

However, we are always *estimating* the values of these variables, so their exact relationship is never known.

One way to think of the relationship that exists between the PCTS constraints is to consider a triangle, as shown in Figure 1.2. P, C, and T are the lengths of the sides, while S is the area. If I know the lengths of the sides, I can compute the area. Or, if I know the area and the lengths of two sides, I can compute the length of the third side.

Figure 1.2   Triangles Showing the PCTS Relationship

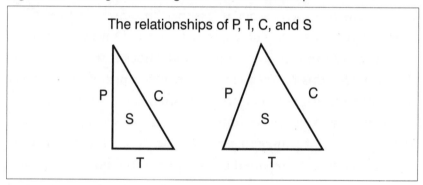

What is important about this illustration is that I cannot arbitrarily assign values to all three sides *and* the area. If three variables are specified, the fourth can be determined, but if you try to assign values to all four, they will "fit" only by accident.

In projects, however, it is common for the project sponsor or some other manager to want to dictate values for all four. This is, in fact, a common cause of project failures, where failure means not hitting all the targets. As a project manager, it is my job to tell the sponsor what I need if I am to do a project, so consider the most common case, in which values for P, T, and S are given.

> **PRINCIPLE:** You can assign values to only three of the constraints. The fourth will be whatever the relationship dictates it will be.

It is my job to tell the sponsor the cost of the project required to achieve those targets.

It is also true that when I do so, the sponsor may have heart failure. The response is often, "My goodness, how can it cost so much!!?" followed by protests—"We can't afford it!"

Then my response is, "Tell me what you can afford, and I'll tell you what I can do." This means that either the scope will be reduced or perhaps the time will be extended. In general, it is not acceptable to reduce performance. In fact, there is a saying that if you are late, overspent, scope is less than specified—but the thing works correctly, you will probably be forgiven. However, if you are late, overspent and reduced scope—and it doesn't work, you are in deep trouble. This means that you can assign priority importance to the constraints, with performance often being number one.

Notice that this is a common trade-off that we make at home. We have a list of things that need to be done. The roof is leaking and needs to be repaired before it ruins the house. The car is making a strange noise. My 13-year-old daughter needs braces on her teeth, which will cost a bundle. And on and on.

Trouble is, I can't afford it all.

What am I going to do? I'm going to establish priorities for the items on the list. If the car quits, I won't be able to get to work to make the money to pay for everything, so perhaps it is number one on the list. The roof comes next. And goodness knows when I'll be able to afford braces for my daughter's teeth. Maybe she will grow up and pay for them herself, but for now, they must wait.

Of course, there is another option in some cases. You get rid of the car and take public transportation. This frees up expense money that can be reallocated. It illustrates that there are often multiple ways to address a problem.

Interestingly, we are forced to prioritize at home, but in organizations, we often try to do it all, thereby spreading our resources too thin, with the result being that nothing gets done well or on time. (We will return to this issue in the section on control.) For now, the point is that you can't have it all, so choices must be made, and my job is to help my boss or sponsor make those choices by providing the best information I can on what is needed to do the project.

THE TIME-COST TRADE-OFF

In today's "hurry-up" world, the heat is on to finish projects in record time. This is due in part to the pressures of competition, especially in developing products, software, or new services. If you take too long to get it done, the competition will get there first, and the first to market with a new product often captures 60 to 70 percent of the market, leaving the rest of the pack to pick up the scraps.

Furthermore, there is pressure to reduce the cost to do the job. Again, this is partly because costs continue to rise over time and also because if you can develop something faster and cheaper while leaving the scope and performance constant, you can recover your investment sooner and protect yourself from the dynamics of the marketplace. (We will examine this in more detail in Chapter 14.)

Look now at the time-cost trade-off curve shown in Figure 1.3. Notice that there is some duration for a project in which costs are at a minimum. That is, there is an optimum duration. The problem is, we seldom know just what that duration is, but we aren't too concerned about it.

What is important is to note that going past that point (extending the duration) causes project costs to rise, because you are being inefficient. You are taking too long to do the work.

Figure 1.3   Time-Cost Trade-Off Curve

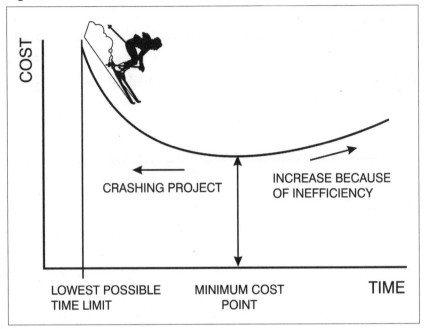

To the left of the minimum cost point, we are trying to reduce the time needed for the job. The common term for this is that we are trying to "crash" the project. That doesn't mean that we are trying to destroy it, but rather that we are trying to do it faster than the optimum time.

You can see that costs start to rise as you reduce time, and they rise very steeply. This is because we usually speed up a project by assigning more resources to it. In common language, we "throw bodies at it."

The difficulty is that, as we throw more bodies at a project, they begin to get in each other's way. The work can be subdivided only so far, and we hit what is called the point of diminishing returns. One way to think of this is that if one person can do something in 10 hours, two people won't be able to do the same job in 5 hours. It may take 6. And four people may take 4 hours. We don't get a linear gain in time.

In addition, there is a lower limit below which you cannot go, no matter how many people you put on the job. I call this the "forbidden zone." Naturally, there is always someone who thinks that if you just put enough people on a project, you can get it done in almost zero time, but that is simply not true.

Further, there is a principle called Brooks's Law, originally specified for software projects, that says, "Adding people to an already late project may only make it later." I believe that this principle applies to all kinds of projects—not just software.

> **BROOKS'S LAW**
>
> Adding people to an already late project may only make it later.
>
> —Fred Brooks, 1975

Worse than that, you can destroy a project by adding people at the wrong time. This is shown in Figure 1.4. If you add someone new to the project, that person must be "brought up to speed."

Figure 1.4   The Rework Spiral

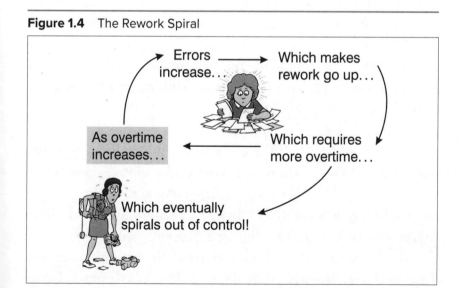

That means that orientation and training are needed. Who is going to do the training?

You, most likely, but perhaps some other member of the team. No matter who does it, that person's productivity will drop. To keep from delaying the job, that person will have to work overtime. In doing so, she will get tired, thus losing more ground. She will probably also make more errors, which means that she will have to correct them. This is called rework. As rework increases, she will have to work more overtime to keep up, thus getting more tired, which causes more errors, which increases rework, *ad nauseum*.

In other words, the project is likely to spiral downward, out of control. The message is, be very careful about adding people to help get the job done on time.

If You Always Do What You've Always Done

Now let's come back to the pressures that we feel to get the job done faster and cheaper at the same time. The time-cost trade-off curve shows that, if you are below the minimum point on the curve, crashing the project costs more money. Yet we are being told to reduce costs *and* time simultaneously! Are we being set up?

> If you always do what you've always done, you'll always get what you've always got.

Maybe.

There is a saying in psychology, "If you always do what you've always done, you'll always get what you've always got."

And there is a corollary. "Insanity is continuing to do what you've always done and hoping for a different result."

The message is that, if what you're doing isn't working, you have to change the way you're doing it. That is, you must change the *process*. In fact, that is what formal project management is all about.

> Insanity is continuing to do what you've always done and hoping for a different result.

Many of you have been managing projects for a long time in an informal way. I call that "seat-of-the-pants" project management, and I know about it because I did project management that way for about 10 years. Why? Because I didn't know any other way.

And I got the job done—usually to everyone's satisfaction.

The trouble is, we didn't know that the work could be done better.

Can formal project management (a change in process) really help you get the job done faster and cheaper at the same time?

I believe so.

It is estimated that about one-third of the cost of doing many projects is rework. As someone has said, that is equivalent to having one of every three people on the job working full time just to redo what the other two people did wrong in the first place. That means, of course, that the cost is extremely high.

> PRINCIPLE: If what you're doing isn't working, you need to change the process by which it is done.

Why all the rework?

I think it is safe to say that it is the result of taking a ready-fire-aim approach to the project. The job is ill conceived, poorly defined, and inadequately planned. Everyone just wants to "get the job done."

It is said that haste makes waste. It is very true. But in our hurry-up-and-get-it-done world, there is little patience with "wasting time" on all that planning. So the result is rework, which is 100 percent waste.

I would suggest that, if you find a way to measure it, you will find that the rework in your projects ranges from 5 to 40 percent.

As I have heard Tom Peters say on a tape (I forget which one), this is a good-news, bad-news story. The bad news is that it can be so high. The good news is that there is lots of room for improvement!

The nice thing about measuring rework is that you can show progress fairly soon. If you try to do baseline comparisons, you often find that baseline data for previous projects does not exist. With rework, you simply plot trend graphs. Such a graph is shown in Figure 1.5.

Figure 1.5 Trend Graph Showing Rework Declining

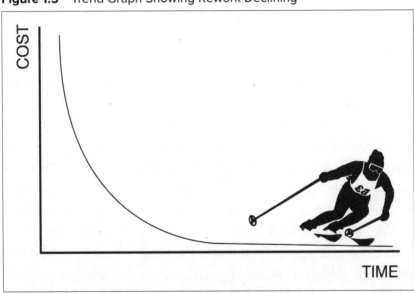

As proof of what I'm saying, I had a client who worked for a large university managing their design and construction department. He had me conduct my training programs on project management and team leadership and then began to practice the methods. One of the rework costs in construction projects is called *change orders*. These are usually the result of inadequate or no planning at all. To see if there were improvements, my client began to track the cost of change orders. He found, over five years, that they dropped so much that they saved $5 million over previous years before they began practicing formal project management.

Quality

I have always considered this to be the forgotten aspect of project management. It has to do with the performance constraint. If the functional and technical requirements of the job are not met, you have done a poor-quality job. Essentially, performance is synonymous with quality.

If you put people under pressure to get the job done fast, and you won't allow them to reduce the scope, then you can almost bet that they will sacrifice quality in the process. Furthermore, as a former quality manager at ITT, I learned that if you improve quality, you get jobs done faster and cheaper, so in addition to improving processes, we must improve quality. In fact, the two go hand in hand.

In the past, quality has been defined in two primary ways. One was that quality was conformance to specifications. Another was that quality was meeting customer requirements or sometimes we say the product is fit for use. Of course, specifications should be written so that if you meet them, you meet customer requirements. Thus, the second definition could be said to be the better of the two.

In the development of the Six Sigma approach to quality at Motorola, a new definition of quality was also developed. This definition says that *quality is a state in which value entitlement is realized for the customer and provider in every aspect of the business relationship* (Harry & Schroeder, 2000, p. 6). This new definition recognizes the profit motive of every for-profit organization, whereas the old definitions focused only on the customer.

Harry and Schroeder say that most organizations are producing product and service quality levels of about three sigma. This refers to the number of errors that occur in a given number of opportunities. For 1,000,000 opportunities, a three sigma level will yield 66,807 errors. At six sigma, there will only be 3.4 errors in 1,000,000 opportunities!

They also say that a three sigma quality level means that of every sales dollar earned by the organization, approximately 25 to 30 percent (or 25 to 30 cents) is lost because of poor quality. This is called the cost of poor quality (COPQ). Most executives think that the COPQ is only a few percent and are horrified to learn that it is this high.

That cost comes from three factors: prevention, appraisal, and failure (PAF). Prevention is anything that we do to keep errors from happening in the first place. As an example of this, Alan Mulally, director of engineering at Boeing when the 777 airplane was being designed (he was CEO at Ford Motor Company from 2006 to 2014), explains how toy company Fisher-Price makes the assembly of their model airplanes *foolproof* so that you can put them together with no hassle. "Fisher-Price makes a little notch in their wheels so that you can only put the right wheel on the right hub, and you can only put the left wheel on the left hub" (Sabbagh, 1996). This approach has been used by the Japanese in manufacturing processes for years.

Appraisal cost results from the inspection of a finished part to be sure that no errors have been made. A basic given in quality is that you cannot inspect quality into a product—it must be designed in and built in to begin with. In fact, the work with Six Sigma programs has shown that "80 percent of quality problems are actually designed into the product without any conscious attempt to do so" (Harry & Schroeder, 2000, p. 36). When the problem is designed into the product, you can't inspect it out.

Failure cost is incurred once the product leaves the plant and reaches the customer. It includes warranty costs, repair costs, and so on. And something that is almost impossible to track, but is a part of failure cost, nonetheless, is lost customers.

The important thing to note is that an increase in the amount of money spent on prevention leads to significant reductions in appraisal and failure costs. This is shown in Figure 1.6. Most of our quality costs should go into prevention so that we reap significant savings in the other two areas. If you want to see how significant these savings can be, I suggest that you read Harry and Schroeder.

Figure 1.6   Reduction in Total Cost of Quality When Prevention Is Increased

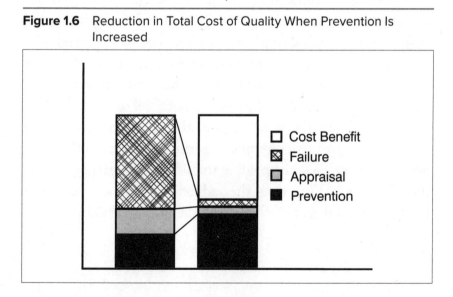

As for projects, if you improve your processes so that quality is improved, then you will also reduce the time and cost of

project work simultaneously. Again, this is because you eliminate rework, which adds no value to the project. Large gains can be made if more attention is paid to quality improvement in projects.

Have Your Cake and Eat It Too

In Figure 1.2, I showed the relationship between P, C, T, and S as a triangle and said that these are the quadruple constraints of a project. There is a problem with using a triangle as an analogy. Suppose I want to hold P, C, and T constant and increase the scope of the job. Based on the triangle analogy, this is impossible. If I increase scope, at least one of the three sides of the triangle must get longer.

However, if I think of the triangle as being drawn on the surface of a sphere, then this is no longer true. If I change the radius of the sphere, it will change the area bounded by P, C, and T.

Figure 1.7 shows a sphere with a spherical triangle drawn on it, and inside the spherical triangle, I have also drawn a plane triangle. If I assume that the sides of both the spherical and the plane triangle are the same lengths, then the spherical triangle has a greater area, which represents project scope, so the scope has been increased while holding the sides of the triangle to constant lengths.* What does the radius of the sphere represent? I suspect it is a measure of how well the process works.

---

* For the mathematically inclined, the drawing is, of course, not correct, but I am trying to explain the concept in simple terms for the benefit of those readers who have no background in spherical geometry.

Figure 1.7   The PCTS Relationship Shown on a Spherical Surface

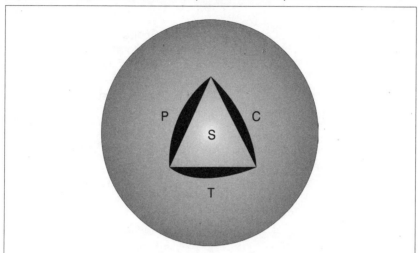

There is still another way to think of the relationship between the variables. Suppose P, C, and T are the sides of the base of a pyramid. This is shown in Figure 1.8. Now the scope is the entire area of the pyramid. What would be the physical meaning of the vertical sides of the pyramid? Perhaps they are factors of P, C, and T. Furthermore, it may be that the height of the pyramid represents how well the process performs. If it is a poor process, the height of the pyramid diminishes until you simply have a conventional triangle (the base of the pyramid).

These figures help us understand that by changing the process by which we do project work, we can get more for our money. We can reduce rework, increase productivity, decrease time, and so on. (A simple example of changing process is to switch from painting a wall with a brush to a roller, or from the roller to spray painting.)

Earlier I mentioned that Alan Mulally wanted the 777 airplane to be designed like a Fisher-Price toy, so that it would

Figure 1.8   The PCTS Relationship Shown as a Pyramid

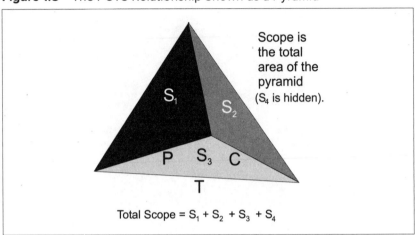

go together easily. In addition, Boeing changed the process by which the airplane was designed. There were two aspects to this change, one technical and the other human.

The technical change was to utilize three-dimensional computer design exclusively. When you design parts in two dimensions, it is impossible to know ahead of time that, for instance, components inside the wing are not going to run into each other. You must build a model to find these problems. Correcting them is extremely expensive. By modeling the plane in three dimensions, these interferences can be detected on the computer screen and corrected before a prototype is built. This approach isn't perfect, and there may still be problems in the design, but it is a vast improvement over the two-dimensional method.

The human change was expressed by the slogan "Working Together." In most organizations, you find various teams building silos around themselves. When conflicts arise, these teams fall into an us-them mode and snipe at each other. The Boeing approach was to tear down those silos and create a climate in which people understood that the success of the project meant that they were totally *interdependent* (Dimancescu, 1992).

Teams were encouraged to discuss their problems freely. Mechanics and assembly workers were involved with the design teams to produce a product that would be easy to build and easy to use. The chief test pilot for Boeing worked closely with the designers to produce a plane that would be accepted by other pilots, because this design departed from the conventional approach of using cables to move the flaps and rudder of the plane, instead using a fly-by-wire method of controlling these components electronically. Because this would cause the plane to lack the "feel" that pilots were accustomed to, it was important to make the difference as unobjectionable as possible.

Most significantly, representatives from the first customer, United Airlines, were part of the team, to make sure that the plane would meet their needs when it was finished. There was ongoing dialogue among all of these parties to ensure that all interests were represented in the design of this twenty-first-century jet (Sabbagh, 1996).

The ultimate result was that United Airlines accepted the 777 airplane on the first test by their own pilots! This had never happened before. It is a world-class example of what good project management can achieve.

Facilitation

Project management is the *facilitation* of planning, scheduling, and control. That word is very important. A project manager does not develop a project plan for a group. The general rule is that *the people who must do the work should participate in developing the plan.*

There are two reasons for this. One is that they know best how they will do their own work and how long it will take. The second is that they are likely to think of everything that must be done, whereas if you plan the project by yourself, you may forget something. And, because they know that your plan is likely to be flawed, if you develop it by yourself and try to "lay it on them," they will most likely reject it. So, if you want to have a valid plan that is accepted by the members of your team, get them involved in the planning process.

How about one-person projects? Well, I suggest that it is very helpful to have someone else review your plan so that they can spot those things that you may have overlooked. Forgetting something is one of the top 12 causes of project failure. If you can't get someone to review your plan for you, then the best alternative (if this is feasible) is to "sleep on it" for a few days. When you do go back to it, you will probably see things that you missed before.

Nature of Projects

Projects often draw on many different disciplines. Consider a simple home-building project. Carpenters, plumbers, electricians, landscapers, roofers, and painters are all involved. These different disciplines often don't talk the same language, see the work of the other disciplines as interfering with their own work, and, in the final analysis, don't cooperate very well. Furthermore, the project manager often does not understand all the disciplines. This is especially true in high-tech projects. That presents problems of evaluating progress and the quality of work.

Projects also have various phases. All too often, the sequence is as shown in Figure 1.9. The project is kicked off with great enthusiasm, but soon things begin to turn sour. The next thing

Figure 1.9 The Typical Project Life Cycle

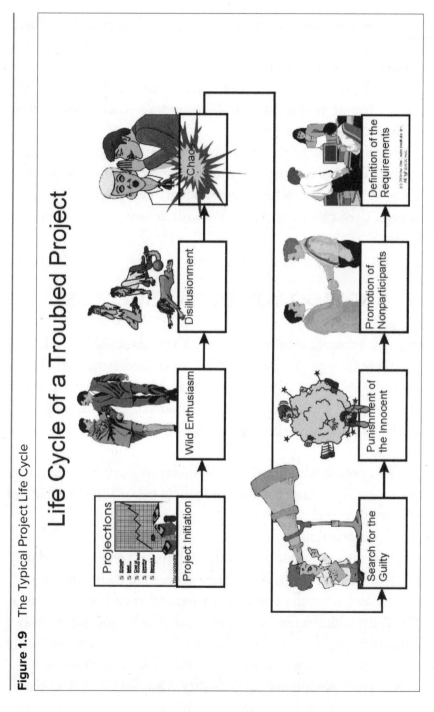

Life Cycle of a Troubled Project

you know, the team is in chaos. After the boiling point is reached, they sit down to define the project requirements. Naturally, this should have been done first!

The PMI model has phases called Initiation, Planning, Executing, Monitoring and Controlling, and Closeout. These will be shown later in this chapter.

In fact, I believe that projects almost always fail in the initiating or definition stage. They may hang around for a long time, going through the other phases, but if the initial definition is wrong, they cannot succeed. We will return to this theme in Chapter 5.

HOW DO YOU DEFINE SUCCESS?

It seems reasonable to believe that, if you meet the P, C, T, and S targets for a project, it would be considered a success. Unfortunately, it doesn't always work that way. There are projects that meet all the targets and are considered failures, and there are those that don't meet any of the targets and are considered successful.

To a person who likes to use numbers to judge outcomes, this is heresy. If you can't use the numbers to gauge success, what *are* you going to use?

Good question.

The answer is that part of the definition process is to clarify the requirements by having stakeholders state their expectations, understand what the results must be, and then determine what the deliverables must be to get those results and satisfy those expectations.

Consider a project in which a vendor has been chosen to provide certain equipment for a facility. One member of the staff preferred a different vendor. His expectation was that the team members would follow his recommendation, but they chose someone else. Even if that vendor meets all of the P, C, T, S targets, this team member will judge the project negatively. So the project manager needs to win this person over. This is the politics of project management, and it will be discussed later in the book.

Consider Figure 1.10. The only truly successful project is one for which you can answer "yes" at each point on the tree. A truly failed project is one for which you have to answer "no" at each point. (Other combinations are logically possible, but they don't make any sense and are highly unlikely.)

> The only truly successful project is the one that delivers what it is supposed to, gets results, and meets stakeholder expectations.

THE PROJECT MANAGEMENT SYSTEM

There are seven components that make up a proper management system. These are shown in Figure 1.11. Note that I have arranged them to show how they interrelate.

Figure 1.10 Expectations, Deliverables, and Results

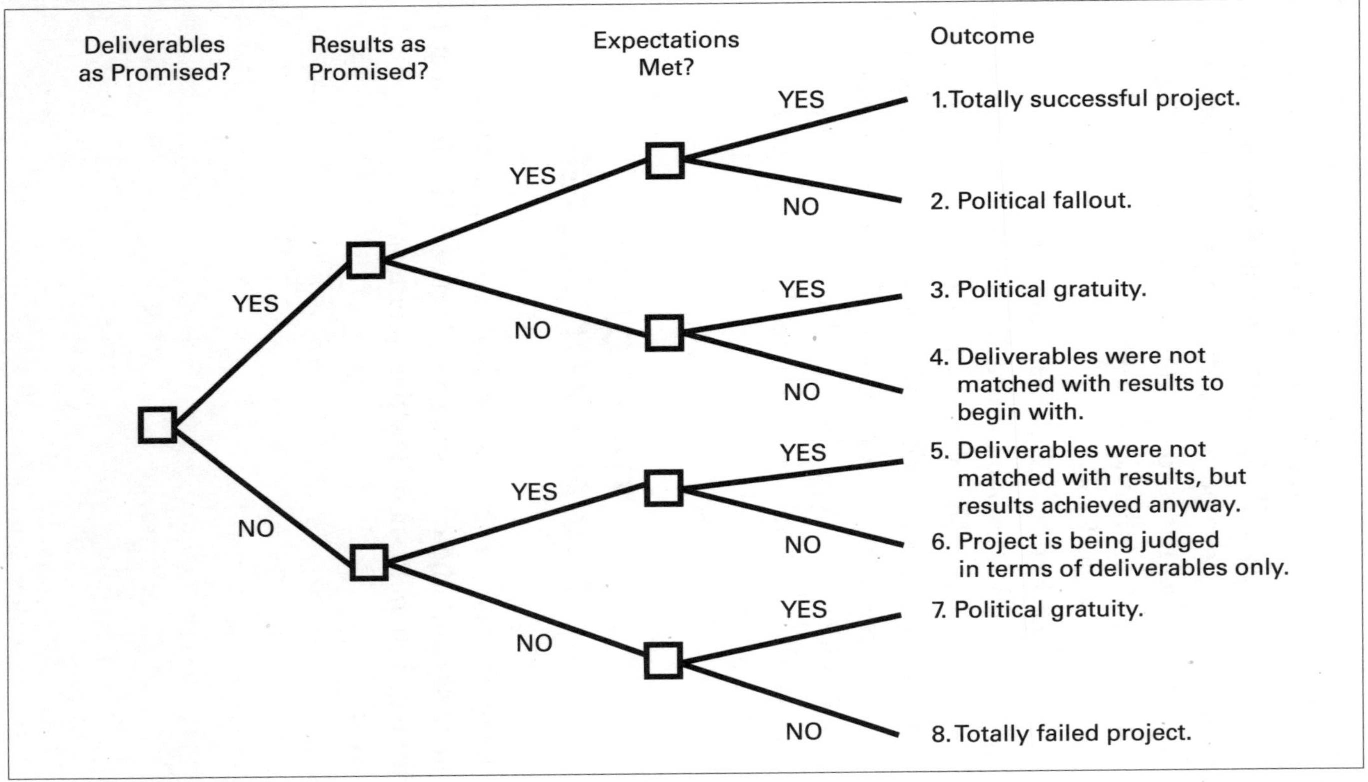

| Deliverables as Promised? | Results as Promised? | Expectations Met? | | Outcome |

Expectations Met?

YES → 1. Totally successful project.

NO → 2. Political fallout.

YES → 3. Political gratuity.

NO → 4. Deliverables were not matched with results to begin with.

YES → 5. Deliverables were not matched with results, but results achieved anyway.

NO → 6. Project is being judged in terms of deliverables only.

YES → 7. Political gratuity.

NO → 8. Totally failed project.

Results as Promised?

YES

NO

Deliverables as Promised?

YES

NO

Figure 1.11 The Project Management System

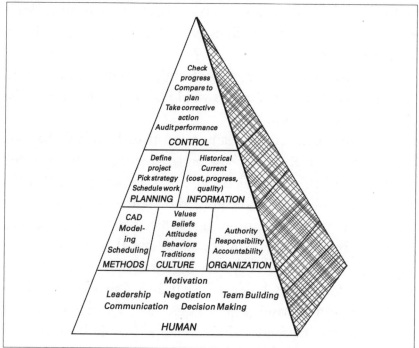

Human Component

The human component is on the bottom of the pyramid, because dealing with people underpins the entire structure.

*Projects are People®!** They are not critical path schedules or Gantt charts. Those are the tools we use to manage projects.

If a project manager cannot deal effectively with people, the project is likely to suffer. In fact, I have never seen a project fail because the manager or her team didn't know how to draw a critical path schedule, but I have certainly seen many of them encounter serious difficulty because of "people problems."

---

* Projects are People is a registered trademark of the Lewis Institute, Inc.

A project manager has to be able to do all of the things listed in the box: deal with communication, conflict, motivation, leadership, decision making, politics, and so on. And the list is by no means complete.

I have had technical people look at the list and say, "Oh, man, I really hate that part! Projects would be okay if you could just get people to be logical!"

I say to them, "If you really mean that, I suggest that you rethink your career. Don't be a project manager—or any other kind of manager." I say this because dealing with people is what leadership is all about, and you need more than management to succeed—you need leadership. If you hate people problems, you probably won't handle them very well, and they will drive you crazy to boot. In my value system, life is too short to spend doing something you hate. Choose to be a technical person instead.

On the other hand, some people say, "I'm not very good at some of the interpersonal skills, but if I could learn them, I would be willing to do so." In that case, I suggest that they set for themselves a learning objective. All the skills identified in the model can be learned, even leadership skills. Everyone may not be equally good at all of them, but everyone can improve.

Culture

On the next level up, we have a component that is related to the human system but is so special that it must be considered separately. This is culture. The word *culture* designates the sum total of the values, attitudes, traditions, and behaviors that exist in an organization. In fact, one way you know when people are talking about their culture is when they say, "We don't do it that way here."

Cultural differences result from geographic differences within a given country, ethnic background, race, religion, and so on. Broadly speaking, there is nothing good or bad about these differences (not everyone would agree with this). However, the differences lead to conflicts, misunderstandings, and disagreements.

Because projects are becoming more global in nature and teams are often more culturally diverse than they were in past years, it is important that project managers learn about and value cultural differences and how to deal with them. A few examples will illustrate.

In Japanese society, it is considered impolite to say "no" directly. Furthermore, the word *hai*, which we interpret to mean "yes," actually means, "I am listening." So, when a foreigner asks a Japanese person, "Do you agree?" and he says, "Yes," it sounds as if an agreement has been reached. Later, when the Japanese individual seems to be violating the agreement, and this is mentioned, he may say, "Well, we agreed to *this*," and it will have a shade of meaning different from what the foreigner thought it had.

Americans like to be very informal and are quick to call each other by first names. When I was a boy, we never called anyone over the age of 25 by his first name, but our culture has changed. So, when we go to countries like Germany on business, we are quick to call managers by their first names. Many Germans find this offensive. I once met a German engineer who had been working for his manager for eight years and still did not call him by his first name.

On one of my first trips to Malaysia, I learned about Malaysian cultural taboos so that I wouldn't offend anyone. A book called *Understanding the Asian Manager* (Bedi, 1992) offered some good tips.

I taught for a company in Kuala Lumpur, and following the program, I had to fly to Singapore. The firm arranged for a company driver to take me to the airport. He was driving a van. As is customary in the United States, I started to get into the back seat. He looked back at me and said, "Sir, you're kind of fat. You would probably be more comfortable up here in the front seat."

It was all I could do to keep from laughing. I could picture this poor fellow coming to the United States and working as a limo driver. He makes this remark to a passenger, who complains, and he is fired. "What's wrong?" he protests. "I was only trying to be helpful."

And he was.

What Bedi's book taught me is that in Asian countries, being fat does not bear the stigma that it does in our twiggy society. It is actually a sign of affluence, because over the years, unless a person was wealthy, he didn't eat a diet that was very fattening. Not knowing this, of course, it would seem insulting to an American to be referred to as fat.

One last example. A German man came to the United States to work with a company in Seattle for a couple of weeks. One day he went to the men's room as it was being cleaned and used the facility. The woman cleaning it was incensed. She filed a sexual harassment grievance, alleging that he had deliberately come in and exposed his private anatomy to her.

Such a furor ensued that the president of the German company had to write a formal letter of apology, explaining that it is common in Europe for women to clean the men's restrooms without closing them. I have experienced this myself in Zurich and Frankfurt, as well as in Malaysia and Singapore.

All these examples show the importance of being sensitive to cultural differences. The difficulty is that you don't know that you are violating someone else's culture until you do it, and people often don't tell you. And unfortunately, there aren't a lot of sources for training or education in such differences. You simply must be sensitive to the cultures of other people, and if things don't seem to be going well, discuss openly what is wrong so that the problem can be corrected. (For an in-depth treatment of cultural differences, see Hampden-Turner & Trompenaars, 2000.)

Methods

The methods component of the model indicates the tools that are used to manage projects. This includes scheduling methods, earned value analysis, work breakdown structures, and so on. I don't find this component to be a significant problem for most people. Tools are easily learned. The biggest struggle seems to be with scheduling software, and the reason this is such a problem is that organizations provide the software to managers without training them in how to use it. Even the most basic scheduling program today has considerable power, and the more power it has, the harder it is to use superficially, much less master. Giving a person a saw and a hammer does not make her a carpenter. She needs training and experience in the art of carpentry. The same goes for the use of scheduling software.

Organization

This component deals with both how a project is organized and how the company is organized. Every organization must delineate the limits of an individual's authority, responsibility, and accountability. A common complaint from project managers is that they have a lot of responsibility but very little authority. I always tell people who say this that they may as well get used to it. As far as I can tell, it isn't likely to change.

However, there are two kinds of authority, and we need to note the differences. One is the right (called *legitimate authority*) to tell people to do something and expect them to do it. This is authority over people, which project managers usually won't have. So you have to get things done through influence—and this is true even for managers who do have authority over people. So concern about having no authority over people is an exaggerated issue, in my opinion.

The second kind of authority is the right to act unilaterally, without having to get one's actions approved by 12 people in advance. This is most evident where spending is concerned. It is still one of my pet peeves that organizations require project managers to get approvals for purchases of over $25 when they are managing projects that have million-dollar budgets. This is ludicrous.

In my system of managing projects, as you will find as you read on, once a plan (which includes a budget) is developed and signed off on, there should be no need for further approvals as long as the project manager is spending in accordance with the preapproved plan. Requiring such approvals simply makes more work, slows down the project, and sends a clear message to the manager that she is not trusted with company money. Then why give her such a large project?

Control

I want to take this one out of order. I will return to planning and information later. The entire reason for managing a project is to make sure that you get the results desired by the organization. This is commonly called "being in control," and it is what is expected of a project manager.

Like many English words, the word *control* has a couple of meanings. One is almost the same as the word *power*.

Authoritarian managers attempt to control people through the use of power.

In management, the word *control* should have another meaning—that of guidance, or an information systems definition. As you can see in the box, control is exercised by comparing where you are to where you are supposed to be and then taking steps to correct for deviations from targeted performance. This can be done only if the two components of the model labeled Planning and Information are functioning correctly.

> **CONTROL:** The act of comparing where you are to where you are supposed to be, so that corrective action can be taken when there is a deviation from the target.

Planning and Information

If you have no plan, by definition, you have no control, because it is your plan that tells you where you are supposed to be in the first place. Furthermore, if you don't know where you are, you can't have control. This knowledge comes from your information system.

Most organizations have difficulties with both. They don't do a very good job of planning. In many cases, this is cultural. The company has grown from a one-person garage-located business into a prosperous concern with hundreds of employees. As the business grows, managers begin to realize that the old "loosey-goosey" way of managing is not working anymore, and they try to impose some structure. This is often resisted. "We've never had to do this before, and we've been successful," people complain.

"Yes, but we can no longer continue to be successful this way," management tries to explain. In fact, there is considerable danger for an organization that is successful, because people tend to become complacent.

Most organizations do a good job of providing information systems to track inventory, payroll, orders, and other measures, but they don't have systems for tracking projects. Why? They didn't realize that they needed such a system. This means that most project managers must track projects manually, which isn't too hard in most cases. Also, most scheduling software provides the capability to do earned-value reporting, so generating your own progress reports is fairly simple.

Note that the information component also includes historical data. This is needed to estimate project time, cost, and resource requirements. If I ask you how long it takes you to clean your house or mow your lawn, you can tell me the approximate time because you have done it so often. The same approach is used for project estimates when history is available. This means that a database must be set up to record task durations.

This works okay on well-defined tasks, but when you try to apply it to engineering, software, or scientific research, it does not work as well. The reason is simple: you seldom do the same task twice, so it is harder to develop good history for knowledge work. Such records do have some value, though, and we will discuss estimating in a later chapter. Additionally, alternative methods of estimating knowledge work will be presented.

PROJECT MANAGEMENT
AND ISO 9000

I am sometimes asked about the relationship between project management and ISO 9000. As I understand ISO, organizations are required to document their processes and procedures so that everyone does them the same way. You need to develop a project management methodology if you want to be ISO certified. Many of my clients have developed a methodology that requires their members to follow The Lewis Method® of project management (as presented in this book).

PROJECT MANAGEMENT AND SIX SIGMA

People also ask about the Six Sigma model, which deals with acceptable errors in processes or products. The idea is to reduce such errors or defects to extremely low levels.

If you draw a normal distribution curve that represents the conformance of a process or product to its requirements, you find that going plus or minus three standard deviations on either side of the mean will contain 99.74 percent of the population. That is, 0.26 percent of the measures you take will fall outside these limits. If you consider only one side of the mean, then 0.13 percent of measures will be unacceptable (assuming that a product that performs better than expected is acceptable). This is shown in Figure 1.12.

If you draw the normal distribution curve to cover plus or minus six standard deviations, then the number of nonconforming measures drops to 3.4 in a million. The Six Sigma system requires that performance targets be set at this level.

Project management and Six Sigma, then, are different. Project management offers tools to help organizations achieve Six Sigma performance targets.

Earlier I said that estimates place rework figures in projects at between 5 and 40 percent. That means that many projects are not even achieving three sigma levels.

If you go one standard deviation below the mean, you have 84 percent of the population conforming to requirements. That

Figure 1.12   Conformance to Requirements

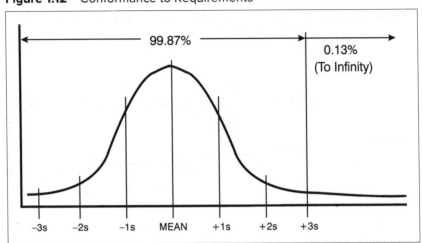

means, of course, that 16 percent of the population does not conform. Thus, we are not achieving even one sigma level if we have rework that exceeds 0.13 percent.

THE LEWIS METHOD OF MANAGING PROJECTS

I attended my first seminar on project management around 1978. Since then, I have looked at project management systems of all kinds and have developed my own model for managing projects. I call it The Lewis Method® and have a trademark for the term. Other models exist. Probably the best known, the Kerzner Approach®, was developed by my colleague Harold Kerzner. If they are valid, all methods are similar. So, you may find that you want to combine characteristics

PRINCIPLE: The thought process can be applied to any project, regardless of its type or size.

from several models to arrive at the one that best fits your project requirements.

Does One Size Fit All?

The question you might ask is, "Does one approach work for all projects?" The answer is "yes—and no." The "yes" part comes from the fact that project management is a disciplined way of thinking about how a job will be done. That disciplined way of thinking is shown by my flowchart, and it can be applied to any kind of project. It can be brain surgery, preparing a meal, developing hardware or software, or constructing a power dam. The overall approach is the same.

What differs is the tools that are used. I believe there are some projects that are so small that to do a critical path schedule would be a waste of time. On the other hand, there are projects that could not possibly succeed without a good schedule. What you need to do is pick and choose what tools you use.

My Projects Are Too Small to Use This Stuff!

For some reason, there are people who think that formal project management techniques are valid only for large projects. What I believe troubles them in many instances is that they are confusing documentation with the thought process. If I were preparing a meal, I would still go through the thought process outlined in my model, but I wouldn't create a lot of paperwork to do the job.

I am a strong advocate of the KISS (Keep It Simple, Stupid) principle in managing projects—don't do any more than you must do if you are to get the job done. (But don't do any less either!) I also like to call this the laziness principle, and I am lazy by nature. I don't want to spend more time or effort than needed to get the job done.

So go through the thought process, and then decide how much of it should be documented and do that. Keep it simple!

An Overview of The Lewis Method

My method conforms to the five processes defined by the *PMBOK® GUIDE*: initiating, planning, execution, control, and closeout. This model has been applied by thousands of project managers and forms the basis of many organization methodologies. It is a practical, no-nonsense approach that, when followed, helps managers avoid many of the pitfalls that cause projects to fail. This even includes some of the more common behavioral issues that seem to plague projects.

The model is presented in Figure 1.13 as a flowchart. This chart can be carried around and used as a memory jogger, rather than carrying the book around. Notice that there is another component of the model, shown in Figure 1.14. This chart is necessary because Step 6 of the model consists of a number of substeps, so rather than make one very large chart, I have broken step six out into a separate diagram.

The model will be covered in depth in the various chapters. For now, I will provide just a summary of the main phases of the model.

Figure 1.13 The Lewis Method of Project Management

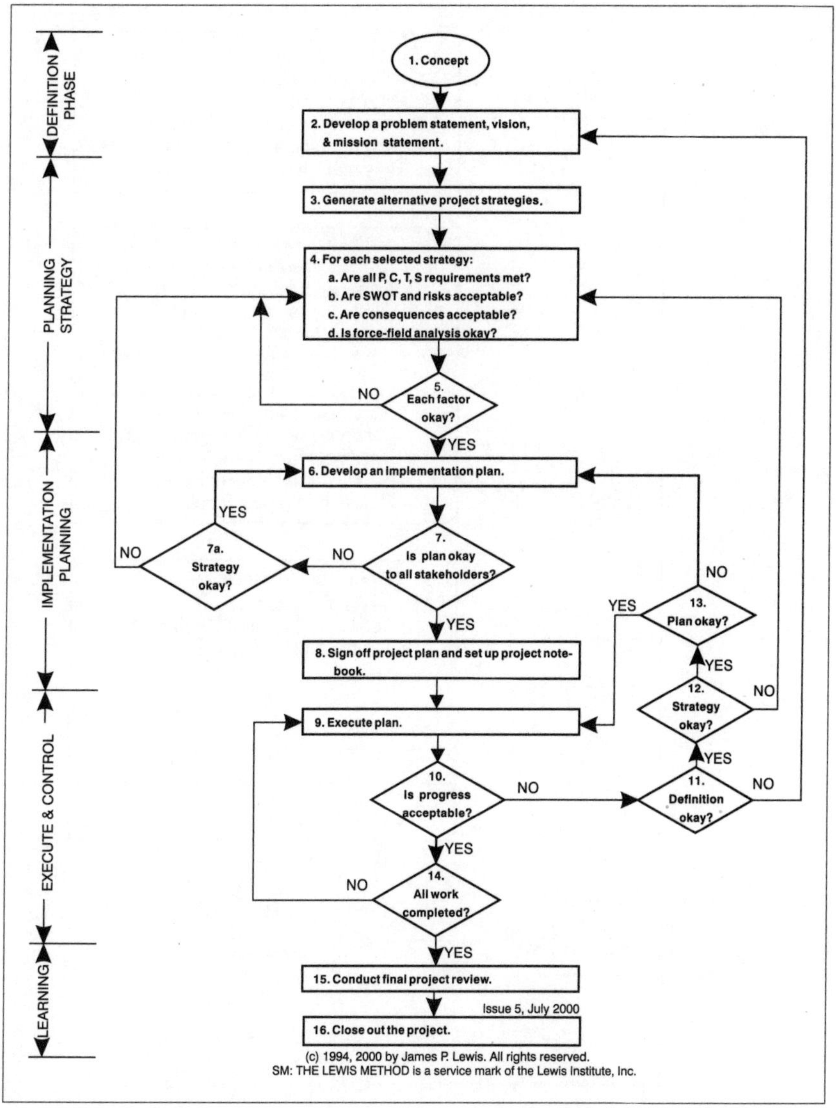

Figure 1.14 Step 6 of The Lewis Method Expanded

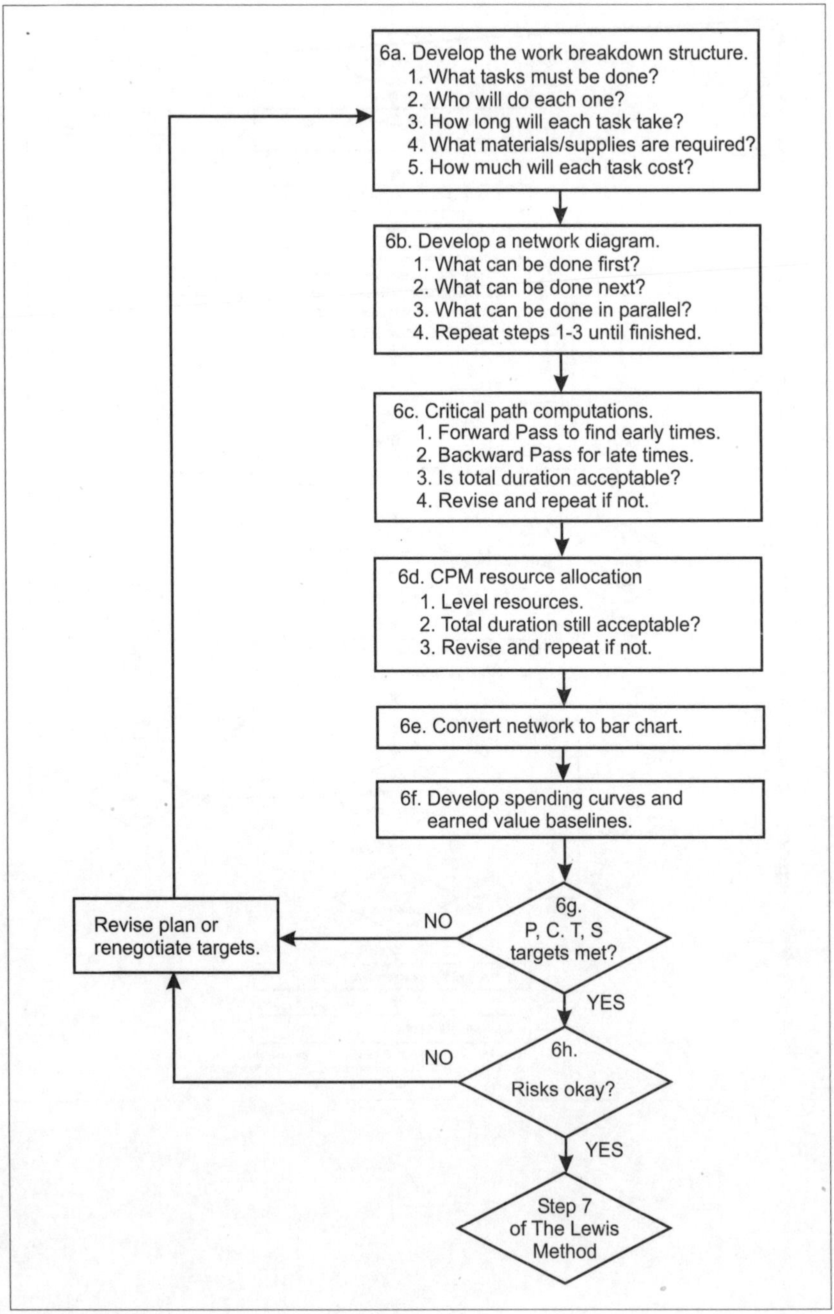

Initiation

As the model shows, a project almost always begins as a concept. We need something. Or we have a problem. The project is designed to solve that problem or meet that need. Remember the definition of projects offered by Dr. Juran? A project is a problem that is scheduled for solution. So, we are solving a problem with a large-scale effort when we do a project.

Where we get into trouble is in forgetting that the way you solve a problem depends on how it is defined. So, the first stage in a project is to make sure that you have defined the problem being solved correctly, that you have developed a vision for what the end result will be, and that you have stated your mission.

This phase is covered in Chapter 5.

Planning: Strategy First

The word *strategy* means that you have an overall approach to running a project. This step is often brushed over lightly. There is always a strategy or "game plan" implied by how a project is run, but that strategy is not chosen by comparison with other approaches. It is simply a default approach. Choosing a proper project strategy can mean the difference between success and failure, and the procedure for doing so is covered in Chapter 7.

Planning for Implementation

This is what most people think of as planning. This is where you dot all your i's and cross all your t's. You work out all the details of how the project will be done—what must be done, who will do it, how it will be done, how long the steps will take, and so on.

Execution and Control

In all too many cases, people jump directly from concept to execution. When they do this, they really have no control, since they have no plan that tells them where they are supposed to be. This was discussed previously. Execution and control will be covered in Chapter 12.

Closeout

This stage is often aborted. At the Frontiers Conference on project management conducted by Boston University, the keynote speaker asked an audience of some 400 people to raise their hands if they conducted regular end-of-project reviews for purposes of learning lessons. About 12 hands were raised. Then he asked a most compelling question.

"How many of you who put up your hands have a mandate that, before you do your next project, you must show your boss how you will avoid the mistakes that you made on your last project?"

Two hands went up.

And that is common. My own surveys in my seminars indicate that this response rate is standard. This topic will be covered in Chapter 14.

IN SUMMARY

There you have it—a concise overview of project management. The rest of this book is aimed at expanding this overview into a complete treatment of how to manage projects. However, I should say that the word *complete* is an exaggeration. The subject is too big to cover in one book. But what you will get in this book are the core methods, principles, and practices of project management.

CHAPTER 2

The Project Management Institute and the *PMBOK® GUIDE*

I f you check the phone book, you will find that there is an association for almost every profession, and project management is no exception. The Project Management Institute (PMI) is the association for those of us who consider managing projects to be more than just a temporary phase that we are going through on our way to maturity. PMI has experienced almost exponential growth over the past several years, as more people have become aware of the value of a structured approach to managing projects. In 2010, PMI had passed the 500,000-member mark, and it continues to grow at about 20 percent a year. You can get more information on PMI by checking their website: http://www.pmi.org.

PMI also attempts to promote project management as a profession, thereby raising the perceived status of project managers, and it has developed a certification process that confers on those who meet the requirements the designation of Project Management Professional, or PMP. As a broad example of the requirements, a candidate must log a certain number of work hours to sit for the exam, which consists of 200 questions. At present, the time limit for the exam is four hours. Applicants are also required to affirm that they will abide by a code of ethics in conducting their work. To find out more about the PMP certification process, check the PMI website.

The exam is based on the contents of the *PMBOK® GUIDE*. With the *PMBOK® GUIDE*, or *Project Management Body of Knowledge*, PMI attempts to define what a project manager should know to be a professional. At present, this knowledge falls into 10 categories, described very briefly here. The *PMBOK® GUIDE* does not attempt to fully document all of these (it would take a tome weighing about a ton to do so!); many volumes from other sources have been written on each topic. The document was revised in 2021 (seventh edition) and a new exam was released.

PROCESSES VERSUS KNOWLEDGE AREAS

A process is some action, or a series of actions, that brings about a result. The *PMBOK® GUIDE* identifies two kinds of processes:

- Project processes are those, such as planning and controlling, that ensure that the *product* produced by the project matches what was intended at the beginning.
- Product processes are those actions taken to produce the product. These may include engineering design, construction, or other such actions.

There are five project processes defined by the *PMBOK® GUIDE*:

- **Initiating:** doing whatever must be done to authorize a project
- **Planning:** identifying all the work that must be done; developing policies, procedures, and other documentation that define the project
- **Executing:** applying labor and materials to develop the product (in this case, *product* is a general term for whatever the project produces—whether an item, a service, or some other result)
- **Controlling:** monitoring progress against the plan and taking whatever actions are necessary to keep the project on *track*
- **Closing:** formal acceptance of the product and documentation of activities throughout the life of the project

KNOWLEDGE AREAS

As mentioned previously, there are currently 10 knowledge areas. These are described briefly in the following text.

Project Integration Management

Every facet of a project needs attention, and integration management is the effort that is made to ensure that everything comes together. This means that scope, cost, control systems, and so on have been defined and set up to function properly. Furthermore, the product that is being produced is inseparable from the project management itself, as managing the job is done to ensure that the product at completion will be what was intended.

Scope Management

Scope essentially defines what is to be done, and not done, in managing the project. In effect, it defines how large the job is. One cause of considerable difficulty for project managers is scope changes. When work is contracted to someone else in a project, scope management takes on a particularly important role: ensuring that the contractor does everything that is called for by the contract.

Time Management

My personal feeling is that this is a most unfortunate choice of terms. To thousands of people, the term *time management* means managing one's personal time, using a paper-based or (more likely) digital planner of some kind. However, in this context, it refers to scheduling.

Because of the importance of project deadlines, scheduling receives a lot of attention, and scheduling software sells in large quantities.

Cost Management

As the term implies, controlling project costs is highly important. The difficulty with cost and schedule management is that durations for tasks are estimated, and these estimates may not be very good—especially for poorly defined work. The net result is that there can be large variances from the estimates when actual work is performed. Organizations should recognize that all processes vary, that the variation can be reduced but never eliminated, and that there will be normal tolerances on all estimates that must be accepted.

Quality Management

As I pointed out in Chapter 1, it has long been customary to talk about the triple constraints in projects, but in doing so, the quality and scope components are combined. While these components may be related, they are not identical, so we should discuss the quadruple constraints. In any event, quality is often the forgotten constraint. When you place people under pressure to finish a project in record time, quality sometimes suffers. Quality management is aimed at preventing this outcome.

Human Resources Management

Although it should be obvious to any thinking person, *projects are people*, and project managers should have a high level of *people skills* before they are allowed to manage projects. In addition, every project must have the right people assigned to do various tasks, and most of the time project managers don't get to choose their team members. Nevertheless, this knowledge area deals with all aspects of managing human resources, including staffing, evaluating, motivating, and so on.

Communications Management

The first thing to be clear about is that communications management does not deal with the processes of communicating, but rather with determining the various stakeholders in the project who need information, at what intervals, and in what formats. Information is vital to the health of a project, and this process is often overlooked in the planning stage of a project.

Risk Management

Someone said to me once, "Project management is really all about managing risks." I think that is a pretty good observation. Because of the need to estimate task durations, resource requirements, and costs, a project faces many risks. And this doesn't even begin to take into account all of the things that can go wrong and shipwreck your project—weather, accidents, contract disputes, illnesses, and so on. It can well be said that either you must manage risks or they will manage you.

Procurement Management

Most projects make use of materials and services that must be procured from outside sources. Note that the common term that people use is *purchasing*, but not everything is purchased. Some things are licensed; others are leased. Clearly, regardless of how they are acquired, project teams can't meet their deadlines if they don't have things when they need them.

Project Stakeholder Management

Studies of project success have determined that if stakeholders are not satisfied with a project, it may be considered a failure.

Therefore, they must be actively managed like any other part of the project. Begin by identifying all the stakeholders. There is more on dealing with stakeholders in Chapter 18. It's not always easy, but it's a crucial part of starting any project, so find out who they are and what concerns they have.

Now plan stakeholder management, which means listing each stakeholder and prioritizing what their concerns are and how they might impact the project. This will lead to managing stakeholders' expectations to make sure their needs are met and that you're in communication with them.

Throughout the project, control stakeholder engagement. This is covered in detail in Chapter 18.

Professional Development Units (PDUs)

One requirement for being a PMP is that you must obtain continuing education credits, called PDUs, both to take the certification exam and to maintain your certification over time. These credits can be obtained through participation in PMI chapter meetings, teaching project management, writing books, and so on. There were various organizations that were designated as Registered Education Providers (REP) with PMI, but this program was terminated on June 30, 2020. For the latest information on the new program, see this FAQ page on the PMI website: https://www.pmi.org/certifications/certification-resources/faq.

IN SUMMARY

There you have it—a 36,000-foot view of PMI and the *PMBOK® GUIDE*. We will now turn our attention to the practical management of projects. Because PMI and the *PMBOK® GUIDE* are constantly changing, please do not depend on this chapter for information. It is included for overview only. Always refer to the PMI website. Even doing a Google search may return outdated information. The site is www.pmi.org.

CHAPTER 3

The Role of the Project Manager

A s I wrote in Chapter 1, the PMI definition of project management does not completely capture the true nature of project management. I don't know if it is possible to convey this. One reason is that project management is a *performing art*, and it is difficult to convey in words what an actor, athlete, or artist does. However, we can describe the various roles of a project manager, and that will be the focus of this chapter. What should be clear is that you can't very well become something if you can't describe and define it, so this is a necessary exercise.

I have been involved in project management for more than 60 years. First, I was a project manager myself. Then, when I decided to start teaching seminars, I taught a program titled Leadership Skills for Project Managers. Altogether, about 60,000 individuals in 30 countries have attended my seminars on project management, and my goal has always been to turn out the best project managers I can develop.

The focus of most management training is on analysis and planning. As I have already said, management is a performing art; it is left-brained in nature and can be learned only through practice. Practice leadership is right-brained, and we will discuss this more as we go.

Perhaps it is my age (80), or maybe I've become jaded, but quite frankly, I am disappointed in the results I've achieved, and I am skeptical about the overall quality of managers in the United States. The focus of management training, whether it is the traditional MBA program or management seminars in general, has always been left-brain-oriented (for more on brain dominance, see Chapter 5). The curriculum teaches tools—especially analytical tools for measuring financial progress—but analyzing data is not the same thing as managing.

> The focus of most management training is on analysis and planning. Leadership is a performing art; it is more right-brained in nature and can be learned only through practice.

Ray and Myers (1986) wrote about this when they published their book *Creativity in Business*. They tried to inject some right-brain thinking into the MBA program at Stanford. Henry Mintzberg (1989) has also criticized the totally analytical focus. One of his suggestions is that people plan on the left side (of the brain) and manage on the right side. I would prefer to say that they plan and manage on the left side and lead on the right side.

IT'S ALL ABOUT PEOPLE!

The first thing you must recognize is that project management is about *people*. It isn't about technology. Yes, technology may be center stage, and yes, you may have to be a techie to manage a given project, but generally speaking you don't need a high level of technical skill. In fact, I believe that being a technical expert can actually be detrimental to a project manager, because such individuals are inclined to get too involved in technology and neglect managing the project. Because managing projects is predominantly about dealing with people, not technology, we should be talking a lot more about project leadership. Given that you know enough about the technology to understand individuals' jobs and problems, the main thing you need to be able to do is deal effectively with people—and not just those on your project team. You must deal with all kinds of stakeholders—customers, suppliers, functional managers, finance people, public officials, and so on. One of the core activities of a project manager is dealing with politics. That's right, politics.

A lot of project managers with technical backgrounds hate the very word. To them, dealing with politics is a fate worse than death. Nevertheless, every act you perform in an organization has political implications, and you may as well recognize this and accept it. You certainly aren't going to change it. Like death and taxes, politics are with us for the long term.

As a project manager, you are constantly bombarded with crises. A vendor shipped the wrong part, and it is going to delay completion of xyz module. A team member from the mechanical engineering group is being a pain, and you must deal with him. A senior manager from another division is demanding that you accommodate his concerns about a market that has almost nothing to do

> Projects are People, and project management is about dealing with people and getting the best possible performance from them. Because managing projects is predominantly about dealing with people, we should be talking a lot more about project leadership.

with your product—but he thinks it does, and he outranks you by about seven levels in the corporate hierarchy, so you must deal with him, too. Then there is the squabble that has broken out between the industrial designers and the marketing department, which is about to escalate to nuclear proportions if you don't defuse it.

So, do you really want to be a project manager?

Not if you hate dealing with these kinds of issues. Life is too short. Go back to your technical job and use my book as a doorstop so that you see it often and remind yourself that you don't want to go that route.

Here's an anecdote to emphasize the importance of what I'm saying. I have a close friend who has about 10 project managers in his department. One of them had to be removed from the position because he was constantly getting into conflicts with various stakeholders to his projects. My friend spent a lot of time doing damage control because the project manager simply did not know how to deal with people. His technical skills were great, but he couldn't get the job done without *people skills*.

What this really boils down to is that you need to be a project *leader*, not just a project *manager*. Leadership is about getting people to follow you. My favorite definition is one by Vance Packard: Leadership is the art of getting others to *want* to do something you believe should be done. The operative word in this definition is *want*. You can get people to do what you want done through coercion or compensation. But getting them to want to do something—now, that's an art!

And, since project managers usually have a lot of responsibility and no authority, you need good leadership skills to get people to do the work that must be done. Again, it's all about people. [For an in-depth treatment of project leadership, see my book by that title (Lewis, 2002).]

SO YOU STILL WANT TO BE A PROJECT MANAGER?

Okay, so you don't mind dealing with people problems. Fine. But do you *really* want to be a project manager—or any kind of manager, for that matter? Or are you following a script that was laid on you by society? In *Scripts People Live By*, Claude Steiner (1990) shows that we often follow a life script that was imposed on us by our parents, our significant others, or society.

One way this works is to recognize that, in American society, success is defined as having status and money (and other countries seem to be rapidly catching up with us in this regard). The two generally go hand in hand. Managers have status, while engineers, clerks, accountants, and those in other positions do not. Thus, based on the American definition of success, these people are less successful than managers. So, if you want to be seen as successful, you must be a manager. At least, that's how it seems to many people (I was once one of them myself).

Another factor that makes people want to be managers is the desire to be in control, rather than being controlled. The need for independence is very strong in some of us, and we think we will gain that freedom if we can just become managers. This turns out to be a myth at midmanagement levels in most organizations, so the individual strives to reach the top—to be CEO, because then real independence will be achieved. That, too, is largely a myth, as any CEO will tell you. CEOs have more bosses than anyone—the stockholders, the board of directors, and every employee in the company.

Please don't misunderstand my message—there is nothing wrong with wanting to be a CEO or a project manager. I am simply pointing out that you should want to be one for the right reasons, not the wrong ones.

There are two kinds of project managers—dedicated and accidental. If you are a dedicated project manager, you own the project from cradle to grave. (Not your grave, but the project's grave.) It is your total responsibility from project initiation to project closeout. If that is not your situation, then you aren't a dedicated project manager, with all the rights and accolades that accrue to that position.

> Management should be proactive, not reactive.

Also, if you are a real project manager, you are proactive, not reactive. I know, I know; you're sick of hearing about people who are proactive. You want to leave as soon as someone uses the term. But it's true, whether you like it or not. A project manager absolutely must take the project and run with it. If you aren't doing so, you need to get with it.

Being proactive means being assertive, as well as taking initiative. The difference between being assertive and being aggressive is important. To be assertive means to stand up for your own rights while simultaneously respecting the rights of others. The aggressive person simply runs over others to get what he wants.

I was recently asked by someone in a seminar, "What do you do when a project is stalled?"

"Tell me what you mean by that," I said.

"Well, we refurbish buildings," he said. "One day you come in and realize that the gas needs to be turned off before some work can be done, and you have no idea how to go about getting it done. What do you do?"

I must confess that I had a hard time keeping a straight face. If you were a true project manager, wouldn't you be thinking ahead about this sort of thing? This person was not being proactive; he was totally reactive. I would say he was a project coordinator at best.

I don't mean to be condescending when I say this. He was an accidental project manager. He may not have wanted to be a project manager in the first place, but the job was thrust upon him, and he didn't fully understand the role. I believe this is true of many individuals who have become project managers in the same way as this person.

A Lesson about Authority

One reason that project managers sometimes fail to be proactive is that they don't have any authority granted to them by virtue of their position, and they think that they must get permission before they can take any action. In fact, organizations tend to establish this as a procedure. You can't purchase anything without having it approved, often by three levels of managers above you.

Naturally, we can't do anything about the red tape. However, we can ask ourselves, "Where could I exercise discretion in my job?" As an example, I once worked for an absentee boss. He traveled all the time, so he was never around when I needed a decision on something. I was fortunate enough to read somewhere that the best approach was to assume the authority when it wasn't given to me, so when I couldn't reach my boss, I

> You have as much authority as you are willing to assume.

would decide what to do and later tell him what I had done. I am convinced that this behavior contributed to my rise in the organization from an entry-level position to chief engineer in seven years. *The lesson was that you have as much authority as you are willing to assume.* If you wait for someone to give you authority, it may never happen, because you haven't demonstrated that you can handle it.

Another aspect of this was taught to me by a colleague. His favorite saying was, "It's always easier to get forgiveness than permission." I think he's right, and in those environments that are so rigidly controlled that this is not true, I would ask myself whether this is a place I really want to be.

DO YOU REALLY WANT TO MANAGE?

In the 60-plus years of my career, I have observed that there are a lot of people who want to be managers, but who don't want to manage! To reiterate, part of the reason is that managers have status, have some authority, and generally make more money than do nonmanagers. Even in technical organizations that claim to have dual career paths, the managerial path usually goes higher than the technical path, in terms of both hierarchical level and salary. In fact, I met a fellow once who had done a study for his MBA degree on organizations with dual career paths, and he had found that the number of companies that had such paths was very small. In many cases, the technical path was a dumping ground for individuals who could not make it in management.

> A lot of people want to be managers, but many of them don't want to manage.

So, before you can really understand project management, you need to understand management in general. One common definition is that management is getting work done through other people. It is easy to see why this definition is inadequate. A guard over a prison work crew gets the prisoners to work, but he would hardly be called a manager. And there are countless people who are called managers who really don't manage very well.

Peter Drucker, who is considered by many to be the father of modern management thinking, has written that *management is making an unsolicited contribution to the organization* (Drucker, 1973). That is, a manager does not wait until a situation exists that requires a reaction; rather, a manager is proactive. Furthermore, a manager is looking for ways to improve the functioning of the organization. He or she is forward thinking.

Mintzberg (1989) has argued that very few managers whom he has shadowed fit the theoretical mold of careful, reflective planners. I agree with him. But I would argue that this is because many managers find themselves caught in the firefighting mode to such a degree that they simply don't have time to do the careful, reflective thinking and planning that they really should be doing. In addition, according to Mintzberg's experience, they are being interrupted at the rate of once every eight minutes, so they can't get their everyday jobs done.

I think of managers as being very similar to pilots. The pilot's job is to get an airplane to a distant destination. She begins with a flight plan. She checks out the plane to ensure that it is functioning properly. Then she practices principles of navigation to guide the plane to that final goal. She compares where she is to where the flight plan says she should be, and she makes course corrections as necessary to get the plane back on target when it has drifted because of crosswinds. The same could be said of managing. (I like this description of flying: Get it in the air. Keep it in the air. Make it go where you want to go.)

A manager has a goal in mind. He makes a plan for how he will reach that goal. Then he sets in motion steps to reach the goal, compares his progress against the plan, and takes corrective action when there are deviations from the plan.

This is called control, and it is a primary function of management. Now note that, if you have no plan, you don't know where you are supposed to be, so control is—by definition—impossible!

So, a manager is like a pilot, guiding his or her organization to a predetermined destination. Of course, a pilot occasionally finds that the airport at the desired destination is fogged in, and he must divert to an alternative until the fog lifts. Managers must sometimes do the same thing, and occasionally they decide that the original destination should be changed because the environment in which they operate has changed, so that pursuing the original goal would be inappropriate.

> Control is exercised by comparing progress against planned performance and taking steps to correct for any deviations from the proper course. If you have no plan, you have no control.

The Law of Requisite Variety

An organization is like an organic system. Such systems attempt to adapt to the changing conditions in the environment so that they can survive. Ross Ashby expressed a law in systems theory that states that *in any system of humans or machines, the element in the system that has the greatest variability in its behavior will control the system.*

We have seen that managing is essentially a process of controlling the behavior of an organization so that it can reach a desired goal. Thus, the law of requisite variety suggests that a manager must have more variability in her behavior than any other element in the system, or she won't be in control; some other element will be.

There are two possibilities for achieving such control. One is to increase your flexibility so that it is greater than that of any other element in the system. The other is to decrease the variability of the other system elements so that you can match or exceed the variation in the system.

> **THE LAW OF REQUISITE VARIETY**
>
> In any system of humans or machines, the element in the system that has the greatest variability in its behavior will control the system.

Any experienced manager knows how difficult it is to be flexible enough to respond to all the variations in the system. There are simply too many of them. We live in a turbulent environment, and chaos theory (Gleick, 2008) has shown that even minute variations in some system element can lead to extremely large excursions in overall system performance. The best expression of this is the premise that a butterfly flapping its wings in San Francisco will, a few days later, affect the weather on the East Coast of the United States.

For this reason, some authors have argued that planning is futile, as the effects of chaos soon wipe out your efforts to control (Wheatley, 1992). I think this goes too far. A more balanced approach is recommended by Stacey (1996), who suggests that long-range planning should be tentative and broad-brush in nature, but day-to-day planning can and should be more detailed.

> You must either increase your flexibility or reduce the variation in the behavior of the organization.

The Negative Approach

Because increasing one's own flexibility is so difficult, I believe that most managers resort to the second approach, which is to try to limit the variation in the system. Unfortunately, they do this in a negative way rather than a positive one.

By this I mean that they try to limit variation with rules, regulations, and procedures that often stifle the variation that the organization needs if it is to survive in its environment. Another way to say this is that they create the ultimate bureaucracy, as bureaucracies are known for being highly rule governed.

> The negative approach (reducing system variation) tends to stifle the system and does not lead to real control.

The rules and regulations are essentially *thou shall nots*. Thou shall not go over budget. Thou shall not go around thy manager to his boss. Thou shall not spend more than $25 of company money without approval from the three lords above you.

Tom Peters (1987) has argued that these policies (as they are usually called) don't guarantee that people will behave in acceptable ways. All they do is give the organization grounds for exercising sanctions against anyone who violates the rule.

The Positive Approach

A better way of reducing the variation in system behavior is through proper planning. If every member of the organization knows what he or she is supposed to be doing and how to do it, then variation in behavior is constrained by the plan, and the manager has control. And this is the only way to gain it. Unless every individual in the organization is in control of his or her own behavior, the manager won't have control. Another more technical way of saying this is that macro-control must be achieved through micro-control.

> Control cannot be achieved through micromanaging.

However, this does not mean micromanaging. In the end analysis, micromanaging means that you can supervise only one person, and I submit that one of you is redundant. Rather, what is required is that conditions exist that allow every employee to be in control of his or her own behavior. How this is accomplished is covered in detail in Chapter 12.

A Word of Caution

It would be easy to conclude that because few managers spend much time planning, this behavior is appropriate for project managers. Every major study that I have seen on the correlations between the project manager's actions and project success have shown planning to be vital. It is important to recognize that good project managers *facilitate* good project planning; they don't do it themselves. As I have written in all my books, the first rule of planning is that the people who must do the work should do the planning. There are two principal reasons why this is true:

> Just because few managers do much planning does not mean that project managers should abandon planning. If you have no plan, you have no control!

1. People have no commitment to someone else's plan—not because of ego, but because it is generally not correct in its estimates, sequencing, or inclusivity.
2. Collectively, the team will think of things that no one individual (namely, the project manager) would think of.

It is a fact that project managers are supposed to be in control, in the sense of getting results from the project team. And since *control* is defined as comparing where you are to where you are supposed to be, so that you can take corrective action when a deviation occurs, it follows that if you have no plan, you have no control, since you have nothing to compare your progress against. (I said this earlier, but it is worth repeating.) For that reason, planning is not an option—it is a *requirement!* Perhaps if more general managers spent time planning, fewer organizations would be operating in crisis mode.

Managing versus Doing

Many managers have risen to their jobs after having first been experts in some field. In their new role as manager, they feel a bit like a fish out of water. They aren't very comfortable with it. I once was told by a woman who had just been promoted, "I sometimes wonder if what I'm doing is what I *should* be doing." Her boss is in another location, so she seldom gets to talk with him, much less receive any guidance from him. I assured her that most of us experience the same anxiety. The only way out of it is to be extremely clear about what you want to accomplish with your department or project team. This means that you have a clear mission and vision in mind.

Even then, however, it is easy to fall into the "doing trap." This happens when someone on your team has a technical problem that you could solve blindfolded. Or perhaps the problem is a bit of a challenge (that's the most dangerous kind). Next thing you know, you're spending a lot of time working on the technical issue and neglecting your management duties.

Or, you may tend to micromanage. You don't fully trust your direct reports or team members to do the job as well as you would do it, so you resort to supervising them very closely. Either way, the managing suffers.

The Working Project Manager

Another trap, one that is imposed on project managers by the organization, is that they are expected to do some of the work that is being done by other members of the project team. They are called *working project managers*. The problem with this setup is that when there is a conflict between getting work done and managing the team, the work always takes priority, and the managing suffers. I personally would rather see a person be given several small projects to manage, with no work responsibility, than to have someone trying to manage the project and do work at the same time. It just never works. Furthermore, the downside is that when performance appraisal time comes, you are trashed for not managing better. It becomes a double bind.

Full-Spectrum Project Management™

Over the past 20 years or so, people working in information systems and software development have developed methods for managing projects that are referred to as Agile or eXtreme (Whitaker, 1994; Wysocki, 2010; DeCarlo, 2004). They argue that traditional methods of managing projects simply don't work well in situations that are poorly defined or that change frequently. Not being knowledgeable about these areas, I can't argue for or against their position, but I know some of these individuals and respect them enough to accept that they are correct.

For that reason, I would suggest that project managers of the future must know both traditional and nontraditional methods of managing projects so that they can apply the appropriate method to their work.

MAKING YOUR CAREER DECISION

Graham and Englund (1997) have written that there will eventually be no more accidental project managers. Rather, project management will be recognized as a true profession, and we will have dedicated project managers with their own special career paths. They also observe that project management will be the proving ground and possibly the path taken to CEO status (as I mentioned earlier in this chapter).

The reasons are that project managers are exposed to almost every facet of the organization; they require exceptional political and interpersonal skills; and if they can manage projects successfully, it is reasonable to assume that they can manage the entire organization.

If, after reading this chapter, you are still undecided about whether you want to pursue project management as a career, you should read *The World-Class Project Manager*, by Bob Wysocki and me (Wysocki & Lewis, 2000). We offer a fuller treatment of project management as a career than is possible in this book, together with diagnostics and other aids to help you make your decision. You can also have someone arrange for you to take the Strong Interest Inventory. It has been used for more than 80 years to help individuals decide what careers are likely to be good choices for them, and I have used it extensively with teens to help them choose career paths in college, with excellent results.

IN SUMMARY

A project manager's role is not singular. You need to be both a manager and a leader. Furthermore, there seem to be project managers who want the title and what goes with it but don't want to manage or lead. This is unfortunate. The job can be rewarding but also challenging, and my suggestion is to refrain from taking the job if dealing with people is something you prefer not doing!

In addition, politics pervade many project environments and cannot be avoided. Many technical people dislike politics and if you are one of them, I would urge careful consideration before accepting a position as project manager.

CHAPTER 4

How to Achieve High-Performance Project Management™

This chapter does not deal directly with how you, as an individual, should manage projects. My intent is that it will serve as a guide that you can present to senior managers on how to make project management a core competence in your organization so that you can thrive in an environment that supports what you are learning from this book.

THE HIGH-PERFORMANCE PROJECT MANAGEMENT MODEL

No doubt you have heard about a quality improvement program called Six Sigma. (I mentioned it briefly in an earlier chapter.) This approach has been adopted by a few companies, one of the most notable being General Electric. According to the Six Sigma providers, most organizations operate at a three sigma quality level. This means that for every 1 million tasks, they will make about 66,807 errors. These errors will cost them about 25 to 30 cents of every sales dollar. This is the cost of poor quality! [For those who are interested in reading more about Six Sigma, see Michael George, *Lean Six Sigma* (New York: McGraw-Hill, 2002).]

> Most organizations and projects function at a three sigma quality level, which means that for every million things they do, they make 66,807 errors. That means they waste 25 to 30 cents of every dollar spent!

When an organization can improve its performance to the six sigma level, it then makes only 3.4 errors for every million operations, and this reduces the cost of poor quality to about three cents on the dollar—a huge improvement that goes directly to the bottom line.

My High-Performance Project Management (HPPM) model defines project management maturity in five levels, with the first two being bare awareness and minimal performance. These two levels are equivalent to the three sigma level mentioned earlier. When an organization reaches the third level, which we call the bronze level, it is probably at around a four sigma quality level. The fourth level, or silver level, is five sigma, and the fifth level, or gold, is a Six Sigma quality level for projects.

In addition to reducing errors, you achieve HPPM only when you consistently meet the PCTS targets for your projects. Remember that three of these can be dictated, and the fourth must be allowed to float. And since these targets are estimated, part of what we are saying is that your ability to estimate has improved considerably.

Given the difficulty of estimating some kinds of work—such as creative design, programming, developing life sciences products, and so on—it is possible that some organizations can never hit their targets consistently, but doing so should be the objective.

As Phil Crosby (1980) said about zero defects, you may never achieve the target, but it should be the target nonetheless.

The Benefits of HPPM

Although most managers know that they need some form of project management in their organizations, I am not yet convinced that all of them distinguish between "seat-of-the-pants" project management and a structured approach that really gets high-performance results. One reason for this is that many senior managers were project managers before being promoted to higher-level management jobs. However, they had no formal training in project management, so many of them used an unstructured approach to managing their projects. They did a good job—good enough, in fact, that they were promoted. And because of this success, they see no need for a structured approach.

Consider, though, that even the most successful sports teams know that if they don't find new and improved ways of playing, they will not maintain their success. Continuous improvement must be the standard approach for all organizations in today's highly competitive world. But just what can a formal, structured approach to project management do for an organization? Following is one such example.

The Four-Hour House

In 1983, the San Diego Building Association sponsored a competition to see just how fast a typical single-family home could be built. They chose as their design a single-story house built on a cement slab, with approximately 2,000 square feet of floor space.

Such houses typically take from three to six months to build. (This time has not changed significantly since 2010.)

Highly detailed plans were developed—plans that defined activities down to 10-minute increments. A practice run was held, in which the two competing teams built identical houses. The best time during the practice run was six hours. The plans were revised based on lessons learned from the practice session. The revised plan predicted that a house could be completed in about 3 hours and 39 minutes, so the competition was called the "four-hour house project."

It is important to bear in mind that these houses were not prefabricated. They were built from "raw" lumber, wallboard, and so on (also called stick-built). The sites had been cleared and the placement for the cement slab was marked, and the slabs were poured when the starting gun for the "race" was fired. The competition ended when the first house was completed; that is, it was ready to move into—fully wired, carpets installed, sod grass in the lawn, shrubs in front, and all appliances (refrigerator, stove, etc.) installed. Each team consisted of 350 workers, all highly motivated to win the contest.

The winning team finished in a time that is recorded in the *Guinness Book of World Records*. They completed their house in an incredible 2 hours and 45 minutes! If you don't believe me, watch the documentary video, which can be ordered by calling the San Diego Building Industry Association at (858) 450–1221 or visiting https://www.biasandiego.org/the-four-hour-house/.

A couple of very important points should be noted. First, as already mentioned, the practice houses required six hours to complete. Through a lessons-learned review, the team was able to reduce this time by more than 50 percent in the competition. This illustrates the importance of lessons-learned reviews on projects! Second, good planning contributed significantly to the winning team's success. Without a truly well-developed plan, there would be no way to build a house in such a short time. But what about the cost? After all, there were 350 workers on each house.

One of my seminar students calculated that the house built in 2 hours and 45 minutes actually cost less (with 350 workers) than a house built with fewer workers over a longer time. Furthermore, if you consider that the house could be sold almost immediately, you have a cost-of-capital advantage. So, while less than three hours may not be the target we should have for all homes of this type, it does show that building times can be reduced significantly.

You may also realize that the planning took far longer than the execution time, and ordinarily this would not be so. This demonstrates the importance of a plan if you want to get a job done very quickly, and thus counters the claim, "We can get it done faster if we don't *waste* time working up a plan."

One last thought. I know some of you are thinking, "I wouldn't want to live in it." You are thinking that they must have cut corners, thereby sacrificing quality, to build a house in such a short time. And you would be justified in thinking this. However, to prevent the workers from sacrificing quality for speed, building inspectors, wearing referee shirts, inspected the work as it was done, and they insisted that each house meet code or they would not consider it a valid completion. In fact, the losing team realized that they had a problem with the roof on their house and had to correct it.

THE NEED FOR A NEW APPROACH

As I mentioned earlier, since I began training people in 1980, I have conducted three-day project management seminars for more than 60,000 individuals. Many of these programs were conducted for companies that were trying to improve project management in their organizations. In one company alone, I taught more than 800 people in sites scattered along the East Coast. Despite this, I learned that very few people actually applied what I taught them. And I have found this to be true of many other clients as well.

This has been a big disappointment to me. I don't want to just deliver training. I want to deliver training that *gets results!* And this simply isn't happening.

> No more than 33 percent of what is taught makes it back to the workplace.

As I pondered this over several years, I learned that it is a typical situation. I once read a study that reported that no more than 33 percent of what is taught ever makes it back to the job (I no longer remember the source of this information). There are several primary reasons for this finding. One is that people are not supported for doing what they learned. Nor are they required to demonstrate what was taught. So, soon after the program, they revert to their old ways, and the learning never "takes."

One of the strongest examples of lack of support was related to me by a fellow who went home from one of my programs feeling very excited about his newfound knowledge. He immediately convened a planning session with his group to develop a project plan. His boss came by the conference room and called him outside.

"What are you doing in there?" his boss wanted to know

"Putting together a plan for our project," said the fellow with enthusiasm.

His boss glared at him. "We don't have time for that nonsense," he said. "Get them out of the conference room so that they can get the job done."

This attitude toward planning is widespread. Managers are task oriented. They want to see people doing work, not drawing work breakdown structures or critical path diagrams. Strangely, this fellow's manager continued sending him to a project management certificate series consisting of six three-day seminars. I have no idea why. He clearly does not understand the benefits of project management.

Solving Problems

Since nearly 30 cents of every dollar spent on projects is wasted due to poor project mismanagement, this represents a problem to be solved by the organization. However, the way a problem is defined affects the solution possibilities, and the typical definition is that people running projects need to be trained. And this is true. However, it is only one component that contributes to poor project management, and if the other components are not addressed, the problem will be only partially solved. The components that must be addressed were introduced in Chapter 1 and are repeated here in Figure 4.1.

People

As shown in Figure 4.1, issues with people must be addressed to develop project management competence in an organization. If you want to understand how to develop the skills of people, you should observe athletic coaches, surgeons, and actors. Coaches have been learning how to improve the performance of athletes for centuries. Surgeons and actors, too, spend years mastering their craft. Can you imagine a surgeon sitting through a lecture

Figure 4.1 Tools, People, Systems

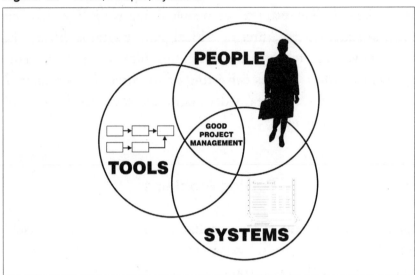

and going directly into the operating room to perform surgery on someone? Of course not! Yet we do something similar when we send people to a seminar and expect them to perform immediately after they return to the job. Fortunately, poor project management skills seldom kill anyone.

Consider athletes. No coach would ever consider a single training session to be adequate to fully develop a player. Rather, players are coached over time. They practice, receive feedback, and practice some more—until they eventually get it right. But notice that this is a lifelong endeavor. No athlete who is any good ever thinks that she is finished with learning or improving. Interestingly, it has been estimated that

> Can you imagine a surgeon sitting through a lecture and going directly into the operating room to perform surgery on someone?

nearly 85 percent of skills are lost in a few months unless the person is coached over time. This means that we must adopt the sports model for coaching athletes to develop the skills of project managers over time.

As I mentioned before, managers in organizations overlook the fact that managing is a *performing art*. It has less to do with knowledge than with behavior—applying skills in dealing with people—because projects are people, not technology. And you only learn these skills through practice, feedback, and more practice—until you get it right. The problem is that thousands of managers have never had any coaching. And there are thousands who are not very good at dealing with people. These managers generally don't understand that behavioral skills are important. After all, they get the job done. Their bosses are happy. The company makes money. And they continue to progress up the corporate ladder. So why all the fuss? All you really need to do (many of them believe) is just kick some behinds, and this will get people moving.

> Managing is a *performing art.* It is learned not through lecture, but by rehearsing.

To use the term from the cartoon strip *Dilbert*, these managers are *clueless!* They don't get it, and they probably never will.

To summarize, we need to provide project managers with training in the tools and techniques of project management, together with skills in dealing with people. And this must be supported by ongoing feedback on how they are performing, together with coaching to improve that performance. Finally, the application of these tools, techniques, and skills must be supported; in fact, senior managers should demand that they be practiced properly. These skills should be assessed as part of the project manager's performance appraisal.

Tools

The next of the three components is tools. Here we find that managers think that the only important tool is a scheduling software program. As I wrote in Chapter 1, this is "instant-pudding" project management—just give a person a copy of Microsoft Project or some other such program, and he will be an instant project manager.

There are two problems with this scenario. First, giving me a saw won't make me a carpenter. I need some training in carpentry first. So people should be given a course in project management first and then taught the software. Second, scheduling software is so complex that it is unrealistic to expect a person to sit down and use it right out of the box. People need at least two days of training to be able to use such software effectively. I have found over the years that most people are simply using the software to develop nice presentation graphics. They have imposed so many "must-start" and "must-finish" dates on tasks that the software can only regurgitate what it has been told—it is unable to do what it is intended to do, which is to tell the user the dates on which tasks can be started and finished.

Systems

Dr. W. Edwards Deming and Peter Senge (1990) have shown that *systems generate behavior*, regardless of the people in the system, and that unless you change the system, you will continue to get the same behavior. A management simulation called the Beer Game shows one such example.

In this simulation, convenience stores sell a beer called Love beer. It's not a big seller—most of them sell only about four cases a month. Suddenly sales of Love beer take off, and the store managers learn that it is because the beer has been mentioned in a popular song. So, they increase their orders for the beer. But because this is going on throughout the region, the beer distributor is soon swamped with orders. The brewery can't fill them fast enough.

The brewery has no choice but to increase capacity, so they initially ask people to work overtime. They also increase orders for grain and hops to make beer, and this puts a strain on the supply chain. But everyone works hard to respond. Still, this is not enough to meet the demand, so the brewery begins hiring for a second shift.

> Systems generate behavior! If the behavior is unacceptable, change the system, not the people.

Unfortunately, the market is fickle. The song loses popularity; the beer isn't a great beer, despite the temporary demand, and so people quit buying. Panic sets in. The stores begin canceling orders for beer, forcing the brewery to cancel orders for supplies and to lay off the newly hired second-shift employees, plus canceling all overtime. It is a snowball effect.

Now for the compelling fact. Senge says that his associates have run this simulation with many groups consisting of members with all kinds of backgrounds—educational, ethnic, and so on—and the result is always the same. The conclusion: *the system generates the behavior, regardless of the people involved.*

This is a profound finding, and one that no manager can ignore with impunity. If the system generates the behavior, then just how accountable can people within the system be? Clearly there is a need for us to examine causality in situations where people don't seem to be performing acceptably.

Another example of the effect of systems on behavior was provided by Deming (1986), who demonstrated the same thing using a bowl of beads, some of which were white and some of which were red. The objective of the person in the demonstration was to insert into the bowl a paddle into which many holes had been drilled, and to extract only white beads. Red beads were regarded as defects. Of course, it is impossible to do this and pull out only white beads consistently. However, what baffled many participants was that Dr. Deming said that there were exactly 10 percent red beads in the bowl and asked the audience what they expected the average defect level to be as the paddle was inserted and withdrawn and the beads were dumped back into the bowl (thus keeping the population constant).

Everyone guessed 10 percent. Deming asked why this number. They asserted that he had told them that the population was 10 percent red beads. Deming then asked what that had to do with anything.

After considerable head scratching, someone usually suggested that maybe the process had something to do with the result. Deming then declared that it did, indeed, affect the outcome. He had three paddles. One would produce an average of 9.8 percent, another 10.0 percent, and the third about 10.2 percent—despite the fact that the bead population was 10 percent red.

As he then told the audience, if you have given workers a system that is going to inherently produce a certain defect level—no matter how they do their jobs—you can admonish them to "do it right the first time," and it will make no difference. They cannot produce results better than those that the system *is capable of producing!*

Because most organizations have been functionally organized for so long, systems to support projects often do not exist. They must be installed if good project management is to be achieved. This includes the reward system, tracking, evaluation, budgeting, and so on. As an example, companies usually budget on a fiscal basis, but projects often span multiple years. It makes no sense to insist that a project manager spend exactly what he was supposed to on an annual basis, but this is what companies do.

Finally, we must examine the reward system in the organization. Most reward systems encourage individuals to maximize their performance, even though it may be at the expense of other people in the group. And functional groups are rewarded for excellent functional performance, rather than for supporting projects. Unless you change the reward systems to support good project performance, you won't get it.

Joint Optimization

One mistake that must be avoided in developing high project management performance is to optimize each of these three factors (tools, people, and systems) independently of the others. You will note that the intersection of the three circles in Figure 4.1 is where good project management occurs. The reason for this is shown by considering how you might build the world's best car. You find the best transmission in the world and combine it with the best auto engine, brakes, body, and so on. The chances are good that you won't have a very good car because these various components have not been designed to work with one another. If the engine is too powerful for the transmission, for example, you will destroy the transmission as soon as you hit the accelerator. For this reason, you must develop your tools and systems to match the capabilities of your people.

STAGES OF DEVELOPMENT

No athlete becomes a star overnight, and no company develops project management competence immediately. Most project management maturity models have five levels of capability, and it takes most companies about one year per level to develop their capability. For the impatient, this is terrible news. Nevertheless, it is reality. Experience cannot be accelerated beyond certain limits. (You can't cram six years of school into a child in one year.) So long as this is recognized and expected, there are very few problems. But when it is not, we find companies abandoning project management because they do not get immediate benefits from it.

> Systems must be jointly optimized. Improving a single system can worsen, rather than improve, the overall organization performance.

Too Many Projects

One of the major reasons that organizations have problems with projects is that they are trying to do too many projects given their resources. The result is that people are constantly jumping from one project to another to keep everything going. In doing so, they must get reoriented each time they shift tasks. This reorientation is called *setup time* in manufacturing, and it adds no value to the work process itself. We have known for a long time that setup time should be reduced as much as possible, as it depresses productivity.

The only way this can be done is to allow a person to work on one thing until it is completed and then move to something else. Heresy, you say? Maybe so, but one company found that its productivity nearly doubled when it quit trying to multitask and prioritized its projects, so that each person had a priority-one project and a backup. The person worked on the priority-one project whenever it was possible to do so and used the backup to fill dead time on the first project. Is it clear that if you double your productivity, you will get everything done in the same calendar time as when you were trying to do everything, but your productivity will be so much higher that your costs will go down dramatically? Multitasking creates the illusion that a lot is getting done. It is, but at low levels of productivity.

> Unless you have unlimited resources, you can't do everything at the same time. Prioritize projects and do them in priority order!

Consider one simple example. Many of you have probably found that you can't get anything done during the day, so you come in early or stay late. Why? Because during the day you are constantly being interrupted. Drop what you're doing and go to a meeting. Answer the random phone calls. Chat with your colleagues who need your help. And report on what you're doing to your boss. Interview candidates for jobs. And on and on goes the list. It is all important "stuff" that must be done, but it takes time that you can't spend doing your work. And it's called multitasking!

The Negative Environment

You can't have high performance in an environment that has a negative climate. This includes a climate of blame and punishment for things that go wrong. Don't get me wrong. It is appropriate to punish people who break rules or act irresponsibly. But when the climate is such that failure to meet project targets is seen as a sign of weakness on the part of people and they are chastised for it, you have an environment that does not support high performance.

Remember, all project targets are estimates (which is a kinder word than guesses, but they are guesses just the same), and they can be expected to be missed often until you have enough history to know how long things really take. And even when you have history, the time it takes to do any given activity will vary because of factors outside a person's control. Variance is a fact of life and must be accepted.

Turf battles are also detrimental to high performance. Team spirit—one of cooperation—must exist, and this must be promoted by senior management. I have known many senior managers who did exactly the opposite. They promoted competition among people in the workplace, believing that this would bring out the best in them. This is a carryover from sports. In sports, competition does tend to bring out the best in people. Unfortunately, it also brings out the worst in them, as we have witnessed in the violence toward fans and other players that sometimes erupts when winning becomes all that matters. And the same thing happens in organizations.

I knew of a textile mill that decided to use competition to improve production. They had a three-shift operation, so the managers told their people that the shift with the highest production for the week would receive an award. All members of that team would get a dinner at a very nice local restaurant. This did initially spark enthusiasm and increase production.

Soon, however, teams became discontented with simply working hard to win. They began to consider how they might create a disadvantage for the other teams—to slow them down. The most obvious thing was to adjust the settings on their machines so that they would not run right. They did this at the end of the shift, so that the people who followed them must waste time resetting the adjustments on all the machines. This gave the preceding team an advantage and enabled it to win.

Of course, it took only a short time for everyone to catch on to what was being done, so each team now left their machines misadjusted at the end of their shift. When management learned what was going on, they established a new rule—a team was eligible for the award only if the team that followed reported that all machines ran properly when the new team came on board!

This is by no means an isolated incident. Alfie Kohn (1999), in a book titled *Punished by Rewards*, wrote that almost all reward systems tend to blow up over time. Employees always try to maximize their rewards, and they will do so at the expense of cooperation and even actual performance. The only legitimate reward system is one in which people are rewarded by true achievement and pride in the work that they do. All carrot-and-stick systems create problems.

This is not a popular notion. Kohn was strongly criticized for his assertions. People want to believe that they can hold carrots in front of people and get them turned on. After more than 50 years of research that demonstrates that money is not an actual motivator, but rather a symbol for those things that really motivate people, there are a lot of people who refuse to accept the results. They cling stubbornly to the belief that you only must pay people well to motivate them.

Daniel Pink (2009) has confirmed what Kohn said in his book. In fact, recent studies have shown that when external incentives are used (pay, and so on), people lose interest in an activity. This means that as soon as those external rewards are no longer available, individuals will no longer engage in the activity. This has profound implications for organizations, including projects. The only true motivation is intrinsic. Write that on your cubicle wall and your bathroom mirror and drill it into your brain. Otherwise, you will go through your career wasting time with motivation methods that *simply don't work!*

I saw this happen in a slightly different setting than industry. One university that I worked with decided to make our project management certificate program more credible, so he announced that you had to pass an exam following each course. When that was announced, students only cared about maximizing their score on the exam. They no longer cared about learning to manage; they just wanted high scores. My perception was that it devalued the courses significantly.

To return to the central premise of this section, a negative environment will not produce good project results. And, while project managers are limited in how much influence they exert over the work environment, they should be aware of those factors that contribute to the environmental climate and do their best to make the project environment as positive as they can. In general, the most important thing they can do is try to match team members with work that they find enjoyable and challenging. And they should strenuously try to create a climate of mutual respect and cooperation.

As a general guideline, I would recommend practicing the principles developed by the former president and CEO of Boeing Commercial Airplanes, Alan Mulally (later, CEO at Ford). These were documented in my book *Working Together* (Lewis, 2002), and I will not repeat them here (as that would require inserting a full book into this chapter!). When applied properly, they mitigate many of the concerns that I have expressed in this chapter. Mulally applied these principles at Ford, and between 2006

> The only legitimate reward system is one in which people are rewarded by true achievement and pride in the work that they do.

and 2009 he moved them from losing $46 million every day of the week to profitability, and he maintained it until he retired in 2014. Three years after his successor was made CEO he was fired; he did not maintain the gains.

Finally, developing High-Performance Project Management does not happen overnight, anymore than a championship team can be developed overnight. It takes time and hard work.

The benefits are worth the investment.

IN SUMMARY

High performance is achieved through the joint optimization of tools, people, and systems, represented in this chapter as a Venn diagram. You must avoid optimizing the individual components without considering the effect this will have on the other two. As an example, we sometimes install rewards that promote behavior that reduces performance in another domain of a project or department.

Senior managers must also support formal approaches to managing projects. Failure to do so has been found to result in project managers leaving the company out of frustration.

Another issue that must be addressed is the capacity of the business to handle the workload that results from doing too many projects simultaneously. Priorities must be established and honored.

CHAPTER 5

Whole-Brain®
Project Management

You can't solve a problem with the
same thinking that caused it.

—ALBERT EINSTEIN

N o doubt most of you have heard about left-brain/right-brain orientations in thinking. Left-brain thinkers are more analytical, logical, and sequential than right-brain thinkers, who are more parallel, intuitive, and global thinkers.

Does this matter to project managers? If so, how do you make use of it?

To answer this question, I'll share an experience with you. I once hired an engineer who worked for a very prestigious company. He was supposed to design communications equipment. During the interview, I asked him a number of questions about communications technology, which he answered flawlessly. Unfortunately, he didn't know how to translate the theory into design practice. In a word, his design work was inadequate.

At the time I had no training in psychology, so I had no idea what was wrong. However, I knew that his former position had been a manufacturing engineering job in which he had helped to solve problems with products that were already in manufacturing. I offered to transfer him to an equivalent job on the basis that if he had done satisfactory work in such a job previously, then he should work well for us.

He saw this transfer as a demotion and refused it. Then he worked for another project manager for a time before returning to my project. The other manager had similar problems with him.

His performance deficit finally came to a head. We gave him the option of finding another job, taking the transfer, or being terminated. He chose to find another job.

What I didn't know then, but do now, is that the design job requires a different type of thinking from the manufacturing support job. The design engineer must be able to think in terms of synthesis, whereas the manufacturing engineer must think more analytically. Synthesis is a right-brain mode, and analysis is a left-brain mode. So I had actually hired the wrong person for the job based on his thinking preferences (and ability). Now, exactly what does this mean?

THINKING STYLES

Ned Herrmann was a training manager at General Electric's Crotonville Management Training Center. Ned was originally educated as a physicist, but he was very interested in the social sciences, especially, in art. He was a gifted painter.

He heard about research that indicated that the two hemispheres of the brain seem to control different kinds of thinking and wondered how those differences might affect learning, management, creativity, and other aspects of human performance. Because the field was in its infancy, Ned had to do a lot of research himself. He found that the left/right dichotomy did not suffice to explain thinking differences, and he postulated another axis based on cerebral/limbic thinking (Herrmann, 1995, 1996). When this dimension is added, you have four pure styles that combine to yield a wide range of different thinking styles. Ned developed an instrument that measures these preferences, called the Herrmann Brain Dominance Instrument (HBDI®),* and the respondent receives a profile like the one shown in Figure 5.1.

Figure 5.1 HBDI® Profile of Thinking Styles

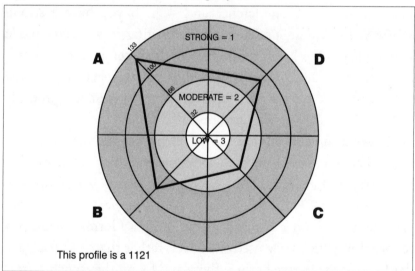

This profile is a 1121

© 2010 by Herrmann International. The profile grid is a trademark of Herrmann International. Used with permission.

In this profile, there are four concentric circles or bands, divided into about 33 points per band, so raw scores range from 0 to 133. However, to give a person a raw score implies a measurement

---

* HBDI® is a registered trademark of the Ned Herrmann Group, Inc.

precision that simply does not exist, so Ned chose to give a ranking instead. The outer two bands have a rank of 1, meaning that the person has a very strong preference for thinking in the specific mode. The next band has a rank of 2, which is weaker but still significant. Finally, the inner band yields a rank of 3, which is a very low preference. In fact, a score in this band indicates that the individual may actually reject this mode of thinking most of the time. There is no such thing as a 0 rank, as everyone uses all four modes to some degree. Note also that the instrument measures *preferences*, not skills or abilities.

> The HBDI® profile measures one's preference for thinking in certain ways, not one's ability to do so.

However, there is a correlation between preference and skill. If you have a strong preference for engaging in a certain mode of thinking, you will tend to do so frequently, and thus you will get pretty good at it. So, over time, preference probably does lead to skill.

Herrmann believed that the preference for the various thinking modes was based on brain physiology, which involves both chemistry and genetics, but whether this is true is still open to question. In the January 2005 issue of *Scientific American*'s special publication on the mind, research by a German team was reported in which they used the MRI, rather than just the standard EEG, to observe brain activity and found that specific areas of the brain do not correlate cleanly with specific kinds of thinking. Rather, various stimuli activated multiple parts of the brain at once. Thus, the idea of left-right hemispheres and limbic versus cerebral as determinants of certain types of thinking may not be accurate, but this is not important for our purposes. The fact is that four distinct modes of thinking have been identified and the HBDI® profile does a good job of measuring them.

At this time the Herrmann International database contains more than a half million profiles of people who have taken the HBDI® assessment. Most find that the measures represent them fairly well. Seldom does anyone say, "That's just not me!"

Profiles

As you might expect, an individual can have a preference for thinking in only one of the four modes. The HBDI® profile for such a person, called *single-dominant*, looks a bit like a kite, so we sometimes refer to a profile as a kite. Only about 5 percent of the population is single-dominant. A sample profile is shown in Figure 5.2.

Figure 5.2   A Single-Dominant HBDI® Profile

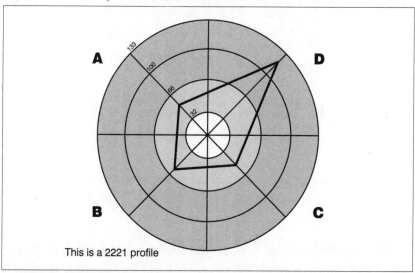

This is a 2221 profile

When an individual likes to think in two modes, the profile is called *double-dominant*, and there are two forms that the kite can take. In one, the two preferred quadrants are side by side; in the other, they are diagonally opposite each other. The two possibilities are shown in Figure 5.3. Naturally, the adjacent preferences can be both left, both right, both top, or both bottom quadrants, and the diagonally opposite can be A to C or B to D. Double-dominant preferences account for about 56 percent of the population.

Figure 5.3   Double-Dominant HBDI® Profiles

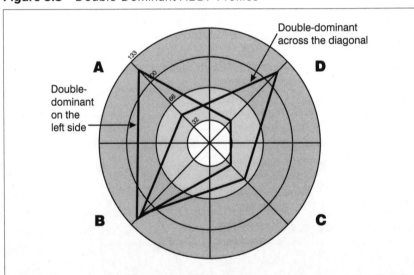

© 2010 by Herrmann International. The profile grid is a trademark of Herrmann International.

The *triple-dominant* profile can be any three adjacent quadrants, and approximately 36 percent of the population falls into this category. A triple-dominant profile is shown in Figure 5.4.

Figure 5.4 The Triple-Dominant HBDI® Profile

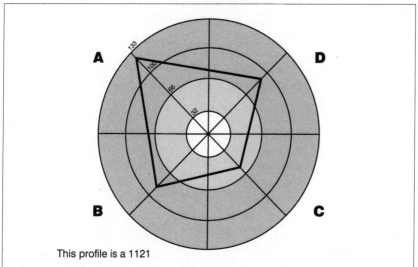

This profile is a 1121

© 2010 by Herrmann International. The profile grid is a trademark of Herrmann International.

Finally, a mere 3 percent of the population prefers to think in all four quadrants, and of course this profile is called *quadruple-dominant*. Such individuals are called multidominant translators, and Ned believed that they should make excellent CEOs, because they can interact effectively with people from each of the quadrants. This may be hard to demonstrate, since the number of people with this profile is so small, and of those people who are quadruple-dominant, only a certain percentage will ever become CEOs, so we may never know if they are good candidates. Furthermore, one's thinking preferences do not guarantee that she will be able to deal effectively with others, so thinking is only part of the picture. A quadruple-dominant profile is shown in Figure 5.5.

Figure 5.5   A Quadruple-Dominant HBDI® Profile

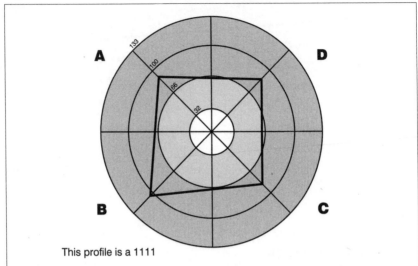

This profile is a 1111

© 2010 by Herrmann International. The profile grid is a trademark of Herrmann International. Used with permission.

What are the differences between the four modes, and how do these differences affect various work functions in a project? Since the model is a grid containing four quadrants, each of which represents a different thought mode, we will begin in the upper left, or A quadrant, and explain each mode by progressing in a counterclockwise direction through the quadrants. Note that the progression is A-B-C-D and that in the profile received by respondents, each quadrant is colored, in the sequence blue-green-red-yellow.

The A Quadrant

The thinking associated with the A quadrant can be described as logical, analytical, technical, mathematical, and problem solving (see Figure 5.6). Such thinking can be thought of as dealing with facts and figures. It seems reasonable that people who like dealing with facts and figures would be attracted to jobs or professions that require such thinking, and this is true. Examples of such careers include technical, legal, and financial areas (including accounting and tax law), engineering, information technology, science, mathematics, and the analytical aspects of management.

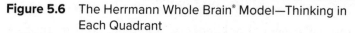

Figure 5.6   The Herrmann Whole Brain® Model—Thinking in Each Quadrant

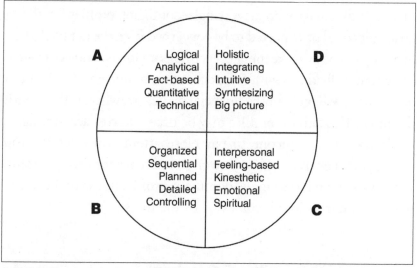

A project manager with a single-dominant profile in quadrant A could be expected to be very logical, interested in technical issues affecting the project, inclined to analyze status reports carefully, and keen on problem solving. Such a project manager may be seen as cold, uncaring, and interested only in the problems presented by the project. However, since only 5 percent of the population is single-dominant, such project managers should be correspondingly rare.

The B Quadrant

The B quadrant is similar to the A quadrant, but with some significant differences. Words that describe B-quadrant thinkers are organizational, administrative, conservative, controlled, and planning. This is the preferred thinking mode of many managers, administrators, planners, bookkeepers, foremen, and manufacturers. Individuals who have single-dominant profiles in the B quadrant could be expected to be concerned with the detailed plans of a project and with keeping everything organized and controlled. Note that individuals with financial interests who are dominant in quadrant A will probably be financial managers, whereas those with dominant B-quadrant profiles may be drawn to cost accounting.

If you want someone to pay close attention to details, you want someone who displays a strong preference for this quadrant. If such a person has a single-dominant profile, however, he or she may see the trees and be unaware of the forest.

The C Quadrant

People with single-dominant profiles in the A or B quadrant probably see individuals with strong C-quadrant preferences as being very "touchy-feely." Words that describe this quadrant are interpersonal, emotional, musical, spiritual, and talkative. Individuals with single-dominant C profiles are very "feeling" and people-oriented. They are often nurses, social workers, musicians, teachers, counselors, or ministers.

A project manager with a single-dominant C profile would naturally be concerned with the interpersonal aspects of the project, perhaps to the detriment of getting the work done. Such an individual would be drawn to the coordination of project activities with people both inside and outside the team and would be a relationship builder. This would be a good bias to have for highly political projects, if other members of the team are attending to the work itself.

In fact, you will remember that we have said several times that projects are people, and dealing with people is one aspect of project management that some individuals find distasteful. So you could expect that this aspect of the job will bother the person who has very low C-quadrant scores on the HBDI® profile. My counsel is that you can develop the skill if you have the desire, but very low scores in the C quadrant naturally mean that this is not your "cup of tea." So you will have to work very hard at this aspect of the job if you want to manage projects.

There is an interesting finding about how we behave in terms of our least preferred thinking styles. I have a very strong D-quadrant preference, with B-quadrant being my least preferred. This means that I love developing concepts and dislike doing detail work. However, if I must do detail work in order to get one of my ideas to see the light of day, then I am very motivated to do so. This means that you can be motivated to deal with the "touchy-feely" stuff if it means achieving success in terms of your other thinking preferences.

The D Quadrant

Words that describe this quadrant are artistic, holistic, imaginative, synthesizers, and conceptualizers. Individuals who have single-dominant D-quadrant profiles are often drawn to careers that involve entrepreneurial effort, facilitation, advising, or consulting, being sales leaders and artists. These are the "idea" people in a team, and they enjoy synthesizing ideas from several sources to create something new from that combination.

This is the natural domain of people who are perceived to be creative. At the beginning of this chapter, we discussed the need for creative thinking in projects. So you may conclude that if you are primarily a left-brain thinker, with strong preferences for A- or B-quadrant thinking and a low preference for thinking in the D quadrant, then you are out of luck. Not so. It turns out that it is easier for left-brain thinkers to learn to do conceptual or "creative" thinking than it is for conceptual thinkers to learn analytical or detail thinking.

Project managers who have single-dominant D-quadrant profiles could be expected to be "big picture" in their thinking—they run the risk of seeing the forest without realizing that it consists of distinct trees. They are generally good at thinking strategically, so in planning a project, the D-quadrant thinker will develop a game plan but will need help from B-quadrant thinkers to make it workable.

Double-Dominant Profiles and Project Management Styles

Since only 5 percent of our population has single-dominant profiles, it would seem more reasonable to examine multidominant profiles. The simplest analysis would be for double-dominant profiles because they comprise 56 percent of the population, and this will give us insight into a host of project managers. A diagram showing the characteristics of each of the adjacent-quadrant double-dominant profiles appears in Figure 5.7.

Figure 5.7 Management Styles of Single- and Double-Dominant
Managers Using the Herrmann Model

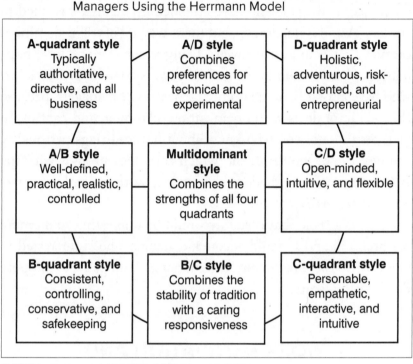

© 2010 by Herrmann International. Used by permission.

Is There a Project Manager Profile?

There are certain profiles that are known to be correlated with specific professions. For example, life scientists tend to have double-dominant profiles that are high in the A and D quadrants. In other words, they are analytical and conceptual thinkers. Social workers tend to have strong preferences for thinking in quadrants C and D, with a slightly stronger preference for C (the interpersonal quadrant) than for D. So it is reasonable to ask if there is a profile that correlates with project management as a profession.

The answer is still unknown. The overall population profile for project managers who have attended my seminars is tilted to the left (A and B quadrants), but there are a lot of triple-dominant profiles that help pull it toward being square for the total population. What we do know is that there is a tendency for people who have strong B-quadrant preferences to be managers, because this quadrant deals with organization, planning, and control. In fact, for those of you who know about Myers-Briggs personality profiles, the SJ temperament, which correlates strongly with the B quadrant, is strongly dominant among both general managers and project managers.

This is a topic that certainly would be interesting to do more research on, and I would encourage anyone who is interested to work with the Herrmann International Company to propose doing such research.

WORK MOTIVATION AND THE HBDI® PROFILE

One aspect of thinking preferences that you should consider is that you probably have a least-preferred thinking style (or several). Mine is the B quadrant, which requires great attention to detail. I would find a project requiring such thinking to be drudgery. When I was an engineer, I disliked the detailed work involved in reviewing drawings or making sure that a bill of materials was exactly right. It was vital work, but I hated it. So knowing your most preferred and least preferred thinking styles should help you determine when a particular kind of project is a good match for you, or what you should do when there is a mismatch.

It is important to note that each quadrant contains five or more clusters of thinking and that each of us may prefer some but not all of them. So for me, doing detail work is not desirable. However, I am very organized when it comes to teaching seminars, and I most definitely want to be sure that all the details have been covered; I just don't want to have to manage them personally. I am also attracted to the idea of being in control, so this part of the quadrant appeals to me, and I am compulsively on time for appointments, whereas the tendency of strong D-quadrant thinkers (which I am) is to be poor time managers and frequently late for appointments.

It is very interesting to note that people's *motivation* to do work is derived from their preferred quadrants. If the preference is single-dominant, you will have a single motivation pattern. If your profile is double-dominant, you will have two patterns, and so on. These patterns of activity motivate a person. As an example, a person with a strong preference for thinking in the D quadrant may be very innovative. A person whose preference is the A quadrant may be a good troubleshooter, which requires analytical thinking.

> People are motivated to engage in various patterns of activity, and these are derived from their preferred thinking modes.

Thus, a person's profile is a pretty good indication of the kind of activities that motivate her. If you understand the characteristics of the job, you will know whether it is likely to motivate the person or not.

Is There a Best Profile?

Ned Herrmann was always careful to say that individuals with almost any profile *can* do most jobs. The HBDI® profile displays one's *preference* for thinking, not one's *ability*. As I pointed out earlier, there is a relationship, but presumably a person with any profile can develop the ability to think in all four modes and become skilled enough to be able to perform in any job.

Also, as I mentioned earlier, Ned did postulate that there may be an ideal profile for a CEO, that being a square—a quadruple-dominant profile. The reason is easy to understand. A CEO must deal with people who think in all four quadrants, and if she prefers to think in all four, then she can translate between them for all parties involved.

I met one such individual, and sure enough, he was a turnaround CEO who specialized in saving hospitals from financial disaster. Unlike some individuals who specialize in turnarounds, this man tried to employ measures that saved as many jobs as possible. The turnaround CEO with very low C-quadrant thinking is often concerned only with the bottom line, and the quickest way to improve financial performance is to eliminate jobs, regardless of the cost in human suffering. Naturally such a CEO will justify such action by saying that sacrificing a few jobs is better for everyone in the long run.

As I mentioned earlier, the Herrmann group pulled a composite profile for all of the project managers that they had in their database, and that overall profile was square. They had 1,250 profiles for project managers, with the population being almost perfectly split 50–50 between men and women. These profiles are shown in Figures 5.8 and 5.9. For the overall population, there is a small tilt toward the A quadrant for men and a small tilt toward the C quadrant for women, and this was also true of the profiles for project managers.

This suggests that project managers come in all shapes and sizes. There has to be a fairly even distribution of profiles to get a composite square, so the distribution for project managers is not very different from that for the population in general.

Figure 5.8 HBDI® Composite Profile for Female Project Managers

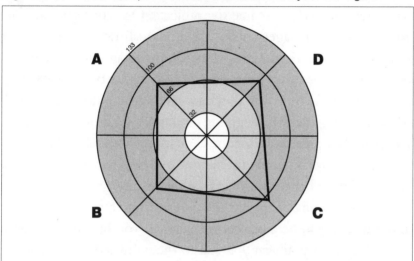

© 2010 by Herrmann International. The profile grid is a trademark of Herrmann International. Used with permission.

Figure 5.9 HBDI® Composite Profile for Male Project Managers

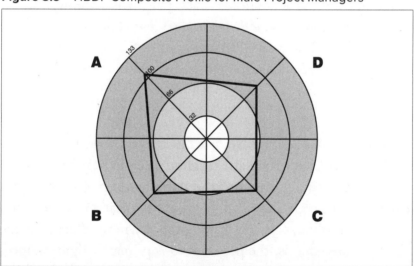

© 2010 by Herrmann International. The profile grid is a trademark of Herrmann International. Used with permission.

As has been stated earlier, an individual's thinking preference will affect his style of managing projects. One concern would be with project managers who have very little preference for C-quadrant thinking, the reason being the age-old problem of project managers: they have a lot of responsibility and very little authority, so the only way they can get anything done is through influence, negotiation, begging, and selling. Project managers with very low preference for the C quadrant are inclined to say, "I hate dealing with people problems," and to them I suggest that they rethink whether they truly want to manage projects. This would be the one deficit that should enter into a person's decision about whether to be a project manager. If you hate dealing with people, then why subject yourself to the daily agony that you are sure to experience as a project manager?

> Your profile will affect your style of managing projects, and this could affect your success in certain environments, but any profile can be effective in project management.
>
> I believe that the project manager with a primarily right-brain preference has an advantage over other profiles in most situations.

Is there a *best* profile? No, not in a universal sense.

In a recent seminar that I taught, titled "Whole Brain® Project Management," I discussed the attributes of project managers having various profiles, and I concluded that of the double-dominant profiles, the one that is probably most effective is the C-D profile—that is, the person who is primarily right-brained. Because project managers must use influence to get things done, they need strong C-quadrant thinking. Furthermore, project managers have a major responsibility to help a team develop a shared understanding of the vision for the project outcome, and this requires a strong D-quadrant focus.

I also believe that a project manager is primarily a leader and facilitator. For that reason, she need not be highly analytical, or be a very strong planner or organizer, as long as she recognizes the need for such thinking and gets the team to do it. In fact, I believe that project managers who are strong in the A and B quadrants may be inclined to get too bogged down in technology or detail, and to possibly do too much of the planning rather than having the team do it, and this is not always good.

As a matter of fact, I have now met quite a few quadruple-dominant individuals, and although they may be good translators between the quadrants, they seem to me to have trouble making decisions. The simple reason is that they try too hard to cover all of the quadrants and to consider all of the issues in each one, and in doing so, they become paralyzed. I'm not certain that this is true, and I would love to hear from any of my readers who can add insight into this question. Write me at lewisinstituteinc@yahoo.com.

FORMING TEAMS USING THE HBDI® PROFILE

One application of the HBDI® profile that is now well documented is its use in assembling teams. A team should collectively represent a "whole brain," meaning that if you overlay the profiles of all members of the team, they will form a composite profile that shows preferences in all four quadrants. If instead they have a strong aversion to one of the quadrants, you could expect that issues requiring thinking in that area may not be handled very well. However, a word of caution is in order. Ned found that whole-brain, gender-balanced teams produce better solutions and work than homogeneous or single-gender teams. However, you can also expect much more debate to take place because people approach each situation from their own perspective, and team members with multiple perspectives have a hard time reaching agreement.

As I've noted, many teams do not collectively represent a whole brain. For example, technical groups often have a profile like that shown in Figure 5.10. They are strong in the A, B, and D quadrants and weak in C—the one having to do with interpersonal matters.

Figure 5.10   HBDI® Average Profile for a Technical Team

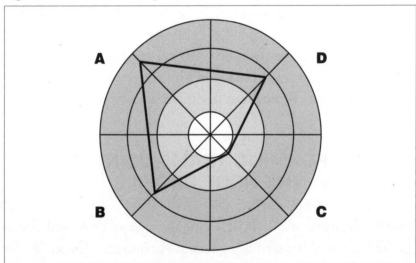

© 2010 by Herrmann International. The profile grid is a trademark of Herrmann International. Used with permission.

This means that they may attend very well to technical issues, are good at details, and generate good ideas, but they neglect the "touchy-feely" attributes, and this may undermine their team's performance. What should they do?

The important thing is that they be aware of the profile and know how to compensate for the low preference in quadrant C. Remember, it is not that they *can't* think in this quadrant but that they simply don't have a strong preference for doing so. If they can understand that failing to deal with quadrant-C issues is going to cause them problems in dealing with what they really care about (namely, technical matters), then they are more likely to spend time working on such issues.

> When a team lacks a "whole brain," members must learn to "walk into" the least-preferred quadrant and cover issues that are relevant to that quadrant.

Figure 5.11 offers another example. This time we have a very creative group of people; they love ideas, are interpersonal, and like doing analytical work—but they dislike detail. We can expect that they will generate good ideas but have trouble executing them, at least as far as the details are concerned. It is said that "the devil is in the details," and the devil may just get this group!

Again, however, if team members are aware of the low quadrant-B score for the team, they can compensate by working hard to ensure that details are not overlooked.

Figure 5.11   HBDI® Average Profile for a Creative Team

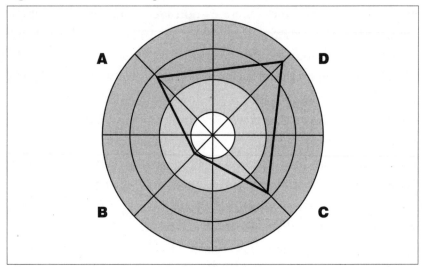

© 2010 by Herrmann International. The profile grid is a trademark of Herrmann International. Used with permission.

Team Dynamics

A project team is meeting to discuss an important project issue—a missed milestone. Everyone is a little apprehensive. They aren't sure how senior management is going to react to their failure to complete project work on schedule.

Wanda says, "I don't see how we could have done any better. We did everything humanly possible to complete the work on time. I feel really bummed out over the whole thing!"

"In looking at the numbers," Chuck says, "I believe we were set up to begin with. We were allocated to the project at a 95 percent rate, which is too high."

"I didn't like the concept we started with in the first place," chimes in Karen. "It was too flaky."

Don had been studying the schedule. "We should have moved these two tasks in parallel," he offers. "Then we could have finished on time."

This sets Wanda off. "You're always changing the plan, Don," she insists. "Can't you see that we did everything we could to meet the deadline?"

"But the schedule is the most important part of the project plan," Don says defensively. "If we don't use the schedule properly, we can't hope to complete the work on time. It's a question of being better organized."

"It doesn't matter how well organized we are if the concept is no good to begin with," Karen interjects.

At this point, the project manager, Beth, interrupts. "Okay, let's calm down for a moment," she says. "And let's look at what's going on."

They all lean back in their chairs and wait for Beth to continue.

"Wanda, you're concerned about the effort you've put into the job, and you're feeling a little guilty that it didn't pay off," Beth says. "In terms of your HBDI® profile, you're thinking in the C quadrant."

Wanda nods in agreement.

"And Karen, you're in the D quadrant, thinking conceptually, as usual," Beth says.

Karen smiles and nods. Beth has her pegged.

Beth continues around the table. "Naturally, Don is concerned about the schedule. He's a predominantly B-quadrant thinker, and Chuck is analyzing the numbers—his normal A-quadrant thinking."

Everyone laughs.

"The bad news is that each of us sees the situation from a different perspective," Beth continues. "And the good news is that each of us sees the situation from a different perspective."

She pauses to let the impact of her comment sink in.

"That's true," Karen says. "If we all saw it the same way, we would probably fall into 'groupthink' and really get into trouble."

"Exactly!" Beth says. "We need every perspective in order to be an effective team, but our different styles make us think that other people don't understand what we're talking about, and we get into conflict."

They all murmur their agreement.

"Now let's see if we can use our varying points of view to get a handle on this project," Beth suggests. "How about if we come back to Karen's contention that the concept is flawed. She's right. If it is, then the detailed plan can't be any good."

From this point on, the meeting proceeds to a solution.

By understanding the fact that each member of the team sees the project in different ways, based on their individual thinking styles, Beth is able to draw on those preferences to the benefit of the project. Were she unaware of these thinking preferences, she would probably see the team as dysfunctional and be tempted to disband it altogether, or perhaps ask a group facilitator to help her keep them in line.

Of course, this scenario has been framed somewhat unrealistically. I have treated each individual team member as though he or she had a single-dominant thinking style. Most of us think in more than one quadrant, but it is true that there may be a quadrant that does dominate our thinking. When we communicate with others who are in different quadrants from our own, we have difficulties.

The opposite is also true. A couple of years ago, I met a fellow with whom I seemed to have almost instant rapport. We saw eye to eye on so many things that it was almost scary. At that time, I was aware of the HBDI® profile, but I had not yet been certified as a practitioner, so it didn't occur to me that this could be the source of our easy communication and understanding. I did know the Myers-Briggs, and I found that we had similar temperaments. In any case, we became good friends.

After I became certified, I sent a survey to my friend, and to our amazement, his profile and mine are congruent to within a few points in every quadrant! No wonder we think so much alike. Naturally, we don't agree on everything, but the similarities are striking.

The danger for us, of course, is that we may agree on an issue too quickly, without exercising the critical thinking that might change our opinions. As Beth told her team, we need opposing points of view to achieve a balanced perspective on issues.

Managing Conflict

If a team is to have creative capacity, it must be able to generate many ideas so that one good one will emerge. These ideas must be screened and the best one selected. During the screening process, various ideas are critiqued, and it is at this point that conflict sometimes turns nasty.

There is a sense that, if you criticize my idea, you are finding fault with me. So I respond by getting angry. Next thing you know, we are locked in an interpersonal conflict. These are often labeled as *personality conflicts*, and in a sense they are. But they have a fundamental cause—we see things differently, and we identify with our points of view and the ideas we have.

A project leader has to get people to generate ideas and manage the critiquing of these conflicting ideas so that they don't develop into interpersonal conflicts. If such conflicts do develop, as they sometimes will, the project manager then has to resolve them, and if people understand the concept of thinking preferences, this will be somewhat easier than it would be otherwise.

THE BALANCED SCORECARD

Kaplan and Norton (1996) developed the concept of using a balanced scorecard to measure the effectiveness of an organization. This concept can also be used to measure project performance. The idea is that most measures focus exclusively on the financial aspects of the business and fail to consider other important factors, such as long-term strategies, developing human resources, knowledge management, and so on.

When you think about this, it is clear that the Herrmann model can be used to measure project performance. Each quadrant represents a domain of concern for project and/or organization performance.

> Develop a whole-brain® balanced scorecard for a project so that you can measure success from the perspective of each quadrant.

The A quadrant deals with the familiar financial measures and other numerical data. The B quadrant focuses on policies, procedures, and controls. The C quadrant provides a focus on people—training and development of employees and maintaining good relations with customers, clients, and key suppliers. The D quadrant concerns long-range planning—positioning the organization or project for the future and dealing with concepts, strategies, and the "big picture."

In planning a project, it is important to decide what outcomes should be achieved in each quadrant, and what evidence will be used to show that these outcomes have been achieved. In other words, you should ask:

- What is the desired outcome?
- How will we know that it has been achieved?

Once you know the desired outcomes and how you will know that they have been achieved, you can develop plans to get you there. This approach will help you avoid focusing only on financials.

As an example, a project may meet all PCTS targets and still be judged negatively by a major stakeholder. This may be because he was not treated as he expected to be treated (C quadrant). By paying attention to C-quadrant factors from the very beginning, such missteps can be avoided.

Figure 5.12 shows a general example of the factors that might be considered in a balanced scorecard for a project.

Figure 5.12   A Balanced Scorecard for a Project, Based on the Herrmann Model

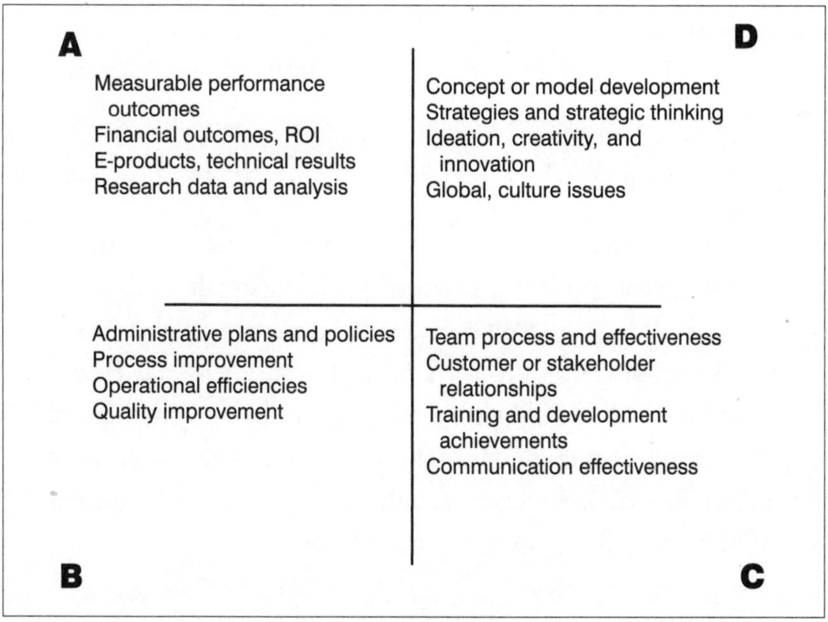

A	**D**
Measurable performance outcomes Financial outcomes, ROI E-products, technical results Research data and analysis	Concept or model development Strategies and strategic thinking Ideation, creativity, and innovation Global, culture issues
Administrative plans and policies Process improvement Operational efficiencies Quality improvement	Team process and effectiveness Customer or stakeholder relationships Training and development achievements Communication effectiveness
B	**C**

© 2010 by Herrmann International. Used by permission.

Creativity and Profiles

It is tempting to think that creativity is primarily derived from the D quadrant, but this is not true. In teaching creative thinking during my HBDI® seminars, I have found that people in every quadrant can be creative—*in line with the preferred thinking of that quadrant!* Thus, people in the A quadrant will be creative in terms of analysis or financial matters, or some other aspect of the quadrant. Similarly, the B quadrant is expressed in developing creative processes, controls, or plans. C can be creative in terms of human interactions, music, or reading people. And of course D can generate lots of ideas for new products, services, businesses, and so on. So don't believe for a moment that you aren't creative because you are low in D-quadrant preference. Give yourself permission to be creative in whatever mode you prefer to think in.

 IN SUMMARY

There are many applications of the Whole-Brain® model in managing projects, because projects involve all kinds of work. We have only scratched the surface in this chapter. I encourage you to read Ned's book, *The Whole Brain® Business Book* (2015), for a more complete exposition of the many applications. And check out the Herrmann International website, www.hbdi.com. It offers a number of resources that you may find useful.

SECTION TWO

PROJECT DEFINITION

CHAPTER 6

Headless-Chicken Projects and How to Prevent Them

W hen I was a boy, we lived in the country for a few years, and my parents kept some chickens around. In those days, if you wanted fried chicken for lunch on Sunday, you didn't go to a grocery store and buy a processed chicken. Instead, you caught one in the backyard and whacked its head off—that was your lunch (after cooking it, of course).

When you cut off a chicken's head, the body runs around spewing blood for a few seconds, then it falls over and quivers a bit, and the chicken is "officially" dead. It is actually dead when you cut off its head, but it takes some time for the message to reach the rest of the body.

Projects can be like that.

We whack off the project's "head" during initiation, and it runs around for a while spewing blood. Then it finally falls over, quivers a bit, and becomes still.

Someone says, "I think that project is dead."

It is. It was dead from the very beginning, but like the chicken, it takes a while for the message to reach the body.

I call these "headless-chicken" projects.

No doubt you have seen one yourself. They're all around us: projects that are doomed before they get started because we whack off their heads at the beginning.

THE COLD, HARD FACTS

Every year, the Standish Group (www.standishgroup.com) surveys software development projects in the United States. How many succeeded, failed, or were changed dramatically? Results from a survey that was done in 1994 by the Standish Group are shown in Figure 6.1. As you can see, 83 percent of all projects suffered serious problems in 1994, with nearly a third of them being bad enough to be canceled. That means that of the $250 billion spent on software development in 1994, about $80 billion was wasted.

Since this data was collected almost 30 years ago, you would expect that the situation must be greatly improved now, but in the most recent report, this figure is more or less unchanged from 1994—less than 20 percent of IT projects succeed.

> Projects are perfectly planned to fail from the beginning.

How can that be? Microsoft has sold millions of copies of Microsoft Project, and thousands of people have been trained in project management. I know of six companies with collective revenues of well over $100 million a year in project management training. So with all that progress, surely the success rate must be higher. Not so. What does seem to have changed is that companies cancel losing projects sooner than they did in 1994.

Figure 6.1   Standish Group Survey Results

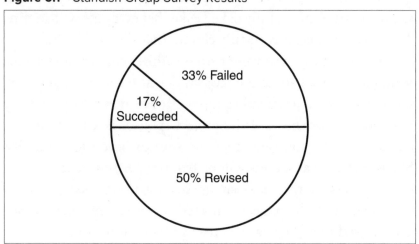

This is a sad situation, to be sure, and it corresponds to what I reported in Chapter 4, namely, that training does not transfer back to the job. This means that hundreds of millions of dollars a year are being wasted on training that does not result in better job performance! It's a scary thought—if I got paid for results, I would have starved long ago, or had to find a new profession.

I have already discussed the reasons why training doesn't transfer (in Chapter 4). So let's focus on the reasons for headless-chicken projects.

THE CAUSES

What causes headless-chicken projects?

First, consider how projects are launched. In many cases, the project sponsor conceives the need for the project. A project manager is recruited to do the job. She is told about the sponsor's concept, which both find very exciting. Of course, the sponsor has only a half-baked idea, but he is certain that the project manager can turn it into a fully baked cake that everyone will admire. The project manager is equally certain that she can do this.

She assembles a team and with breathless enthusiasm tells the team members all about the project. She also congratulates them on being selected for membership on this team, for they are truly the chosen ones; because the project sponsor is a high-ranking manager in the company, they are sure to have high visibility. She is certain that success will be handsomely rewarded.

Members of the team sit in rapt attention, nodding their agreement with the project manager's words of anticipation. She is overjoyed that they have so readily "bought in" to the general concept of the job, and she sends them forth to do the work, fully confident that they are bound for glory.

They leave the room, walking side by side down the hall, going back to their desks. Unknown to the project manager, one of the chosen team members, Matthew, asks Karen, "Did you understand what Heather was talking about?"

"I don't have a clue," Karen says, shaking her head.

"Boy, I was hoping you understood her," Matthew says. "Because I didn't get it at all. Maybe Susan got it," he says, as he notices Susan walking ahead of them.

"Hey, Susan, can we ask you a question?" Matthew asks.

"Sure." Susan pauses to wait for them.

"We were wondering if you understood what Heather wants us to do," Karen tells her. "Neither Matthew nor I have a clue."

Susan shakes her head, an obvious expression of dismay on her face. "I don't either," she admits. "But I was sure I was the only one in the group who was confused, so that's why I didn't say anything."

"I thought the same thing," Matthew confesses. "I guess none of us really understood, but we were all afraid to say so."

The Abilene Paradox

This is an example of what Jerry Harvey (1988) calls the Abilene Paradox. Harvey made up a story about a family that lives in Texas. One hot Sunday morning, the family members are sitting around, bored to death because they have nothing to do.

Someone asks, "What do you want to do today?"

Another member of the family suggests, "How about if we go to Abilene and have lunch at the cafeteria?"

Next thing you know, they all pile into an old car with no air conditioning. It's 110 degrees in the shade, but driving 75 miles an hour with the windows down creates enough of a breeze to make the 90-mile drive bearable.

They have lunch. Not a very good lunch. A cafeteria lunch.

Following the mediocre meal, they go out onto the streets of Abilene, only to find that there is nothing to do.

Now they are bored in Abilene.

There's nothing to do at this point but go home, so they make the 90-mile blast-furnace trek back home.

They park the car, and as they walk back to the house, someone says, "Boy, that was a waste of time!"

"I thought you wanted to go," another person protests.

"No, I just went because the rest of you wanted to go," replies the first person.

They look at each other sheepishly and take a poll.

It turns out that nobody *really* wanted to go to Abilene—not even the person who first suggested it. She was only thinking out loud.

They have all made a 180-mile round trip to Abilene for a mediocre meal, when nobody really wanted to go at all! A paradox, to say the least.

Harvey makes a highly significant point about this. He says it appears to be a failure to manage agreement.

It is not. It is a failure to manage *disagreement*!

The reason? They never knew that there *was* any disagreement, because no one said anything. They have fallen into the trap called, "Silence means consent." This is the nature of the Abilene Paradox.

Notice that the same thing happened to our project team. Because no one said anything, the project manager assumed that they were all in agreement and all understood the mission.

They didn't. But they were afraid to say so.

Why?

Probably because they did not individually want to appear stupid to other members of the group. After all, *they could tell* from the smiling faces of their peers on the team that *they* all understood. "Surely," each of them was thinking, "I must be the only team member who doesn't understand."

Overcoming the Abilene Paradox

Notice that the way a project team falls into the Abilene Paradox trap is that the message is delivered in a way that allows the team members to remain passive. Furthermore, they are not yet a true team. They have been brought together to be *told* about the project, and in most cases the project manager does nothing to make them feel that they are a team. She is so excited about the project that she wants to dive right in and get them started. She is completely *task focused*.

This is a pervasive problem. We forget that there are two aspects to all projects—the *what* and the *how*. The *what* is called the task to be performed. *How* it is to be performed is called process. But process also applies to how the team functions in total—how their members communicate, interact, solve problems, deal with conflict, make decisions, make work assignments, run meetings, and every other aspect of team performance.

And the lesson that many managers have not learned is that *process will always affect task performance!* We have understood this in manufacturing for many years. We have applied statistical process control (SPC) to manufacturing to detect process problems. We have worked to improve processes, to eliminate non-value-added steps, and to reduce scrap and rework, and we have even begun to recognize that nonmanufacturing processes should be improved. But we haven't gone far enough. We need to pay as much attention to project processes as we do to task outcomes. If the process is broken or defective, it can't get a positive task outcome.

> Process will *always* affect task performance.

For that reason, we must employ a process that will avoid the Abilene Paradox. The best approach that I know of is to get the team members actively involved in defining the project, which includes examining the problem to be solved and then developing a mission statement that tells where the team is going and a vision for the end result that the members wish to achieve. I have found that the steps in Figure 6.2 meet this requirement.

In this procedure, the team members are told the mission, but are then asked to put it into their own words. Each member writes out what he or she believes the mission to be. They then try to consolidate their individual statements into one that they can all support. This statement is then polished and published. From that point on, every time a question about the team's performance comes up, you ask how to answer the question, take the step, make a decision, or solve a problem in such a way that you support the attainment of the team's mission.

Figure 6.2 The Steps in Developing a Mission Statement

Notice that this procedure makes team members active participants in drafting the statement. Furthermore, once the statement is written, it is used to keep the team on track and to guide them on how to address various issues as they arise. This makes the mission statement an operational, living document.

This is in sharp contrast to what is usually done. In many cases, the mission statement is drafted and then forgotten, leaving everyone wondering what all the fuss was about. In fact, more often than not, the mission is handed to the team and no one ever questions whether it is valid—until the project fails to solve the problem that it is supposed to solve.

Furthermore, I have found that almost every team will have at least one member who is initially going the wrong way, compared to where the team is going. This is shown in Figure 6.3. Ideally, when the team members write out their individual statements and compare them, they will all be going in the same direction— the one represented by the big arrow. This means that they are aligned with the direction to be taken by the project. However, you usually find that someone has a different idea about what the team is supposed to be doing, and unless this discrepancy is resolved, the team will fail.

There are only three things that can be done to resolve the disconnect. The first response is to convince the person to go in the same direction as the others. This may be done through discussions in which any of the individual's misunderstandings are corrected. Or he may need to be convinced of the proper direction.

> Suffer fools gladly. They may be right.
> —Holbrook Jackson

The second response is to change the direction of the entire team. It may well be that the "errant" person has thought of the mission in a way that everyone else

Figure 6.3   Misalignment of One Team Member with the Others

missed. In this case, the team agrees to go in the direction advocated by the individual. This can happen when a paradigm shift occurs. You may recall that the Swiss invented the digital watch. However, they weren't impressed with it—in the eyes of "real" watchmakers, it was just a toy. So they didn't even patent it. When Seiko and Texas Instruments learned about it, they began producing digital watches, and over the next several years the Swiss lost thousands of watchmakers.

Now imagine a team getting ready to design a new watch. One lone member thinks that the team should design a digital watch. The others think he is crazy—a nonteam player who should be thrown off the project. But this is the one person who has it right, and unless they realize this and go in his direction, they will produce another product that is not wanted by the market.

If neither of these responses is possible, the only remaining step is to remove the person from the team. You simply cannot have a successful project when a core team member disagrees with the mission as it is seen by the other members. This may be the most difficult step you will be called upon to take, since you often do not get to choose core team members, but it really is necessary. And you can't kid yourself by thinking that it isn't important. Ensuring that you have a shared understanding of the mission, vision, and problem is the most important action you can take as a project manager. Otherwise, you are certain to have a headless-chicken project.

> The first objective for a project manager is to achieve *a shared understanding* of the team's mission.

But beyond the process offered to avoid the Abilene Paradox, just how do you integrate the problem, mission, and vision statements for a project?

MISSION AND VISION

I have found that there is considerable confusion between the terms *mission* and *vision*. The reason seems to be that we use the terms almost interchangeably. So before we go much further, we should clarify the difference.

Let's begin with something simple. Suppose you have decided to change jobs and are moving to another city, far enough away that you don't plan to commute from where you presently live. So you will have to find a new home, apartment, or condominium. You turn in your resignation, and soon everyone knows that you are leaving. One of your friends passes you in the hallway and says, "Charlie, I hear you're leaving." You acknowledge that this is true.

"You look a bit distracted," says your friend.

"Yes, I have to find a new place to live," you say.

Your friend has apparently been to a project management seminar, because she says, "What is your mission?"

"To find a place to live," you say.

"And how about your vision?" she persists.

"To have a place to live," you reply, somewhat confused.

"Well, those sound the same," she says. She pulls you over to a nearby desk and begins to draw on a sheet of paper. "Suppose we think of it this way. Your problem is that you don't have a place to live in your new town, right?"

You agree. She then sketches the diagram shown in Figure 6.4.

Figure 6.4   The Empty Chevron

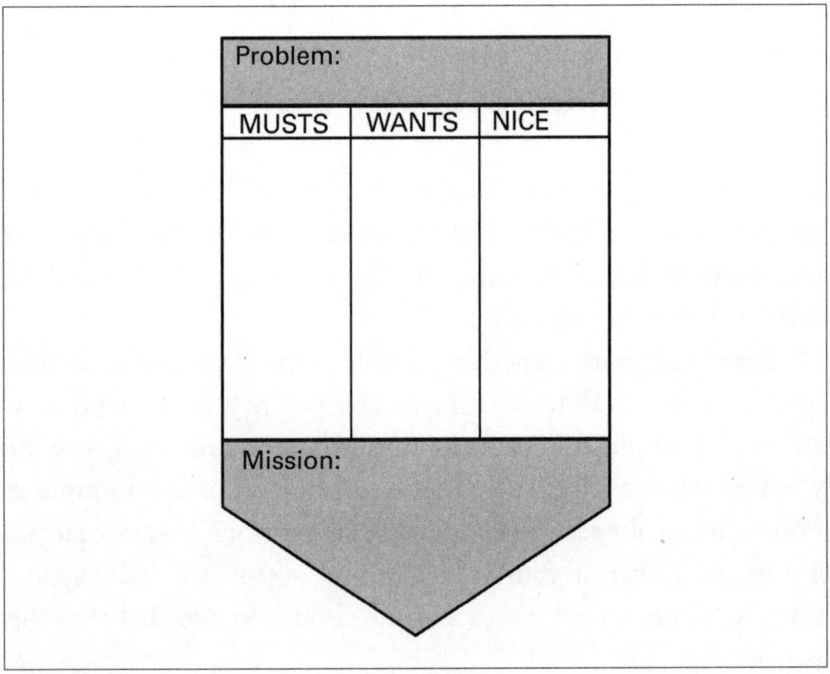

"Let's put your problem statement here," she continues. "And let's state it as a negative. I'll explain why in a moment." She fills in the problem statement as *I have no place to live* (Figure 6.5).

Figure 6.5 Chevron with Problem Statement Entered

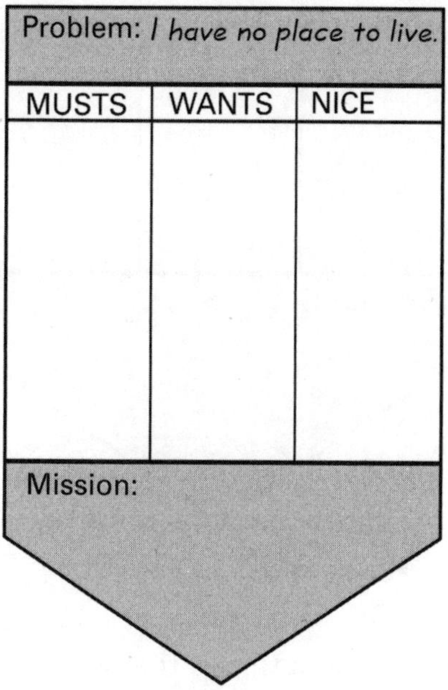

That done, she asks, "Now, do you have an idea in mind for what kind of place you're looking for?"

"Yes, I plan to buy a house," you say.

"Okay. Let's fill in the chevron. What are the characteristics of the house that are nonnegotiable? In other words, what are your must-have features?"

You name several features, and she fills in the must-have section of the chevron (Figure 6.6).

Figure 6.6   Chevron with Must-Have Features Entered

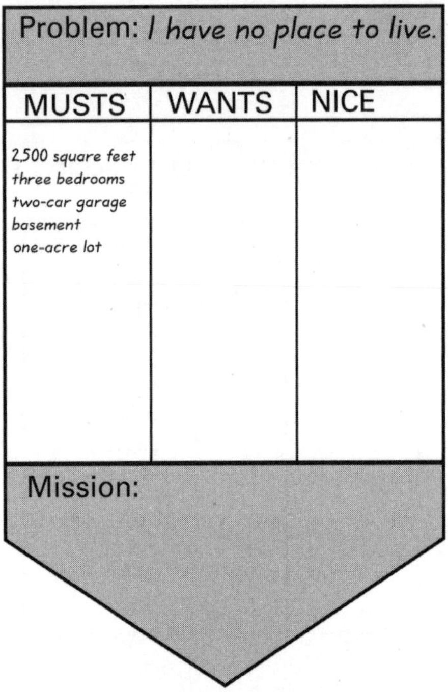

MUSTS	WANTS	NICE

Problem: *I have no place to live.*

2,500 square feet
three bedrooms
two-car garage
basement
one-acre lot

Mission:

"Now, how about some things that you want, but you would be willing to give up if you had to?" she continues.

You name a few such features, and she enters them into the wants section. Then she asks about things that would simply be nice to have and enters these into that part of the diagram. The final result is shown in Figure 6.7

Figure 6.7   Chevron with Wants and Nice-to-Have Features Added

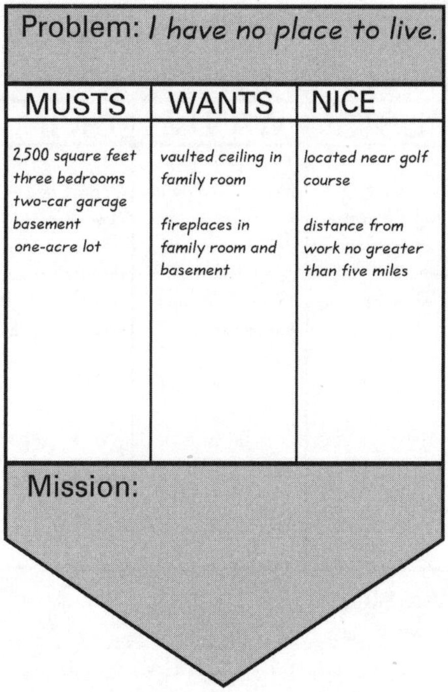

Problem: *I have no place to live.*		
MUSTS	**WANTS**	**NICE**
2,500 square feet three bedrooms two-car garage basement one-acre lot	vaulted ceiling in family room fireplaces in family room and basement	located near golf course distance from work no greater than five miles
Mission:		

She says, "These features constitute your vision for the kind of home you want to buy. And your mission is to find such a place, thereby achieving your vision." She pauses for you to think and then adds, "If you do these two things, then your problem is solved, agreed?"

You do agree. And the result is as shown in Figure 6.8.

Figure 6.8   Chevron with Everything Filled In

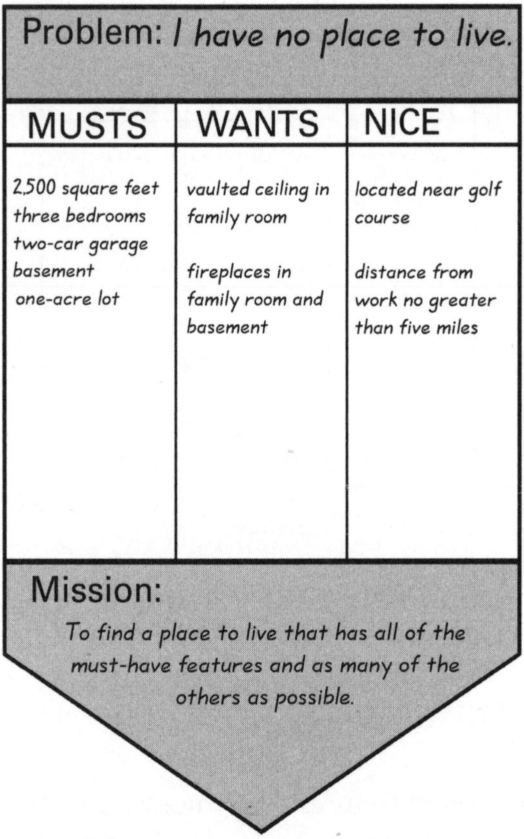

This is a simple way to understand the difference between the problem, mission, and vision for a project. It isn't always so easy to fill in all the parts, but if you can do this with your sponsor and your team, the battle is half won.

I do have one suggestion. Once you have filled in the nice-to-have features for your project, you should burn that list. Unfortunately, these things become tempting distractions for a project team, and the team members will often spend too much time on them and neglect the musts and wants. Do be careful. What is a nice feature for one stakeholder may be a must feature for another. So you may have to spend some time getting consensus on your final list. Let's summarize what we have learned.

You must have a statement that tells everyone where they are going, and if you don't like the word *mission*, then call it a goal, objective, or target. I'm going to stay with the mission because it is the correct term. And the mission is always to achieve the vision for the project outcome.

And the vision, quite simply, is a definition of the characteristics of that outcome. It may be truly visual for tangible things like houses or hardware. But it may be simply a concept for something like software. In fact, the vision for software has more to do with how it functions than it does with actual visual effects. For example, a photo-editing software program would allow you to crop a photo just by dragging a rectangle around the part of the overall photo that you want to retain and clicking your mouse button; the unwanted part disappears. Can you "visualize" this functionality? If you have used PhotoShop® or other editing programs with this feature, you know what I'm talking about. But if you have not, I would expect my description to still allow you to "see" it in your mind, and that is what we are talking about.

> Where there is no vision, the people perish.
>
> —Proverbs 29:18

So a vision depicts the final result of the team's efforts. It's that simple. If you know what the result is supposed to be, you will know when you're finished with the job. Otherwise, you may not be certain that the job is done.

Writing problem, mission, and vision statements is not a popular exercise. People often see it as a waste of time. When you have one member of a team who thinks that you should be going in one direction and others who have their own ideas of the right direction, you can't expect to have a cohesive result. People will take you where they think you are going, not where you want to go.

Now that we have seen the difference between problem, mission, and vision, let's take a closer look at problems and how they are defined, because this is where many headless-chicken projects are created.

PROBLEMS, PROBLEMS

Dr. Juran defined a project as a problem scheduled for solution. That is, we are solving a problem on a large scale when we do a project. Building a bridge solves the problem of not being able to get across a river or gorge easily. Developing an automobile solves the problem of not being able to transport people from one place to another easily.

> The uncreative mind can spot wrong answers, but it takes a creative mind to spot wrong questions.
>
> —Anthony Jay

Developing an insurance package provides protection against financial ruin for people. Financial ruin would be a major problem—a problem that is solved by the insurance package.

In the same way, every project solves a problem for the organization, but we often make the mistake of assuming that we understand the problem when in fact we do not. As an example, let us suppose that you have a headache. You assume that the cause is stress, so you take some capsules for pain, and the headache goes away. The next day it returns, so you again take some pain pills. It retreats.

This is repeated for an extended period until you finally become concerned and go to the doctor. After some exhaustive tests, the doctor reports that you have a brain tumor that can be removed only by surgery.

You have been treating the *symptom*—not the cause—of the problem. The symptom is the headache itself. The cause is the tumor.

This is typical of many attempts to solve problems. The way we define the problem always determines how we try to solve it. If the definition is incorrect, the solution won't work.

> The way a problem is defined determines how we attempt to solve it.

This is the major cause of headless-chicken projects.

We don't spend enough time working out the actual definition, and so we may very well develop the *right solution to the wrong problem*, leaving the organization with the original problem that the project was intended to solve.

If we are to ensure that our projects don't solve the wrong problem, clearly, we must spend more time on the definition stage. Furthermore, we need to have a clear understanding of what is meant by a problem, because the word is used so loosely that it means many things. We say that the headache is a problem when it is actually a symptom of the underlying cause. We claim that the problem is slow sales, when this again is but a symptom of some larger cause. So there is a tendency to equate symptoms with problems, guess at the cause, and go off on a happy hunt for the witch that we think caused the symptom.

Every project is conducted to solve a problem for someone. Usually, the sponsor has an idea in mind of what things will be like when the problem is solved. This is his or her vision for the final project outcome. The mission of the project team is to achieve that vision, which will presumably solve the problem.

However, you seldom receive a statement of the problem when you are assigned a project to manage. Rather, you are given a description of the outcome you are supposed to achieve. Perhaps it is to develop software or a product. Maybe it is to build an office building. It may be a fund-raising campaign. Whatever the nature of the job, you will be told that you are expected to make it happen—whatever "it" is.

> **MISSION: The goal or objective that the team must achieve. The mission is *always* to achieve the vision for the final project outcome.**

In many cases, this is fine. If you do what you have been told to do, it will solve whatever problem your sponsor has. However, if the sponsor has misdefined the problem to be solved, then you may do what you are told to do, but the organization will still have the original problem. For that reason, when you are assigned a project, you should examine the problem to be solved and determine whether doing the project as assigned will achieve the desired result. If it won't, then you need to discuss this with the project sponsor, being careful to express your concerns diplomatically, of course. If the sponsor insists that you do the job assigned, even though you are convinced that it won't solve the intended problem, then you may have to acquiesce, but in that case, I suggest that you have an up-to-date résumé handy.

A problem is defined as a gap between where you are and where you want to be, confronted with obstacles that make closing the gap difficult. It is actually the obstacles that make the gap a problem. As an example, if you are at one end of a long hallway and you want to go to the other end, that is a simple goal. However, if someone puts a large alligator in the hall, and you know that the alligator will bite off your leg if you try to pass, then you truly have a problem. The essence of all problems is dealing with alligators! You must remove them, get around them, or momentarily neutralize them if you want to reach the other end of the hall.

There is another alternative. It may be that you want to reach a room just off the end of the hallway, so instead of going down the hallway that contains the alligator, you detour to another path to get to the desired destination. You have avoided the alligator altogether. This is the essence of creative thinking—finding another route to the solution that can be easily navigated.

Open- and Closed-Ended Problems

There are two categories of problems—those that have single solutions and those that have multiple solutions. Those with single solutions are called *closed-ended problems*. Those with multiple solutions are called *open-ended problems*.

Solving problems in each category requires a different approach. Closed-ended problems are best solved using a left-brain analytical approach, whereas open-ended problems are best solved by applying a right-brain synthesis approach. In terms of the Herrmann brain dominance model, we would expect quadrant-A thinking to be required for solving closed-ended problems and quadrant-D thinking to be required for solving open-ended ones. Remember, of course, that a preference for thinking in a certain quadrant does not indicate *ability*. We all have a whole brain. However, if your preference is very strong for the A quadrant and very weak for the D quadrant, you will probably be drawn to analytical problems, and vice versa.

> Closed-ended problems have single solutions.
>
> Open-ended problems have multiple solutions.

Interestingly, American education is largely focused on solving closed-ended problems. Very little attention is given to solving open-ended ones, yet there are far more open-ended problems in the world than there are closed-ended ones. The result is that we leave school with a mindset that all problems are closed-ended, and we have limited skills for solving open-ended problems. Of course, projects demand that we deal with both kinds of problems.

As an example, an environmental cleanup project is closed ended. So is a project to overhaul a piece of equipment, repair a car, or discover the cause of a disease. On the other hand, a project to develop new software or hardware is open ended, as are projects to build a house, improve a process, sell a product, or develop a project-based organization. One way to think of these is that closed-ended problems are oriented to the past, while open-ended ones are oriented to the future.

> Solving closed-ended problems requires an analytical, left-brain approach, while solving open-ended ones requires a right-brain approach.

Repairing a car is an attempt to return it to a condition that existed previously. Math problems are closed ended; the solution exists already. We are simply trying to discover it.

Building a house, however, is open ended. The house does not yet exist. There are several ways to build it. You may say that one approach is better than another, but that does not negate the fact that there is more than one way to go about it. The same is true for developing a new product; it does not yet exist, and there are several approaches to designing it.

> Closed-ended problems are oriented to the past, while open-ended ones are oriented to the future.

DEFINING CLOSED-ENDED PROBLEMS

For closed-ended problems, the best approach to defining the problem is to use what is commonly called the scientific method, which consists of the following steps:

- Ask questions.
- Develop a plan of inquiry.
- Formulate hypotheses.
- Gather data to test those hypotheses.
- Draw conclusions from hypothesis testing.
- Test the conclusions.

Constructing a Good Problem Statement

Also, at this point, it is essential to develop a solid problem statement. The guidelines for doing this are as follows:

1. The problem statement should reflect shared values and a clear purpose.
2. The problem statement should not mention either causes or remedies.
3. The problem statement should define problems and processes of manageable size.
4. The problem statement should, if possible, mention measurable characteristics.
5. The problem statement should be refined (if appropriate) as knowledge is gained.

Defining Closed-Ended Problems
with Problem Analysis

As was previously stated, closed-ended problems have single solutions. Something that used to work is now broken. The remedy is to determine what has broken and repair it—a single solution. To solve closed-ended problems, we use a general approach called problem analysis.

The diagram in Figure 6.9 shows the steps in the problem analysis process.

Identification

The first step in the problem analysis process is identification. "How do I know I have a problem?" In general, you know that you have a problem because a system that previously performed properly suddenly ceases to do so. *Symptoms* of this misperformance will tell you that something is amiss. In the case of mechanical systems, strange noises may be coming from within the machine. Or the level of performance changes—an automobile quits running, for example, or a tire on your bicycle goes flat.

In biological systems (people, plants, and animals), illness occurs. You have a severe headache. That is a symptom that something is wrong with your body. It is not performing as it usually does.

As previously stated, a problem is a gap between a desired state and a present state, confronted by obstacles that prevent easy closure of the gap. As just described, when a process is involved, that gap is a *deviation* from standard performance. In monitoring progress in a project, there is an index called a *critical ratio*, which should have a value between 0.8 and 1.1. When the

Figure 6.9   Problem Analysis Steps

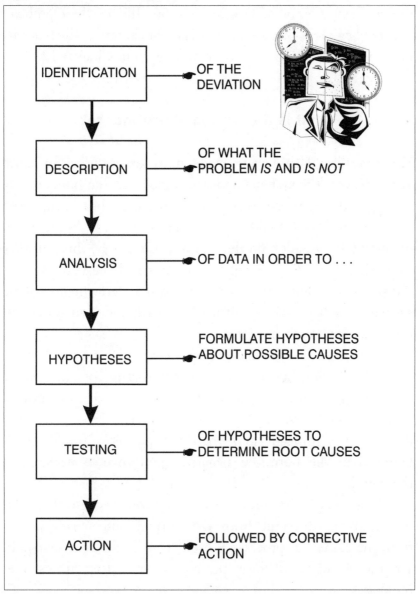

critical ratio falls outside these limits, it's a signal that a potential problem exists with the task in question. This is where problem analysis begins in that situation. (The critical ratio, which is part of earned value analysis, is covered in depth in Chapter 12.)

What Is the Normal Performance?

When dealing with deviations, we must know the performance *norm*. How is the system supposed to behave? The human body is supposed to perform pain-free. Your automobile is supposed to accelerate from 0 to 60 mph in a certain time. It should get so many miles per gallon on the highway. Of course, this will vary somewhat depending on road conditions and the driver's style. All systems exhibit variation around normal performance. Some systems will have very small levels of variation, and some will have large levels of variation.

In the same way, some project work will have much more variability than other project work. For that reason, the critical ratio limits might be set tighter for some tasks than for others. Once the normal variability is known, we can determine if the deviation is significant, and whether it is positive (performance better than the norm) or negative (performance worse than the norm).

To summarize: A problem is recognized because the *effects* produced are different from the normal outcomes expected from the system or process. Those effects might be a change in scrap level, higher or lower production, or a drop in customer purchases.

Determining the Cause

To correct for the deviation, we need to find its *cause*. For a desirable deviation, we must know the cause so that we can replicate it. For an undesirable deviation, the cause must be remedied. To determine the cause of the deviation, we employ a process called *description* of the problem.

Description Using Is/Is-Not Analysis and Stratification

Stratification and is/is-not analysis are ways to localize a problem by exposing underlying patterns. This analysis is done both before collecting data (so that the team will know what kind of differences to look for) as well as after it (so that the team can determine which factors represent the root cause).

To stratify data, examine the process to see what characteristics could lead to biases in the data. For example, could different shifts account for differences in results? Are mistakes made by new employees very different from those made by experienced individuals? Does output from one machine have fewer defects than that from another?

Begin by making a list of the characteristics that could cause differences in results (use brainstorming here). Make data collection forms that incorporate those factors and collect the data. Look for patterns related to time or sequence. Then check for systematic differences between days of the week, shifts, operators, and so on.

The is/is-not matrix in Figure 6.10 is a structured form of stratification, based on the ideas of Charles Kepner and Benjamin Tregoe (1965).

Figure 6.10   The Is/Is-Not Matrix

	Is	Is Not	Therefore
	Where, when, to what extent, or regarding whom does this situation occur?	Where does this situation NOT occur, though it reasonably might have?	What might explain the pattern of occurrence and nonoccurrence?
Where The physical or geographical location of the event or situation. Where it occurs or is noticed.			
When The hour/time of day/ day of week, month/ time of year of the event or situation. Its relationship (before, during, after) to other events.			
What Kind or How Much The type or category of event or situation. The extent, degree, dimensions, or duration of occurrence.			
Who What relationships do various individuals or groups have to the situation/event? To whom, by whom, near whom, etc., does this occur? (Do not use these questions to place blame.)			

Instructions: Identify the problem to be analyzed. Use this matrix to organize your knowledge and information. The answers will assist you in pinpointing the occurrence of the problem and in verifying conclusions or suspicions.

Analysis

Once stratified data has been collected, the differences can be analyzed so that hypotheses concerning causes of the problem can be formulated. The following questions are designed to help identify differences:

What is different, distinctive, or unique between *what* the problem is and what it is not?

What is different, distinctive, or unique between *where* the problem is and where it is not?

What is different, distinctive, or unique between *when* the problem is seen and when it is not?

The focus of these questions is to help us determine what has changed about the process. If nothing had changed, there would be no problem. Our search should be limited to focusing on the following question: What has changed about each of these differences?

Noting the date of each change may also help us relate the start of the problem to some specific change that was made to the process. Perhaps a different person was doing the job when the change in performance occurred. Maybe there was an electrical storm. Perhaps a new shipment of raw materials came in.

Hypotheses

A hypothesis is simply a conjecture or guess about the possible cause of a problem. We form hypotheses based on our data collection and analysis. Then we test them to determine if we have guessed correctly. At this point, *all* reasonable hypotheses should be listed. Nothing should be excluded because it seems improbable or because it was suggested by someone who is not deemed credible as an expert on the subject.

One of my favorite stories about solving problems came from a Japanese semiconductor plant. The plant was experiencing low-yield problems in making a new chip. The engineers were working frantically to determine the cause of the problem, but they were making no progress. One morning an 18-year-old woman who had only recently taken a job at the plant was on her way to work. She rode a bicycle, and as she approached the plant, a train passed by. She had to wait until the crossing was clear before she could proceed.

As she stood watching the train, she noticed that the ground was shaking. She had heard about the yield problem and wondered if the vibration from the train might be a factor. She posed this question to her supervisor, who passed it on to the engineering group. A member of the group decided to test the hypothesis. He rented a ditching machine, dug a large trench between the building and the railroad track, and filled it with water to absorb some of the vibration, and the yield problem was solved! (Subsequently the firm shock-mounted their equipment—the ditch was a temporary fix.)

An important point about this story is that in many cultures, this young woman's idea would have been totally dismissed because she was not an expert in engineering. In Japan, however, contributions from anyone tend to be welcomed.

Cause-Effect Diagrams

One of the most used tools for formulating hypotheses is the Ishikawa, or cause-effect, diagram, also called the fishbone diagram because it resembles the skeleton of a fish. An example is shown in Figure 6.11. It can be used separately or in conjunction with is/is-not analysis to help formulate hypotheses. As shown in the diagram, four general categories of causes are standard. Here we use *manpower, machines, methods,* and *materials* (there are other possibilities, but these four are common). For each category, we ask whether some change has occurred that might explain the problem. Has a person who is not properly trained been assigned to the job? Was someone sick on the day the problem began? Are people not following standard operating procedures? Is a machine out of adjustment? Is an improper method being used to do something? Are materials defective or incorrect?

Figure 6.11   An Ishikawa Diagram

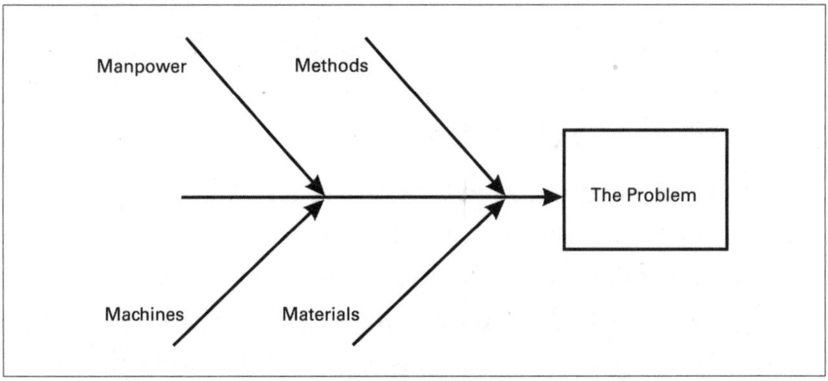

Using brainstorming by a group to generate ideas, all possible causes are listed on the branches. Again, it must be emphasized that censoring ideas is not allowed.

Test Hypotheses

Once ideas have been generated, they must be tested. To test hypotheses, we first ask if the suspected cause can explain both sides of the description. That is, the cause must explain both the is and the is-not effects. If it cannot explain both, it is unlikely to be a real cause.

To save time, the group will usually try to determine which of many causes is the most likely one. This may be done simply through intuition. Headaches are most frequently caused by stress; thus, a doctor might ask a patient if she has been under a lot of stress recently. If this is not the case, then other possible causes would be examined, possibly by having the person undergo a number of tests, such as brain scans, blood tests, and so on.

The testing method follows:

- Test each possible cause through the description, especially the sharp contrast areas.
- Note all "only-if" assumptions.

The most likely cause will be the one that best explains the description or the one with the fewest assumptions. To be certain, you must now verify the hypothesis quickly and cheaply.

One test is whether you can make the effects come and go by manipulating the factor that is supposedly causing the deviation. If you can, you have probably found the true root cause. If a doctor believed that you were having headaches because of an allergy, tests would be run to determine if the allergy existed. If it did, you would be advised to avoid that allergen. If the headaches ceased, then the allergen was the most likely cause. Note that we could test this by deliberately exposing you to the allergen, but most people are happy to have the headaches go away and are unwilling to submit to this second part of the test. In testing hypotheses in general, however, this is a valid method of confirming that a cause is *the* one we are looking for.

Action

While we are testing hypotheses, or trying to determine the root cause, there are three possible types of action that we might take:

Interim action. You buy time while the root cause of the problem is sought. This action is only a "patch" for correcting symptoms. You may, for example, take painkillers while doctors try to determine the cause of your headaches.

Adaptive action. You decide to live with the problem or adapt to it. There are people who learn that they are allergic to certain foods and should give them up, but they love these foods so much that they decide to live with the symptoms instead.

Corrective action. This is the only action that will truly solve the problem. It is aimed at the actual cause of the problem, rather than simply alleviating symptoms.

Design of Experiments

There are times when single causes do not account for problems. As an example, a biotech product may have many ingredients, each of which must have a concentration that falls within a certain range or the final product won't perform correctly. I know of one such case in which the cause of product misperformance was believed to be an enzyme, but it turned out to be the concentration of a buffer that was incorrect. This was determined by running an experiment in which various factors could be changed simultaneously and observing the outcome. This approach allows testing of both first-order and second-order (interaction) effects. Second-order effects are particularly difficult to identify unless such an approach is used. For example, it may be that both the temperature and the concentration of a buffer must be off for the defect in performance to occur.

It is outside the scope of this book to explain the design of experiments. The interested reader should consult a good book on the subject, such as Walpole (1974).

DEFINING OPEN-ENDED PROBLEMS

There are generally more open-ended problems than closed-ended ones. This is especially true of projects. The problem being solved by a project is likely to require different methods from those presented previously for solving closed-ended problems. Even the approach used to define the problem is different. For closed-ended problems, the scientific approach to analyzing data can be used. A closed-ended problem has a *cause*. There is no cause of an open-ended problem, so we need different methods for defining it. The techniques that follow are intended to help you develop good definitions for open-ended problems.

Remember also that open-ended problems do not have single solutions. When there is a cause of a problem, the solution is to remove the cause. For open-ended problems, no such action is possible. We often refer to these as creative problems, and they are characterized by the question, "How do I make something happen?" As examples:

- How do we design a product to perform in a certain way?
- How can I pay for my child's college education?

- How do we send someone to the moon and bring him back safely?
- How do we penetrate a certain market?

I should mention here that Dr. Edward de Bono is considered by many people to be one of the leading experts on creative problem solving, and his book *Serious Creativity* (2015) covers the subject in more detail than this chapter can possibly do. I heartily recommend that you consult Dr. de Bono's works.

The procedure outlined in Table 6.1 is designed to help you develop a good definition for an open-ended problem. However, it is only one approach, and others are presented following the table. Note that you are not trying to solve the problem with this approach, even though there are questions that begin "If I could solve the problem . . ." You are simply trying to understand what the problem is. You are really trying to understand the nature of your desired outcome. That is, when the problem is solved, where will you be, or what condition will exist?

TABLE 6.1   An Exercise to Develop a Good Problem Definition

1. Describe an open-ended problem that is important to you and for which you need answers that could lead to action. Take as long as you wish for this.

2. Again taking your time, complete the following statements about the problem you have chosen. If you cannot think of anything to write for a particular statement, move on to the next one.

   a. There is usually more than one way of looking at problems. You could also define this one as . . .

   b. . . . but the main point of the problem is . . .

   c. What I would really like to do is . . .

   d. If I could break all laws of reality (physical, social, etc.), I would try to solve it by . . .

   e. The problem, put another way, could be likened to . . .

   f. Another, even stranger, way of looking at it might be . . .

3. Now return to your original definition (Step 1). Write down whether any of the redefinitions have helped you see the problem in a different way.

I have had people do this exercise many times, and through this process, they often find that the problem they thought they were solving was, in fact, not the correct problem. For example, a person might begin by stating the problem as needing to buy a new car and wondering how to afford it. On closer examination, she finds that what she really wants is reliable transportation to work every day; a car is only one way of accomplishing this goal.

The Goal-Orientation Technique

Unless you are clear about your goal, you are certainly not likely to achieve it. Most important, there is little value in achieving the wrong goal—as would be true if a person bought a car, only to realize that the real goal was getting to work, and that this could have been achieved with less expense.

Goal orientation is an attitude, first. Second, it is a technique to encourage that attitude. Open-ended problems are situations in which the boundaries are unclear, but in which there may be well-defined needs and obstacles to progress.

The goal-oriented person tries to recognize the desired end state ("what I want") and obstacles ("what's stopping me from getting the result I want").

To illustrate the goal-orientation technique, consider the problem outlined in Table 6.2.

TABLE 6.2 Use of the Goal-Orientation Technique

Original problem statement

Adult illiteracy has reached alarming proportions. In 2004 Ford Motor Company said that it was having to train almost 25 percent of their workforce in basic reading, writing, and arithmetic, at considerable cost.

Redefinitions:

1. (How to) efficiently and effectively teach adults to read.
2. (How to) keep kids from getting through school without being able to read.
3. (How to) get parents to take an interest in their kids so that they will learn to read in school.
4. (How to) eliminate the influences that cause kids to take no interest in school.

The Successive Abstractions Technique

Suppose a company that makes lawn mowers is looking for new business ideas. Their first definition of the problem is to "develop a new lawn mower." A higher level of abstraction would be to define the problem as "develop new grass-cutting machines." An even higher level of abstraction yields "get rid of unwanted grass" (see Table 6.3).

TABLE 6.3 Successive Abstractions

Highest level	Get rid of unwanted grass
Intermediate level	Develop new grass-cutting machines
Lower level	Develop new lawn mower

Another definition of the problem, of course, might be to "develop grass that grows to a height of only 'x' inches above the ground."

Analogy and Metaphor Procedures

One interesting way of describing problems is through the use of analogy or metaphor. Such definitions help increase the chances of finding creative solutions to problems and are especially useful in group techniques, such as brainstorming. In fact, they are preferable to literal statements, since they tend to be extremely effective in stimulating creative thinking. For example:

"How to improve the efficiency of a factory" is a down-to-earth statement.

"How to make a factory run as smoothly as a well-oiled machine" is an analogical redefinition.

"How to reduce organizational friction or viscosity" is a metaphoric definition.

Wishful Thinking

Many left-brained, rational people do not appreciate the value of wishful thinking. However, wishful thinking can provide a rich source of new ideas. Dr. Edward de Bono, in his work on creative thinking, talks about an "intermediate impossible"—a concept that can be used as a stepping-stone between conventional thinking and realistic new insights. Wishful thinking is a great device for producing such intermediate impossibles.

Rickards (1975) cites the example of a food technologist working on new methods of preparing artificial protein. As a fantasy, she considers the problem to be "how to build an artificial cow." Although the metaphor is wishful, it suggests that she might look closely at biological systems and perhaps look for a way of converting cellulose into protein, which is what takes place in nature.

Remember the statement from Table 6.1: "What I would really like to do is . . ." Or try this approach: "If I could break all constraints, I would . . ."

Nonlogical Stimuli

One good way of generating ideas is through forced comparisons. This method can be used for developing ideas for solving a problem, or as an aid to redefinition. Table 6.4 is an example of the procedure, used in conjunction with a dictionary.

TABLE 6.4   An Exercise in Nonlogical Stimuli

For this exercise, you will need paper, pencil, and a dictionary.
1. Write down as many uses as you can think of for a piece of chalk.
2. When you can think of no more ideas, let your eyes wander to some object in your range of vision that has no immediate connection to a piece of chalk.
3. Try to develop new ideas stimulated by the object.
4. Now repeat Stages 2 and 3 with a second randomly selected object.
5. Open the dictionary and jot down the first three nouns or verbs that you see.
6. Try to develop new ideas stimulated by these words in turn.
7. Examine your ideas produced with and without stimuli for differences in variety (flexibility) and total numbers (fluency).

Design Tree

Another phrase for a design tree is "Mind Map®," which is a trademark of Tony Buzan. The design tree has been used by many people to illustrate associations of ideas. For example, you can use the design tree to outline a book. You begin by writing a single word—representing the issue you want to deal with—and then draw a circle around it. Next list all the ideas that come to you, connect them to the first word with lines, and continue by examining each new word in turn for the ideas it might trigger. I used the word *transportation* to illustrate the approach (see Figure 6.12).

Figure 6.12   Design Tree for Transportation

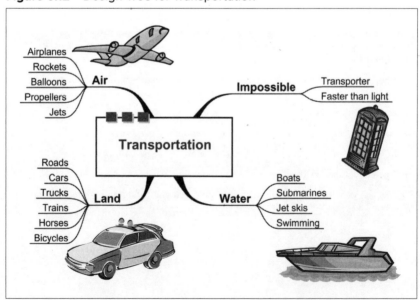

Expectations, Deliverables, and Results

It would be nice if all we had to worry about was meeting PCTS targets in a project, but this is not the case. We also must deal with the expectations of stakeholders, as I explained in Chapter 1. Clarifying stakeholder expectations is as much a part of project definition as anything else, and meeting those expectations is necessary for the project to be judged a success.

In addition, you must ask, what results is this project intended to get, and what must we deliver to achieve those results? The answers to these questions should help you in developing a crisp, shared mission and vision for your project.

Be aware that if a stakeholder changes midway through the project, you will have to go through the process of clarifying the new stakeholder's expectations. You can't just assume that if you meet the expectations of the former stakeholder, everything will be okay. The new person will see the job differently from his or her predecessor, and you will have to negotiate those things that can be accommodated and those that cannot. The new stakeholder may have totally unrealistic expectations about deliverables and results, and you must bring the new stakeholder in line with reality.

You may think of this as one of the political aspects of the project management job, and it is. Ignore it at your own risk!

THE FALLACY OF PROJECT MANAGEMENT ASSUMPTIONS

Everything I have written about managing projects would be ideal—if the process could be made to work the way I have suggested. However, there is a huge fallacy in the assumptions we make about managing projects, and that is that the world will stand still while we execute our carefully constructed project plan. This simply isn't true, and we know it.

As I discussed earlier, stakeholders change, and with new stakeholders come new expectations, requiring us to adapt our project to meet those expectations or be judged negatively when the project ends. Furthermore, as projects evolve, we learn things that we didn't know at the beginning. If we are developing software or hardware, we have new ideas about how the final product should function. For that reason, many products are *adaptive* in nature and cannot be planned *deterministically*.

I believe this is a major reason why software development projects have such high percentages of missed targets. Remember the Standish Group study that shows that only 17 percent of software projects meet the original PCTS targets? It's no wonder. The targets are constantly moving. (This is one reason why Agile and eXtreme management methods are being adopted by IT and software project managers.)

I speak from experience. I once developed an online training program for my website. I began by defining what I wanted it to do. As I neared completion of the project and started testing the program on a temporary dummy site, I began to realize that I could make the program far more effective by making some changes. I also thought of functions that had never occurred to me a year before. So the job took nearly twice as many programming hours as originally estimated, but I wound up with a significantly better product as a result.

Could I have used the product in the form originally defined? Yes, but it would not have had the utility of the present version.

You must exercise caution, of course. If you continually make changes to a product in response to new ideas, you will never release it. This is the trap into which perfectionists fall. They can never finish a design because they can always make it better.

You must decide if a change is needed to make the result as functional as it must be in the final application. If the change is not made, can the resulting product be sold? Will it be accepted by the customer? If the change is made, will it delay product introduction to the marketplace so much that competitors will seize the market share and cost you all of your profits? These are not easy questions to answer, and they should never be answered unilaterally by technologists. Many technologists have very little grasp of market dynamics and will opt for technical improvements even if the product never sells.

The message here is that project planning must be done with the understanding that there must be flexibility enough to respond to legitimate environmental forces, without going so far as to become aimless. On construction projects and other well-defined jobs, this is not such a big issue. Software, hardware, and scientific work (such as drug development), however, are more likely to require an adaptive, rather than a deterministic, management approach.

 IN SUMMARY

In this chapter, I pointed out that a project often fails at the definition stage because it is not handled properly. A project always solves a problem on a large scale, and unless the problem is correctly defined the result will be to develop a solution for the wrong problem.

The *vision* for a project is a result that solves the problem as effectively and efficiently as possible. The *mission* is to achieve the vision. Time spent on this phase of a project can avert missteps and lead to positive outcomes and should not be avoided or regarded as unnecessary.

PROJECT PLANNING

CHAPTER 7

Developing Project Strategy

n this chapter, we will discuss developing a strategy for a project. This involves Steps 3 to 5 of my method, and these steps are repeated in Figure 7.1 for your convenience.

As I have written previously, there is a strong tendency for people to skip from Step 1 in my model down to Step 9. They want to just get on with it and get the job done. As a result, they fail to properly define the problem being solved and establish a proper mission and vision for the job. Consequently, the project fails.

Another mistake is to want to jump from Step 2 down to Step 6. People who do this understand that they must deal with Step 2, but they fail to consider project strategy. They simply want to construct a working plan—usually a schedule that is developed with software.

Figure 7.1 Steps 3 to 5 of The Lewis Method

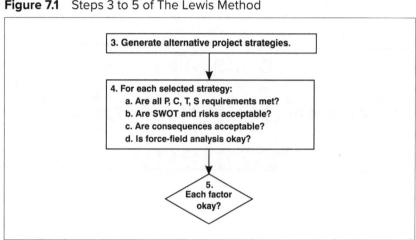

WHAT IS STRATEGY?

Strategy is an overall approach to a project. It is sometimes called a *game plan*. The difference between strategy and tactics is that tactics get you down to the "nitty-gritty" details of exactly how you are going to do the work, thus executing the strategy. For example, if I have decided that the best way to build a house (strategy) is to use prefabricated components, then I must work out how I am going to make the components (tactics). Do I assemble an entire wall and send it to the job site, or do I make it in small sections that can be joined together at the site?

Logistics involves how I am going to get the prefab parts out to the site, how I will supply the workers with tools and other equipment, how I will feed them, and so on. Tactics and logistics will be worked out in Step 6 of the flowchart during detailed implementation planning.

The Importance of Strategy

A manager once told me that he could not keep engineers because the big manufacturers in his area could pay more, and no sooner would he get a young engineer trained than a big company would steal that person. He decided to adopt a new strategy. Instead of recruiting engineers, he would hire technical-school graduates and teach them to be engineers. Since the big companies generally preferred engineers with four-year degrees, he very seldom lost a tech-school graduate to them. Certainly his tech-school engineers may not have been quite as qualified as those with full degrees, but they were capable enough for his needs, and the cost of constantly replacing engineers dropped dramatically.

In a similar vein, about 1995 the United States had a shortage of programmers for several years, and many companies found that they could get programming done in India at considerably less cost than if they had used local programmers do the work. The programmers in India speak good English, are well educated, and work for considerably less than American programmers since their cost of living is much lower than that in the United States. This strategy has been used for several years to get projects done on time and at less expense than would otherwise be possible.

> I became a good pitcher when I stopped trying to make them miss the ball and started trying to make them hit it.
>
> —Sandy Koufax

When the Chunnel was built to connect France with England, the strategy was to start digging from both sides. Using laser-surveying methods, the crews met in the middle with only negligible error in position. This strategy allowed the project to be completed in about half the time it would have taken to dig from one side to the other, because you can dig only so many feet per day. By going in both directions, the digging speed was essentially doubled.

My first engineering job was with a very small company that designed and built land mobile communications equipment. We had only 150 employees, and of course our engineering staff was very small. There was no way that we could compete directly with the big players in the game, because they had far more resources than we did.

So one of our engineers conceived the idea of doing modular design of radios. Instead of having to design every new radio "from scratch," we would design some circuits that could be used in all models. Good examples are audio amplifiers and intermediate-frequency (IF) strips. By employing this method, we were able to develop a family of products in a relatively short time. We were leveraging our limited resources.

Air Industries has employed a similar strategy in its Airbus line of aircraft. In most cases, pilots are trained to fly a single kind of airplane. Thus, a crew that can fly one plane can't fly one with the same design but a slightly different configuration. Airbus has several planes with different seating capacities that can all be flown by the same crews. The cockpit layouts are the same, and the planes handle so similarly that the crews don't have to be retrained to switch from one to the other. In addition, the airline does not have to stock as many different spare parts because the planes all use the same ones. This represents a significant savings in inventory costs, pilot training, and so on.

Boeing designed the 757 and 767 airplanes so that the same pilots can fly them as well. As is true for Airbus, this saves money for the airlines.

Project Strategy and Technical Strategy

There are often two aspects to project strategy. As an example, suppose you must feed a group, and you are considering how to do it. You could (1) cook the meal yourself, (2) take everyone to a restaurant, (3) have a potluck dinner, in which everyone brings something, or (4) have a caterer deliver the food. You examine the alternatives and decide that you will cook the meal yourself. This is your project strategy. But how will you cook the food?

You could (1) cook it conventionally on your stove, (2) microwave it, or (3) have a backyard barbecue. These three approaches would be called *technical strategy*. Your preference is to have a backyard barbecue, but you discover that your grill is kaput. You don't want to cook on the stove or microwave, so you decide to have the meal catered. In other words, your choice of technical strategy may determine your project strategy (see Figure 7.2).

Figure 7.2 The Difference between Project and Technical Strategy

In a technological company, for example, you are considering developing a product by employing a new technology. However, no one in the company knows anything about that technology, so you will have to either contract out that part of the work (a project strategy) or develop the capability.

A general guideline in selecting a technical strategy is that you don't want to have a very tight project deadline. Of course, this rule is violated frequently in high-tech industries, but deadlines are also missed occasionally, and sometimes products are released that later have field problems. This can seriously damage a company's reputation.

Related to this rule is that you should separate discovery from development in a project. That is, you don't want to be trying to make some technology work when you are supposed to be developing a product. The best approach is to do a feasibility study, and then, based on the outcome, launch a development project. If you are trying to prove feasibility and develop a product at the same time and you can't make the technology work, that project will be judged a failure. However, no matter what result you get with a feasibility study—yes, it works, or no, it doesn't—that should be judged a successful project, as you have conclusively answered a question.

GENERATING AND CHOOSING THE CORRECT STRATEGY

As you can see from my model, in Step 3 you generate a list of alternative project and technical strategies that may apply to your project. In Step 4 you select the combination that you judge to be best. Generating the list may be as simple as looking at existing strategies and listing them, or you may need to invent a new strategy. Note that this step requires strategic or conceptual thinking. Individuals with a strong preference for quadrant-D thinking will be invaluable at this step, but if they aren't available, members with other thinking preferences will have to "step into" the D quadrant to brainstorm strategies (see Figure 7.3).

Figure 7.3 Quadrant-D Thinking Is Needed at This Step

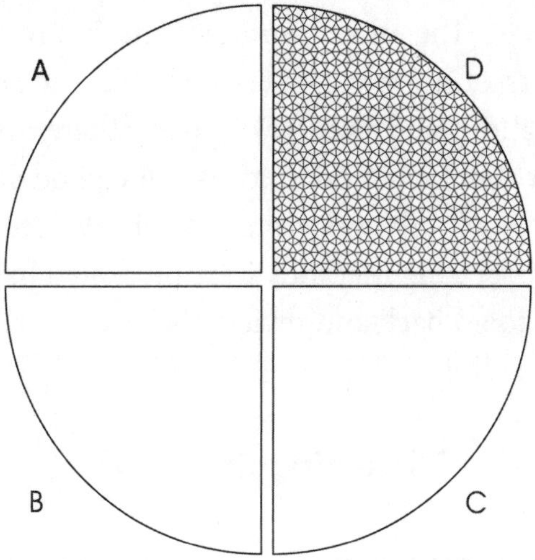

Inventing a Strategy

As an example of this, Charles Kepner and Benjamin Tregoe developed an approach to problem solving that was very rigorous. They convinced managers at General Motors to adopt it. In fact, GM wanted most of its employees to be trained in the new method. Kepner and Tregoe knew that they could not possibly train all those people themselves, so they were almost destroyed by their success. So they conceived a new approach. They would train individuals within GM to deliver the training. They conducted a series of train-the-trainer workshops and made GM self-sufficient in doing its own internal training. All Kepner and Tregoe had to do from that point on was sell the classroom materials to GM, and that was how they made their income. This was an invented strategy at the time. It has become common since then.

If you must invent a strategy, you should use creative problem-solving methods. The most common one is brainstorming, in which members of a group generate as many ideas as they can without evaluation, and then select one. There are many other approaches for developing good ideas. One good source of techniques is the book *Thinkertoys* by Michael Michalko (1995). Several idea-generating methods were presented in Chapter 6, so you may want to go back and review those.

Selecting Strategy

Sometimes choosing a strategy is a simple matter. However, if several issues are involved, the choice may not be so easy to make. A step-by-step procedure that will guide you through the process is presented at the end of this chapter, but you should understand why the steps are followed, not just apply them in a rote way.

When you were generating ideas for project strategy, you were in quadrant D of the Herrmann model. To select the best combination of project and technical strategy, quadrant-A thinking is needed. Critical analysis is required to sort through the facts and details of the various choices, so if you have no one on your team who is good at such thinking, you should temporarily bring in someone who is.

Ranking the Alternatives

To select the best combination of strategies, you should rank both lists (project and technical strategies). The easiest way to do this is to use a priority matrix, as shown in Figure 7.4. There are several ways to go about this. One is to make each choice binary. Suppose, for example, that I have four strategies. If I had some way to rank them quantitatively, it would be easy to make a choice, but there may be several factors involved that affect the "measure" that each one would yield, and it gets too complicated to work out. So I simply ask myself if one strategy is better than another. If the answer is "yes," I put a one in the cell, and if it is "no," I put a zero. If I proceed across Row 1 and ask this question for Strategy 1 compared to each of the others, I get the result shown in Figure 7.4. This technique is called *paired comparisons*.

Figure 7.4   Priority Matrix for Four Strategies with Row 1 Filled In

STRATEGY	1	2	3	4	TOTAL	RANK
1	X	1	0	1		
2		X				
3			X			
4				X		

Next, I ask if Strategy 2 is better than each of the others. However, you will note that when I ask if Strategy 2 is better than Strategy 1, I have already asked that question in Row 1, but in reverse. So whatever I put in Row 1 under Strategy 2 must now be the inverse in Row 2, Column 1. This is shown in Figure 7.5.

Figure 7.5   Priority Matrix with Row 2 and Column 1 Filled In

STRATEGY	1	2	3	4	TOTAL	RANK
1	X	1	0	1		
2	0	X	1	1		
3	1		X			
4	0			X		

In fact, as you continue with the matrix, you will find that every entry in Column 1 is going to be the inverse of what is in Row 1, and that the same will be true of every column entry below the diagonal, so you can save time by simply filling in the rows of the matrix above the diagonal and then filling in the columns with the inverse of their rows. The result is shown in Figure 7.6.

Figure 7.6   Priority Matrix with All Entries Filled In

STRATEGY	1	2	3	4	TOTAL	RANK
1	X	1	0	1		
2	0	X	1	1		
3	1	0	X	0		
4	0	0	1	X		

Next, you total each row, and the row with the highest total will be your first choice, that with the next-highest total will be your second choice, and so on. If you find that two rows add up to the same total, just look in the matrix to see which of the two choices outranks the other, since that decision has already been made. The result for this matrix is shown in Figure 7.7.

Figure 7.7   Priority Matrix with Totals and Ranks Filled In

STRATEGY	1	2	3	4	TOTAL	RANK
1	X	1	0	1	2	1
2	0	X	1	1	2	2
3	1	0	X	0	1	4
4	0	0	1	X	1	3

This ranking should ideally be done by a team. When this is the case, you can still deal with the strategies in a binary fashion, but now you ask your team members how many of them think that Strategy 1 is better than Strategy 2, and you count the votes. Suppose, for example, that you have 10 team members, counting yourself, and you ask for a comparison of Strategy 1 versus Strategy 2. When you enter the votes, you put the votes for Strategy 1 in Row 1 and the votes for Strategy 2 in Row 2. This is shown in Figure 7.8.

Figure 7.8   Matrix with Votes Tallied for Strategy 1 versus Strategy 2

STRATEGY	1	2	3	4	TOTAL	RANK
1	X	8	6	1		
2	2	X				
3	4		X			
4	9			X		

Continue in this manner until you have completed all voting, and then total the votes in each row. This gives the result shown in Figure 7.9. This is a more finely tuned approach than using ones and zeros as you did previously.

Figure 7.9   Matrix Completely Filled In and Totaled

STRATEGY	1	2	3	4	TOTAL	RANK
1	X	8	6	1	15	2
2	2	X	5	1	8	4
3	4	5	X	2	11	3
4	9	9	8	X	26	1

The Analytical Hierarchy

The priority matrix can be enhanced by evaluating various attributes of each choice. As you can see in Step 4 of The Lewis Method, the first question is whether a given strategy can meet our PCTS targets. It may be that one choice will meet the CTS targets but is not as good as another choice in meeting the performance objective. But are P, C, T, and S all of equal importance to the project?

It could be that performance is most important and time is second. Graham and Englund (1997) have written that *mind share* is what you want to achieve with a product to capture *market share*. For example, when someone mentions laser jet printers, Hewlett-Packard wants everyone to think of its units as the best available. So performance may be the foremost requirement to be met. Then may come time, scope, and cost. If weights are assigned to these, you would then have a more complicated situation to analyze.

Now you would have to ask the question, is Strategy 1 better than Strategy 2 in terms of performance? In terms of cost? Time? Scope? And you would tally the votes for all four criteria for each paired comparison. To arrive at a numerical weight for each choice involves matrix algebra, which I long ago forgot and which is best done with a software program called Expert Choice®. The program allows comparisons between quantitative and qualitative facets of a choice, making it an extremely powerful way of arriving at a correct decision. To find out more about the software, check out the website at www.expertchoice.com.

Conducting SWOT and Risk Analysis

In choosing the best project strategy, it is a good idea to do a SWOT and risk analysis. The acronym SWOT stands for *strengths, weaknesses, opportunities,* and *threats.* It is a technique that was originally used in marketing analysis. Before entering a new market, it is useful to ask the following questions:

What are our strengths? How can we take advantage of them?

What weaknesses do we have? How do we minimize the effect of them?

What opportunities does this market offer us? How can we capitalize on them?

What threats exist that may impact our success? How can we deal effectively with them?

The best way to do a SWOT analysis is to simply fill in the form shown in Figure 7.10. I do suggest that you identify *all* the strengths you can think of and then answer the question of how to take advantage of them, rather than identifying a given strength followed immediately by how to deal with it. This procedure goes faster as a rule. The same goes for the other three concerns.

Figure 7.10 A SWOT Analysis Form

SWOT Analysis Form

Project:	Prepared by:
Date:	Strategy, goal, or objective being considered:

List strengths of your team.	How can you best take advantage of these?	List weaknesses of your team.	How can you minimize the impact of these?

What opportunities does this project/strategy/goal present?	How can you best take advantage of them?	List those threats that might keep you from succeeding.	How can you deal with each identified threat?

Threats versus Risks

Notice that Question 2 in Step 4 asks if SWOT and risks are okay. The difference between risks and threats is that a risk is something that can simply happen—an accident, an act of nature, or a missed deadline—whereas a threat is something that may be posed by another entity. It may be a competitor who beats you to market, for example.

For practical purposes, it is okay to combine threats and risks, because either way you look at it, they both jeopardize the project if they happen. However, the downside to this approach is that dealing with threats is done differently than dealing with risks.

Furthermore, it is not enough to simply identify risks and threats. The question is, what are you going to do about them? The essential point is that threats and risks should be managed so that they do not cause the project to fail.

There are two points in planning a project where risks should be analyzed and managed. The first is to address risks to the strategy itself. For example, employing cutting-edge technology in a product development project is riskier than using proven technology. Unless the benefits to be gained far exceed the cost of failure, the cutting-edge approach would be undesirable. Even if the cutting-edge strategy is chosen, it is a good idea to have a contingency plan in place in case the strategy proves to be unworkable.

You also need to manage risks during implementation planning. Many things can go wrong in the execution of a project plan, and if these are identified ahead of time, plans can be developed to deal with them. You can sometimes eliminate a risk altogether with a small change in your approach to the project. As my colleague, Harvey Levine, says, it is better to avoid risks than to have to deal with them.

Risk management is covered in detail in Chapter 11. For now, suffice it to say that there are four primary responses to risk:

1. **Mitigation:** you do something to correct for the damage done by the event.
2. **Avoidance:** you attempt to avoid the risk in the first place.
3. **Transfer:** you transfer the risk to someone else. Insurance is an example of risk transfer. Contracting work to another party is also a form of risk transfer.
4. **Accommodate:** you accept the risk and take no steps to deal with it. We do this when we drive our cars (though wearing seat belts is an attempt to minimize the impact of an accident should you have one).

Unintended Consequences

An unintended consequence is something that happens because of the action you have taken to solve one problem. For example, you decide to contract work to an outside vendor, and the consequence is that you lose control of that part of the project. Or you push everyone to complete a project by a certain date, and they unintentionally sacrifice quality (performance) in the process.

Unintended consequences are all around us. It has been said that most of today's environmental problems are the consequence of solutions to yesterday's problems. I also believe that many organizational problems are the consequences of actions and decisions made previously to solve problems. For that reason, it is important to ask yourself if your chosen project strategy is going to lead to serious consequences that may actually be worse than the problem you were trying to solve when you selected that strategy.

As an example, several years ago, I decided to change my way of printing seminar workbooks. Previously, I had typed the text on my computer and left space for illustrations. We then pasted the art into the placeholders. These masters were copied and used to reproduce the workbooks in quantity. The problem was that the final workbook, a second-generation copy, had lost some quality. It was also difficult to revise the copy. A significant change could cause page numbers to change, requiring new paste-up. This was time-consuming.

To remedy this, I decided to utilize desktop publishing for the workbooks. In doing so, I found that some of the art wouldn't scan without being degraded. Also, the computer would occasionally crash for some reason, costing time to redo the files. To make a long story short, although there were times when I questioned the wisdom of my decision, I'm convinced that this was the right strategy for the long run. (When I first wrote this, desktop publishing was to some degree in its infancy. It is now the only method that anyone in her right mind would consider, and with the prevalence of digital cameras and high-bandwidth Internet connections, it is very easy to obtain and process digital images. Not to mention the easy access to stock photographs, art, and infographics. I have left the example in here to illustrate how rapidly our technology is changing, and it is certainly having its effect on the management of projects.)

Force-Field Analysis

Psychologist Kurt Lewin invented the process that he called force-field analysis in the 1930s. It is a process by which you look at psychological forces. However, the term causes people to include risks and threats in the analysis, and threats are external to the organization, while the forces we want to examine are internal. I prefer to call it *stakeholder analysis*. In the discussion that follows, please keep in mind this distinction. Also, even though some stakeholders are external to the company, they are directly involved in the project, while threats from other entities are not.

The Concept

Organizations and projects are, by nature, political. The basic nature of politics is that people try to gain and keep power. They choose sides on various issues and then try to have their side "win." This can affect a project when a certain strategy is not acceptable to certain individuals or groups.

As an example, a facilities engineer once told me about an experience he had in refurbishing an office. He arranged to do the job over the plant shutdown that occurred for about a week around Christmas. He convinced some people from the plant to help move furniture, lay carpet, and paint walls, and paid them triple time because they were working during a holiday period. They completely overhauled the office, and it was ready for occupancy when the plant resumed its normal operation.

To his chagrin, when he walked into the office on the first day, the union steward was talking with the engineer's boss. He was outraged. "We would normally have taken several months to do that job," he snarled. "Now management knows that it can be done in less time."

I asked him the boss' response.

"You should have known better," his boss told him.

This is a good example of a strategy that would have been rejected if it had been suggested to the union steward before the fact.

Stakeholder analysis is a process by which you consider all the attitudes of those stakeholders that may cause your strategy to succeed or fail because of its acceptance or rejection by the parties involved. Essentially, this entails paying attention to the politics of the project, and this is sometimes overlooked by project managers. Acceptance or support creates a *supporting force*, while rejection creates a *resisting force*.

The process is to identify stakeholders that may accept or reject a strategy, assess the strength of their support or resistance, and determine whether your strategy can succeed. The basic idea is that the total strength of the supporting forces must exceed the strength of the resisting forces, or you can't make your strategy work. Such an analysis is shown in Figure 7.11.

Figure 7.11 Force-Field Analysis

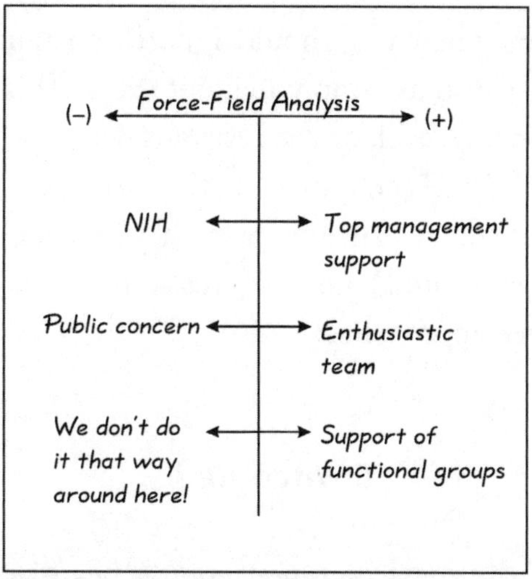

Notes: NIH means "not invented here."
Also, the forces across from each other are not opposites of each other. They are just drawn this way for appearance.

The difficulty with this approach lies in trying to quantify the forces. I consider an attempt to do so a very iffy proposition. On top of that, when we sum the resisting forces to get a total, we assume that all resistance is the same, and this may not be valid. You may be adding apples and oranges. I suggest that you forget about trying to quantify the forces and concentrate instead on managing resistance. After all, the positive forces are going to help you.

There are four approaches to dealing with resistance:

1. Ignore it.
2. Overcome it.
3. Go around it.
4. Neutralize it.

Ignore It

There are times when you should ignore resistance. If you pay attention to it, you may simply make it grow. This is valid when the resistance is low level, or the resistant person is in no position to do you any harm. The danger is that you may underestimate the level of resistance. In any case, if you later find that you should not have ignored someone's resistance, you can adopt one of the next three approaches.

Overcome It

This is one of the most common approaches to resistance. You try to counter the person's resistance by arguing against it. Suppose, for example, that a person objects to a strategy for reasons of safety. You try to convince him that his concerns are unwarranted. He counters your argument with expressions of strong fear that someone will be injured and bring a lawsuit against the company.

You go back and forth, offering argument and counterargument, until you are convinced that he is a stubborn opponent who will never "see the light." Of course, he thinks the same thing about you. What has happened is that the strength of your opposing arguments has simply grown, and neither of you has been able to convince the other of the correctness of your position.

The nature of this conflict is a move-countermove exchange, which is called a *game without end*. This means that there is almost no way that the game can end because there are no rules within the system for changing its own behavior. (For more on this, see Watzlawick et al., 1974.)

When you see that you are getting into a game-without-end interaction, I suggest that you try another approach. Otherwise, you may simply strengthen your opponent. In addition, even if you were able to convince him of your position, he has invested so much energy in his own point of view that to change now would make him lose face, which he may be very reluctant to do.

Much has been written about the effects of fighting resistance in the past decade. An example is that waging war on drugs has magnified the problem, creating a lucrative business for the drug dealers and generating a "drug-fighting" machine with thousands of officers. It is a war that we probably can never end, and it seems to have a secondary outcome that is very undesirable— when something is prohibited, it becomes even more desirable. We should have learned this in the days of prohibition of alcohol, but unfortunately, such lessons seem to be hard to learn.

Go Around It

To go around someone means that you go to that person's boss and ask that the boss have a "heart-to-heart" talk with your opponent. This might work, but you might very well regret your action in the long run. It is generally not considered a very wise choice. The only exception would be when some serious safety issue is involved, and you have made no headway with other tactics. Otherwise, this should be a last resort.

Neutralize It

The word suggests that you are going to blast your opponent off the face of the earth—and you may well wish you could do so— but that is not the meaning of *neutralize* in this case. Here it means that you try to find a way to dispel the person's resistance.

The simplest approach is to ask the individual, "What would I have to do to convince you that this is a good strategy?"

The person has two possible responses. One is to tell you to forget about trying to convince her. She is never going to accept this strategy.

When I get this very negative response, I ask, "Really? There's absolutely nothing I can do to convince you?"

If the person is willing to meet you even partway, you will usually get the second response, which is, "Oh, I suppose if you could do (whatever it is), I would be convinced." The nice thing about this is that you no longer must try to find out how to convince the individual, because she has told you.

I suggest that, even if you can do what the person suggests, you ask if there is anything else you need to do. The reason is that you may do what was originally requested, only to have the person say, "Well, I still have this concern . . ." By taking care of all her concerns at one time, you avoid the sense of playing games later.

People, Problems, and Projects

I find that very few people take stakeholder analysis seriously. I'm not sure why. Perhaps they don't feel that they have the skills to deal with resistance. Maybe they think that the resistance will go away once the person sees the logic of the strategy. Or it could be that they are simply underestimating its importance.

This is a serious error of judgment. I once met with a company that sells heavy equipment and has developed software that allows users to get maximum advantage from the equipment. The user, recognizing this almost immediately, is eager to purchase the software.

The difficulty is with the company's own sales force. For years they have sold heavy equipment. They don't know or care anything about software. They are resisting the new system.

This is a good example of a paradigm shift. The old paradigm is that the company sells equipment. The new one is that it sells a system in which the software makes the equipment more useful.

The initial response to all paradigm shifts is rejection. For example, when Henry Ford first set about popularizing the automobile, people thought it was very impractical. After all, they argued, where was anyone going to get gasoline for it? Indeed, the infrastructure needed to support the auto did not exist at that time.

How many people ignored the impact of the personal computer, believing that it could never replace a mainframe unit?

Overcoming resistance to a paradigm shift is very difficult. Usually, evidence of the validity of the new paradigm grows to such a point that people can no longer reject it, and then there is a landslide of acceptance. This is shown in Figure 7.12.

Figure 7.12   Acceptance of a Paradigm Shift

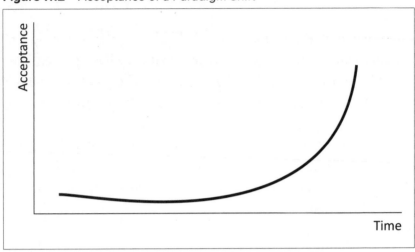

Some organizations must acknowledge that there will be a few employees who will not accept the new paradigm. These people become casualties of the changing direction of the business. This is unfortunate, but given the potential strength of resistance to change, it may be unavoidable. However, it is always worth trying the strategy that I outlined earlier—ask the person what you must do to convince her of the soundness of the new paradigm. If you are unable to get a positive response, you can resort to some other action.

The important point is that projects often get into far more trouble because of these "people" issues than they do because the schedule was incorrect or because someone didn't plan properly. As I said at the beginning of the book, successful projects can be achieved only when tools, people, and systems are jointly optimized. Unfortunately, the people side of the equation is more often overlooked than the other two.

IN SUMMARY

Following is a step-by-step procedure for developing and selecting project strategy.

Steps 3 to 5 of The Lewis Method

Project strategy describes, overall, how the job will be done. This is sometimes called a game plan. You should consider both project strategies and technical strategies when appropriate. Since these may interact, the choice of a technical strategy may affect your project strategy, and vice versa.

1. Brainstorm a list of alternative project and technical strategies. Remember, in brainstorming, there is no evaluation or criticism until after all ideas have been listed.

2. Once the project strategies have been listed, rank them using the priority matrix presented in this chapter. Do the same for technical strategies.

3. Is the number one technical strategy compatible with the number one project strategy? If not, decide which pair of the two will be compatible before continuing.

4. For the chosen strategies, can you meet your performance, cost, time, and scope targets? If yes, continue to Step 5. If no, then select another

(continued)

strategy to evaluate. Continue this process until the answer is yes.

5. Fill in a SWOT form, in which you combine threats and risks. Don't bother to fill in the right panel of the threat portion of the form at this time. Note that you are doing this for strategy only, not for implementation steps.

6. Next, fill in a risk analysis form in which you calculate RPNs (risk priority numbers) for all threats and risks. (You will have to read Chapter 11 to do this.)

7. For all risks that have a severity of 8 to 10 points, you *must* find a contingency to deal with the risk. Remember, you can avoid, mitigate, or transfer risk.

8. For all risks that have high products (regardless of severity), you should identify ways in which these RPNs can be reduced, either by reducing probability or severity or by improving detection.

9. Are any risks serious enough that the strategy may not work? If so, you may have to select the next strategy in your priority matrix.

10. Are any identified weaknesses serious enough that they may jeopardize the strategy? Can they be overcome? If not, then you may need to select the next strategy in your matrix.

11. Now consider consequences. Will the chosen strategy lead to unacceptable consequences? If so, you may have to reject the strategy.

(continued)

12. Finally, conduct a force-field analysis in which you identify the positive forces in the environment that will help your strategy succeed and the negative forces that may do the opposite. These forces can be political, social, or paradigm issues. Then ask yourself:

a. Can I ignore any resisting forces? If yes, cross them off your list. If not, then ask:

b. Can the remaining forces be overcome? If not, then ask:

c. Can I go around them without creating enemies for life? If not, then ask:

d. Can I neutralize them by asking the following question: "What must I do to convince you that this strategy is okay?"

CHAPTER 8

Implementation Planning

W e are now ready to discuss detailed implementation planning, Steps 6 to 8 of The Lewis Method. These steps are shown in Figure 8.1.

In the previous chapter, I wrote that people are inclined to jump from Step 1 of my model down to Step 9. When I can convince them not to skip the definition phase, they then want to jump from Step 2 to Step 6. They tend to think of planning as detailed planning, omitting strategy from their thinking altogether.

In fact, I still find many individuals thinking about detailed planning while they are trying to define the project. The inclination to do detailed planning seems to be virtually genetic! In terms of the HBDI® profile, this is the place for quadrant-B thinking. You want people to work out exactly how to execute the strategy chosen in Steps 4 and 5. In case you have forgotten where quadrant B is, the model is shown in Figure 8.2, with quadrant B highlighted.

Figure 8.1   Steps 6 to 8 of The Lewis Method

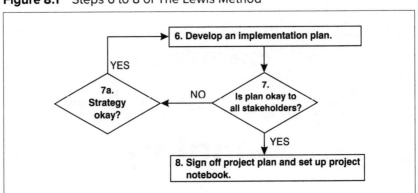

Figure 8.2   Quadrant B Highlighted

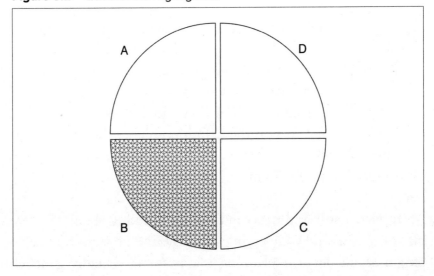

Please note that, even though a great deal of B-quadrant thinking is required in this step, this does not mean that you don't need the other quadrants. It is just that planning is particularly a B-quadrant activity. Nevertheless, you may need creative thinking (the D quadrant), and you especially should consider the C quadrant, which deals with interpersonal issues, in putting together a plan. Whole-brain thinking would be very helpful at this stage of the project.

You are now ready to work out the details of how a job will be done. For example, if you were building the Chunnel, knowing that you will go in both directions and meet in the middle, you must now determine all the steps that will get you there. Since there are many contractors performing various parts of the project, you must decide *who* does what, *when* it will be done, *how much* each step will cost, *what* will be needed, and so on. In fact, this illustrates the definition of planning. It is answering all the who, what, when, and how questions, much as a reporter asks when writing an article.

This is not to say that planning is easy. In fact, I believe it is some of the hardest work that we ever do. One reason is that estimating is involved. How long will a step take? Who knows? As one of my engineers told me once when I asked how long some work would take, "You can't schedule creativity."

I agreed with him at the time, but as I told him, "We have to pretend that we can, because they won't fund the project unless we tell them how long it will take."

Since then, I have changed my mind. You can schedule creativity (within reason, of course). In fact, the most motivating factor in creative thinking is a deadline. Ad agencies live with this all the time. So do journalists. And so do engineers and programmers.

Dr. Edward de Bono, one of the world's leading gurus on creative thinking, has written that when he teaches creative thinking to children, if he gives them a deadline, they produce great results. Otherwise, if they have no time limit, they just mess around.

> Prediction is very difficult, especially about the future.
>
> —Neils Bohr

I know a creativity consultant who took an engineering group to the mountains for a weekend to develop a design for a new device. They started on Friday afternoon, and by Sunday afternoon they had developed a device that was later patented. Using a structured approach to creativity enabled them to do this.

MISTAKES IN PLANNING

Before we go any further, it may be helpful to discuss the more common mistakes that people make in planning so that you can avoid them. There are five common ones.

Unilateral Planning

This mistake is made when the project manager plans a project for the group and turns it over to the group members to execute. The major reason that this is a mistake is that no one individual can possibly think of everything in a project. Even a one-person project can benefit from the thinking of other individuals.

Furthermore, when you plan the project by yourself, you must estimate task durations yourself, and your estimates are likely to be wrong. Specifically, your estimate is very likely to be optimistic because you forget about all the details that consume most of the time. For this reason, the person who eventually must do the work is not likely to be very committed to the time you have specified. If he misses the mark, he is likely to say, "It was your number, not mine. I knew it couldn't be done that fast."

> **MISTAKE 1:** Not involving in the planning process the people who must do the work.

No project can succeed when the team members have no commitment to the plan, so the first rule of project planning is that the people who must do the work should help plan that part of the project. Not only will you gain their commitment to the plan, but they will most likely cover all the important issues that you personally may have forgotten.

I want to point out that one reason for this mistake (or trap) is that we confuse the thought process with documentation. I explained in Chapter 1 that my flowchart shows the *thought process* that you must follow to manage a project. Even if the project is to prepare a meal (it is a small project, after all), you should *think* through every step in my flowchart. If you don't believe this, try it out. You will find that all the steps apply.

For example, when you get to Step 6, where you would prepare a schedule in a large project, do you develop a critical path schedule? No. Do you consider the order in which various steps must be done? You bet. Otherwise, the meal will not come together properly. Your steak will be ready, but you'll be sitting around for a half-hour waiting for the baked potatoes to get done.

> The first rule of planning is that the people who must do the work should participate in the planning.

The Ready-Fire-Aim Mistake

One reason that people don't plan projects is that they are convinced that they could have finished the work by the time they could do the plan. The complaint is, "We don't have time to plan; we need to get the job done." However, this is a counterintuitive situation. Especially if you have a critical deadline, you must have a good plan.

As a simple example, suppose I have flown to Chicago for a meeting, and because of bad weather, my plane lands very late. I have never been to Chicago before. I rush off the plane, dash to the rental car counter, and get my car. The agent asks, "Mr. Lewis, do you need a map?"

"I don't have time for that," I say. "I must get to my meeting. I'm already late!"

> The more important a project deadline, the more important the plan.

We can easily see the fault in that logic. But we can't seem to see the same fault in the logic that says that we don't have time to plan projects!

Another example is the 1983 San Diego Building Industry Association's contest that I touched upon earlier. This example illustrates a project in which the planning time far exceeded the execution time.

Planning in Too Little Detail

One major cause of project failures is that ballpark estimates become targets. For the benefit of my readers outside the United States who may not understand the idiom "ballpark estimate," the expression comes from baseball. If the ball is hit over the wall, it is out of the ballpark. If it does not go over the wall, then it is in the ballpark. So we use the term *ballpark estimate* to mean one that is approximately correct. (It is within acceptable boundaries or limits.)

The problem is that a ballpark estimate is done by comparing one project to another similar one, adding a bit for this, taking off a bit for that, then inserting some money for unknowns (called *contingency*). The tolerances on ballpark estimates can be extremely large. Imagine being asked what it would cost to develop a vaccine for AIDS, as an example. A person could offer only a guesstimate with a huge range. There are simply too many unknown factors to be able to give a precise number.

This is an example of planning a project in too little detail. If a better estimate is desired, you must identify the major tasks to be performed, and probably some of the subtasks as well.

> **MISTAKE 3:**
> **Broad-brush**
> **planning.**

I once worked with a defense contracting company. Its projects were bid at a fixed price. To estimate the cost to do the job, the person preparing the bid would ask various individuals how much his or her part would cost. Each person would do a ballpark estimate. The company would then be awarded the bid (based on being the low bidder) and would lose money on the job.

I explained that the company was planning in too little detail. It needed more detailed project planning to get a realistic estimate.

Three years later, in a follow-up interview, I asked, "How are your projects going now?"

The response was very positive. "We don't get as many jobs as we used to," said my contact, "but when we get one, we make money on it."

Isn't that the name of the game?

As a way of indicating the level of detail that you should incorporate into a final project plan, consider a client I worked with that had never done very much project planning. Most of their planning was done on the backs of envelopes. Nevertheless, the company had been very successful.

A new manager inherited the company and explained to everyone that the company had to do a better job of planning. The reason was survival. A Japanese competitor had just entered the market and was selling its product at a lower price than my client's. The new manager explained that he didn't know the cost to develop his product, so in order to ensure that the company would make a profit, he had to sell at a higher margin than the Japanese company, which had a fairly accurate measure of its development costs. That being the case, the company could use a lower profit margin because it knew how many units it had to sell to reach breakeven, and therefore when it became profitable. His point was that good project management could give the firm a competitive advantage in the marketplace.

His proposal was met with considerable resistance. The engineers had never had to do this "administrative stuff" before and saw no need for it now. In part, they were afraid of being held accountable for estimates that might not be correct. This seemed to be "policing" them.

The frustrated manager told them that he at least wanted them to give him a bar chart schedule. They responded by giving him a schedule that had bars 26 weeks long for individual tasks. His response was that they would never complete a 26-week task on time. They would back-end load it and ultimately fail. The term *back-end loading* means that they were going to push their work out toward the end of the task, and then, if they encountered technical problems, they would ultimately fail.

His reasoning was that they would delay starting on time, fully convinced that they could always make up one day. After all, they had 26 Saturdays to make up the lost day. Next day, still busy, they would convince themselves that they could always make up two days, then three days, and so on, until they had slipped an entire week. It is incredibly hard to make up a week of lost work.

He suggested that they should always follow the rule that no task ever have a duration greater than 4 to 6 weeks. Thus, a 26-week task should be subdivided or "chunked down" into increments of about 4 weeks. Furthermore, they needed a marker that told them that they were finished, and such markers can be difficult to apply to knowledge work. Another term, *exit criteria*, also refers to some way of knowing that the work is complete.

RULES FOR PLANNING
- No task should have a duration greater than four to six weeks.
- Engineering and software tasks should have durations no greater than one to three weeks.
- All tasks must have markers that enable everyone to tell that the work is actually complete.

Had I known then what I know now, I would have told him that engineering and programming work should be chunked down even further, so that durations fall in the range of one to three weeks. Otherwise, you find that such work gets to 90 percent complete and stays there forever.

Planning in Too Much Detail

Unfortunately, the reverse of too little detail also causes problems. Some people get carried away and microplan. I know. I did it myself once and lived to regret it.

The basic principle is that you should never plan in more detail than you can control. In engineering software, that means no more than the nearest day. You simply can't control much better than that.

However, people who do maintenance work can sometimes control the work to

MISTAKE 4: Microplanning.

the nearest hour. It is common practice to schedule jobs to refuel a nuclear reactor or overhaul a power generator to the nearest hour. The schedules will be revised at the end of the shift, or once a day when they need to be. These jobs would not be scheduled to the nearest 15 minutes, however, because they can't be controlled that closely. If you make the mistake of scheduling in too much detail, you will spend all your time keeping your schedule up to date, and that is a waste of time.

> Never plan in more detail than you can control.

Apparently, people sometimes fall into the microplanning trap because their scheduling software permits them to plan down to minutes. If you *can* do it, goes the thinking, then maybe you *should* do it.

Failing to Plan for Risks

A "can-do" attitude is far preferable to a "can't do" attitude—up to a point. That point is when the person ignores probable risks. I once had a manager tell me that he didn't want me to suggest that his people pad their schedules. He wanted their schedules to be *aggressive*. I appreciate his concern, but there is a difference between aggressive and foolhardy.

> **MISTAKE 5:**
> Failing to plan for risks.

If you are doing construction work and that work may be delayed by weather, it is common risk management practice to allow for weather delays by padding your schedule. If the weather delay doesn't happen, you get ahead. If more delay occurs than you anticipated, you will have to work hard to recover. But to ignore the possibility of weather delays altogether is foolhardy.

Murphy's Law states that whatever can go wrong will go wrong. Stated in terms of probability, this means that there is a higher probability that things will accidentally go wrong than that they will accidentally go right. And of course, we know that even Murphy was an optimist.

Risk management is an integral part of good project management and will be discussed in Chapter 11.

> There is a higher probability that things will accidentally go wrong than that they will accidentally go right.

DEVELOPING THE WORK BREAKDOWN STRUCTURE

At the beginning of this chapter, I showed that we are now down to Step 6 of my overall flowchart. Step 6 actually consists of a number of substeps, as shown in Figure 8.3.

As we saw earlier, implementation planning answers the questions shown in Step 6a of Figure 8.3 and repeated here:

1. What tasks must be done?
2. Who will do each one?
3. How long will each task take?
4. What materials, supplies, and equipment are required?
5. How much will each task cost?

Notice that we don't worry about the order in which tasks will be done until we get to Step 6b. This is the scheduling problem, and it will be fully covered in Chapter 9.

> The first step in implementation planning is to answer the question, "What must be done?"

Figure 8.3   Step 6 of The Lewis Method Expanded

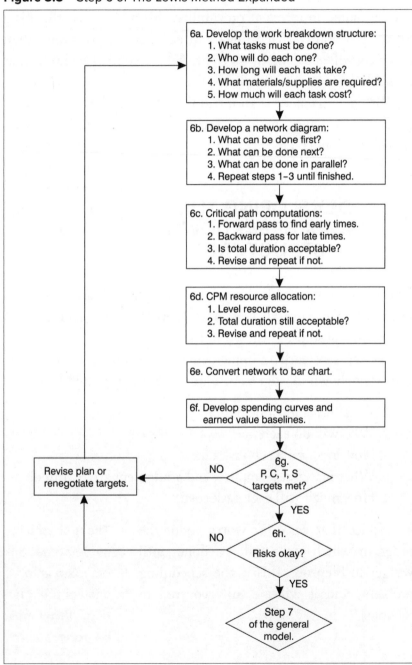

For now, we will concentrate on the first question: What must be done? The tool of choice for doing this is the work breakdown structure (WBS), which is constructed in Step 6a. An example of a very simple WBS, a small project in your yard, is shown in Figure 8.4.

Figure 8.4 Work Breakdown Structure for Yard Project

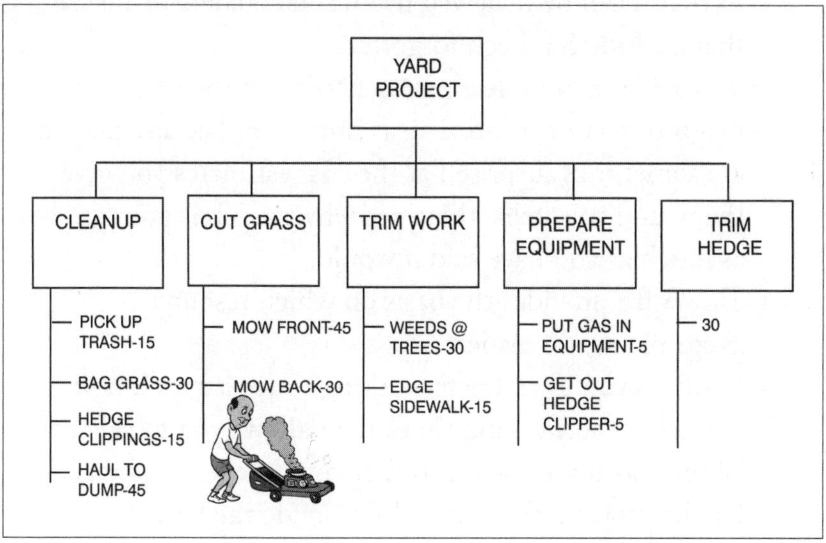

As you can see, there are five major tasks to be done: cut the grass, do trim work, and so on. Some of these tasks also have subtasks underneath. The terminology will be explained shortly.

But what use is this? First, one of the major causes of project failure is that something is forgotten until the project is underway, and then it is discovered. The forgotten work has a serious impact on the project, in terms of either schedule or cost. The WBS is one device that helps us ensure that nothing significant has been forgotten.

As a matter of fact, I consider the WBS to be the most valuable tool of project management, as it ties the entire project together. This position is contrary to the popular belief that project management is just scheduling. There are some projects that are so small that developing a schedule would be a waste of time, but a WBS is *always* useful. Here's why:

- It identifies all work to be done in the project graphically, so that it can be reviewed by all stakeholders to ensure that nothing has been forgotten.
- It provides a graphical representation of the scope (or magnitude) of the job. This is important because people are sometimes surprised at the cost estimates you give them, and this helps them see why the job is going to cost as much as you have said it would.
- The WBS provides the basis on which resource assignments are made.
- It allows you to estimate working times for each task.
- Knowing the working times then allows you to calculate labor costs for all work, so that you develop a *labor budget* for the project. The times also provide the basis for developing a schedule.
- You can also identify material, capital equipment, and other costs associated with each activity (such as insurance costs).

Terminology

Now let's discuss terminology. In Figure 8.5 you will see that each level of the WBS is given a name. The first level is called *program*, and the next is called *project*. This explains the difference between program management and project management. A program is a very large job that consists of several projects. A good example is a program to develop a new airplane. A partial WBS for such a job is shown in Figure 8.6.

Figure 8.5   Names of Levels in a WBS

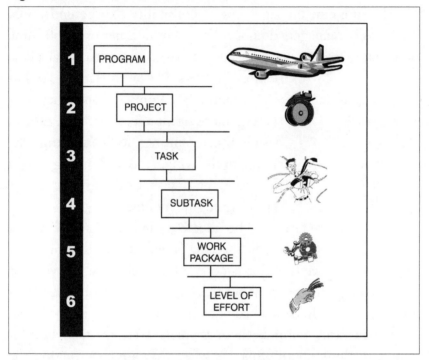

Figure 8.6   WBS for an Airplane Development Program

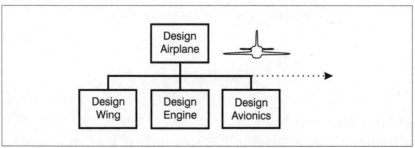

The engine design is a project in its own right, with a project manager and a project team. The wing design, avionics design, and so on, are also large projects. In fact, the wing design would probably be done by the aircraft company, and the engine and avionics would be contracted to other companies, such as General Electric, Rolls-Royce, or Collins Radio.

The program manager has responsibility for the entire job. The project managers do not report to him or her on a solid-line basis but do report on a dotted-line basis. Note that an airplane such as Boeing's 777 or an Airbus 319 has wing-mounted engines. Somewhere in the engine design project will be a task to design the mountings for connecting the engine to the wing. And in the wing design there will be a task to design the corresponding engine mounts.

> Don't worry about the sequence of tasks while constructing the WBS.

Clearly, these tasks will be interactive in nature and will have to be coordinated between the two project teams. The program manager must see that this is done. However, when the WBS is drawn, we do not worry about the sequence in which these tasks are done. This will be worked out when the schedule is developed.

I make this point because there is a strong tendency for people to think about sequence when they are constructing the WBS. "You can't do that until you have done this," they say. You must keep telling them, "That's true; you can't do this until that is done, but we're not trying to work that out yet."

Work Package

What exactly does "work package" mean? It is simply a label that identifies a specific level in the structure. If I ask you about a work package in the engine project for the airplane, you would know that it is something at level 5 in the structure. Whether something goes at level 5 or 6 (or whatever) can be known only by breaking work down in progressive steps until you reach a point of diminishing returns. And wherever an activity falls, it falls. It is not a matter of something absolutely being a level 3 subtask. It is a function of how the work is structured. You will see this in the example that follows later in this chapter.

The Steps in the Process

How do you go about developing a WBS? I'm going to use a simple example. We're planning a family camping trip. It is for a family of four—two adults, a boy who is 12 years old, and a girl who is 8. They have set aside a two-week period for the trip, and they have already arranged with their employers to be away during that time. Furthermore, they have a budget. They don't want to spend more than a certain amount for this trip.

Notice what has been specified so far in terms of the PCTS constraints. We have specified time and cost. Scope and performance are undefined.

What would scope mean in a camping trip? Things like what the family members want to do while they are away; that is, a list of activities in which they want to engage. It may also involve whether they are tent camping or taking a Winnebago. As for performance, remember that this is the quality of work done. In the camping example, it means the quality of the family members' experience. If they try to cram too much into the trip, as people sometimes do when they go abroad and want to see 12 cities in three days, they will sacrifice quality in the process.

The family members make a list of everything they want to do. It doesn't appear that quality will be sacrificed, but when they add up the costs, they realize that they will exceed their budget. What do they do?

Two possibilities exist. First, they can decide that this is a once-in-a-lifetime trip, and they will just put a little more on the credit card than they had intended. Or they may decide that the budget is very important and delete some activities from the list.

The importance of this example is that you can never escape the PCTS constraints in *any* project—not even a simple thing like a family camping trip. Trade-offs are always being made to balance project requirements.

The First Step

When I draw a WBS, I begin by identifying major tasks. My first pass would look like the one shown in Figure 8.7. As I continue, this may change. For that reason, it is convenient to do this on a whiteboard or to use Post-it® notes so that things can easily be moved around.

Once I have listed all the tasks, I begin breaking them down. For example, "Select Site" can be broken down as shown in Figure 8.8.

Now note that the task of listing activities during the trip can be a stand-alone task, or it may be part of the family meeting. That is, if the family is going to make the list during the family meeting, we can remove it as a task and put it there as a subtask. This is shown in Figure 8.9.

Figure 8.7 First Pass on a WBS for a Camping Trip

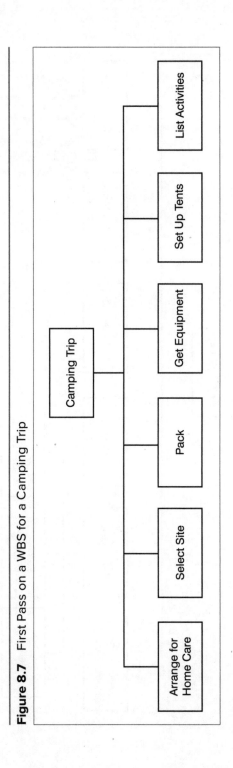

224

Figure 8.8 WBS with "Select Site" Broken Down

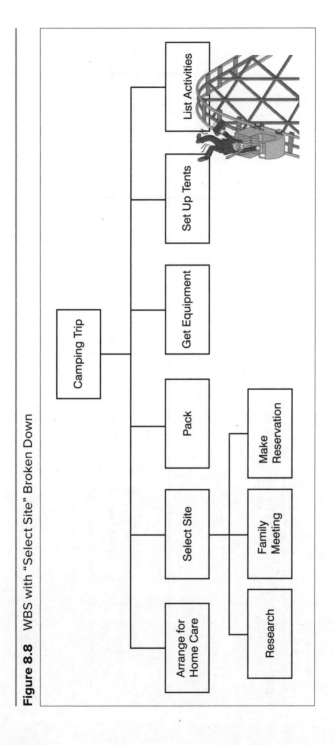

Figure 8.9 WBS with "List Activities" Moved under "Family Meeting"

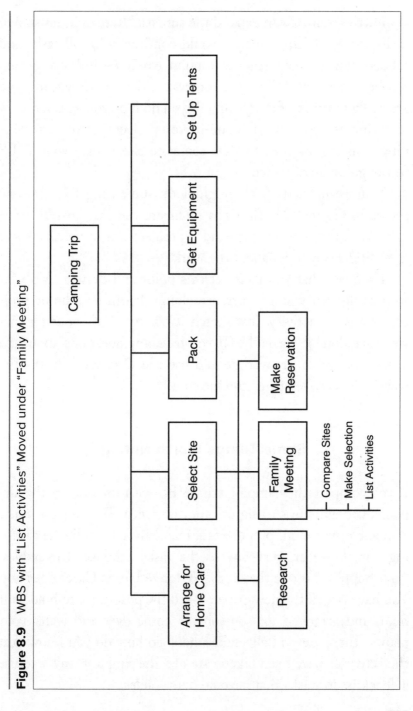

Furthermore, I can expand the subtask "Research," as shown in Figure 8.10. This process would continue with all tasks and subtasks until I have reached a point where I think everything has been covered. When this process is done with a team, you are likely to think of everything. If you do it by yourself, you may miss something, so if it is a one-person project that you are planning, it is a good idea to have someone else review your WBS before going any further.

Your completed WBS might look something like the one shown in Figure 8.11. This is by no means the only possible solution. Most projects are open-ended problems, meaning that there is no single way to go about the work.

I suggest that you pause at this point and draw a WBS for something that you are currently doing. It can be a home project or a work activity. Just sketch it out to satisfy yourself that you have done it correctly. (If you have any questions about the procedure, go to my website and use the *Contact Us* form. The website is www.lewisinstituteinc.com.)

Some Things Worth Noting

If you compare the camping trip WBS with the one for the airplane, you will notice a significant difference. The projects in the airplane program all produce tangible deliverables. In the camping trip, however, very few of the tasks produce deliverables. "Get Supplies" is one that does. "Arrange Home Care" does not. You have cut off the newspaper, asked the post office to hold your mail, and arranged for someone to come over and water your plants. There are no deliverables here, so how do you know that the activities have been taken care of? The simplest way is to use a checklist for tasks that have no deliverables.

Figure 8.10 WBS with "Research" Expanded

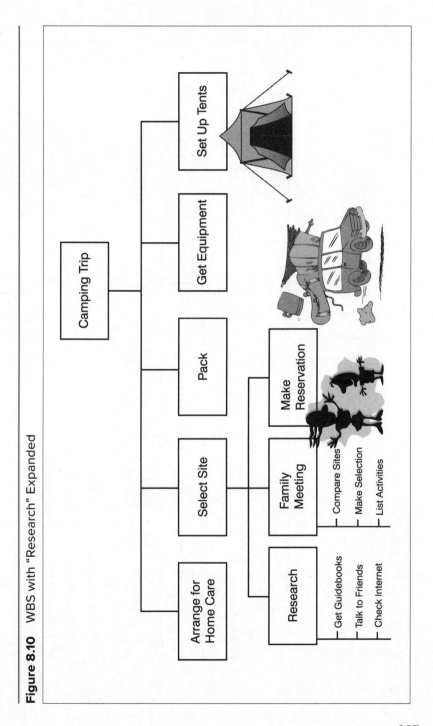

Figure 8.11 Completed WBS for Camping Trip

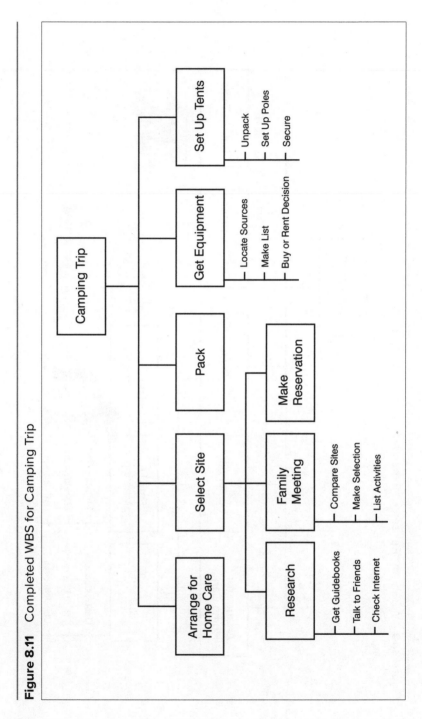

I consider the camping trip WBS to be primarily process oriented. The airplane WBS is deliverables oriented at the top level. However, as you get further down into the structure, you will find several process-oriented activities. As an example, you will have to test the engine. There is no hardware deliverable, but you will produce a test report. That is your deliverable, and it is evidence that the test has been conducted.

In many cases, you don't even produce reports, so how do you know that the work has been done? You use exit criteria. As a simple example, if you change the oil in your car and I ask if you are sure that you've done it correctly, you could show me that the dipstick registers "Full" and shows clean oil. One of these is *quantitative*, and the other is *qualitative*. I would also look under the car and inspect to see whether any oil is dripping out, which would mean that the plug had not been correctly reinstalled, another qualitative exit criterion.

I know of a situation where a company produced a prototype product and called one of the vice presidents to examine it. He didn't like a major feature of the product and insisted that it be redesigned. The prototype had been built with tooling, which had to be scrapped. The total cost to redesign the product was huge.

In this case, the exit criterion was that the vice president approved the product. Knowing that, it would have been best to get him to look at preliminary drawings, rather than wait so long. In fact, I wouldn't be surprised if they had tried to do so and were unable to get him to review the design because he had a heavy schedule and felt that he couldn't afford the time. The lesson is that corrections should always be made as early in a process as possible because each succeeding step magnifies the cost to correct an error by about 10 times; the progression goes 1, 10, 100, 1,000, and so on.

Suggestions on How to Proceed

When you develop a project plan, you are determining the who, what, when, and how, as I have previously explained. It may be helpful to approach a WBS by answering questions in this order:

1. What must be done? Example: The house must be cleaned. This would be the project.
2. What must be done to clean the house? Wash the windows. Clean the floors. Put everything in its proper place. Dust the furniture. Carry out the garbage. These would be major tasks in the project.
3. Who will do each one? Mom will clean the floors. Tommy will put everything in its place. Sue will dust the furniture. Dad will carry out the garbage. Donnie will wash the windows. This assigns roles and responsibilities.
4. How will each task be done? Mom will clean the floors by vacuuming the carpets and mopping the tile floors. Sue will dust the furniture using furniture polish. These will be subtasks.
5. What is needed to do each subtask? A vacuum cleaner. Furniture polish. Rags. Paper towels. Garbage bags. Identifying these allows you to develop costs for equipment and materials. This is a major part of the budget.
6. How long will each subtask take? These estimates provide the basis for the labor budget (see Step 8) and for developing the schedule.
7. What is required for each subtask to be considered complete? This will constitute exit criteria for each activity.
8. In a normal work project, how much will each subtask cost for labor? This gives you the labor budget, which, when combined with the equipment and materials budget, yields the total project budget.

Guidelines to Follow

The following are some guidelines that you should follow in developing a WBS:

- Up to 20 levels can be used. More than 20 is considered overkill.
- All paths on a WBS do not have to go down to the same level. One path may go down five levels and another only three levels. When you have reached a point that allows you to manage the work, you stop. Don't force the structure to be symmetrical.
- The WBS does not show the sequencing of work except in the sense that all level 5 work packages hanging below a given subtask must be complete for the subtask to be complete, and so on. However, the work packages below that subtask might be performed in series or in parallel. Sequencing is determined when schedules are developed.
- A WBS should be developed before scheduling and resource allocation. Identify the tasks first, then come back and decide who will do them, and estimate how long they will take.
- The WBS should be developed by individuals who are knowledgeable about the work. Different parts of the WBS will be developed by various groups. Then the separate parts will be combined. Remember, the first rule of project planning is that the people who will ultimately do the work should develop the plan.

> A work breakdown structure *does not show the sequence in which work is performed!* Such sequencing is determined when a schedule is developed.

- Break down a project only to a level that is sufficient to produce an estimate of the required accuracy. This should be explained. One of the big advantages that a WBS offers is greater accuracy of cost and time estimates than you would get by simply comparing one project to another. A project-to-project estimate is called a *ballpark estimate*, as was mentioned previously, and we saw that its accuracy is lacking.

  If you break a project down to the level that can be controlled, you can develop a working estimate. But what does this mean? Ask yourself what level of detail you can control in your work. Can you predict to the nearest hour when a task will be finished? The nearest day? The nearest week? If you break work down into such small units that they take only hours to perform and you can't control work to that degree, you will spend all of your time updating your schedule and get no work done! I know. I've done it.

  It isn't any fun. So when you reach a level that you can control, stop there.

  > A WBS is a list of activities. It is not a grocery list.

  It may be that an estimate is needed to decide if a project should be done. It may be possible to make that decision if the accuracy of the estimate is ±50 percent. You may have to break the project down only two levels to achieve that accuracy. Going further at this point would be a waste of time if the decision is to not do the work.

- A WBS is a list of activities, not a grocery list. Imagine that I am doing a home project—some yard work, some repairs, and some grocery shopping. I draw a WBS like that in Figure 8.12.

Figure 8.12 WBS for Home Project

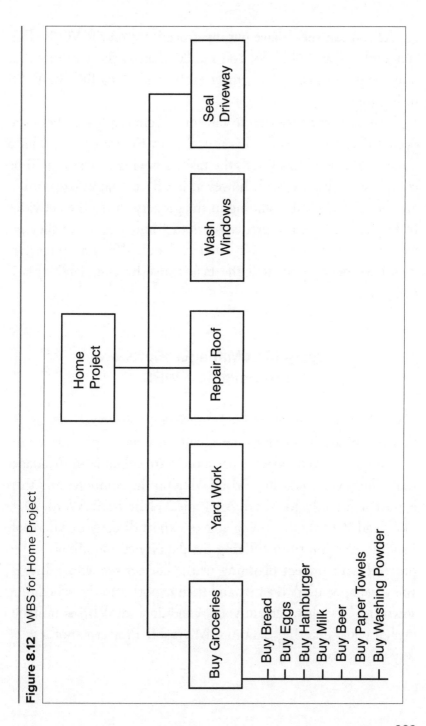

As you can see, I have put my grocery list on the WBS. That is not what you should do. You should identify the activities that must be performed to buy groceries. It would look like the WBS in Figure 8.13.

This is a very easy trap to fall into. Here is a test to help you decide if you have made this mistake. In Figure 8.13, if I have done all the activities listed, the task of buying groceries will be complete. In Figure 8.12, however, if I have bought eggs, milk, and bread, I am still standing in the grocery store. The activities in Figure 8.12 are not predecessors to "Buy Groceries"; they *are* the components of that task listed in detail. When all the activities have been done, will the task above be complete? This is your test.

Using MindManager® Software to Develop a WBS

If you have ever developed a Mind Map, you know how useful this technique is for thinking about an issue, especially brainstorming. Mindjet software has a program called MindManager that allows you to create a Mind Map on the computer and then export it directly to Microsoft Project, Microsoft Word, Outlook, and PowerPoint. Being able to export directly to Microsoft Project saves you from entering the data twice and allows you to proceed with project planning in the correct sequence. That is, you develop your WBS first and then export it to the scheduling software. Trying to create your schedule and WBS simultaneously by just entering data into Microsoft Project is not a good way to go about it.

Figure 8.13 WBS with Proper Activities Shown for Buying Groceries

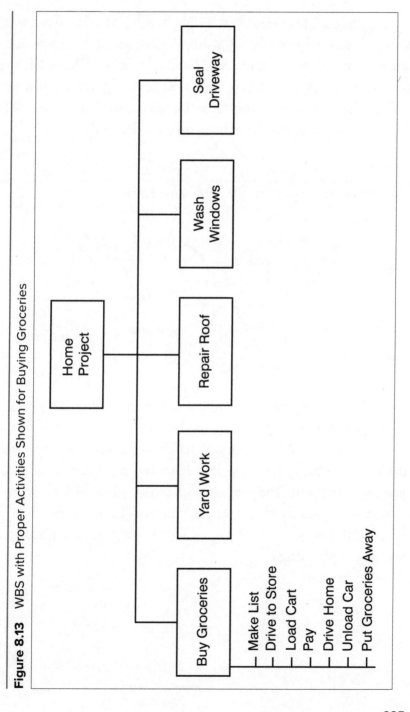

Figure 8.14 provides an example of a Mind Map developed with MindManager. This is a simple example of a yard project, shown previously in Figure 8.4. Note that, while I have left the format of this Mind Map in its standard configuration, you can format the display as an organization chart, so that it looks like the box structures that have been presented already.

Figure 8.14   Mind Map Using MindManager Software

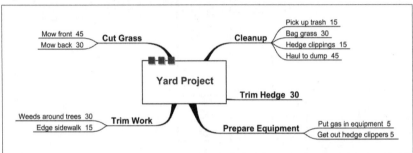

Using a computer projector, you can develop a Mind Map with a group in brainstorming mode, and everyone can see what you're doing. In addition, if you decide you don't like where you placed something, you can drag it to another location without having to retype it. The program can be downloaded for a 30-day evaluation by going to www.mindjet.com. (I am not receiving a fee for this endorsement; I just think the program is a great tool for project planning.)

ESTIMATING TIME, COST, AND RESOURCE REQUIREMENTS

Once you have your WBS completed, you are ready to use it for estimating. This step scares the daylights out of a lot of people. They don't know how long something will take, but they know that if they give their manager a number, they will be held to it. So they try to waffle or avoid committing to a number altogether. As I pointed out earlier in this chapter, people think you can't schedule creative tasks, but you can.

You *cannot*, however, schedule pure discovery work, and you should always separate discovery from development in a product development environment. As an example, the CFO at Merck Pharmaceuticals wrote an article in the *Harvard Business Review* reporting that the company examines approximately 10,000 compounds before one makes it as a drug. There's no way you can schedule such work.

That does not mean that you can't plan research projects, however. I've been told that by several scientists. What confuses them is that research projects have conditional branches. You do a series of studies or experiments, and, depending on the results you get, you go in one direction or another. This is shown in Figure 8.15.

You may not know at the beginning of the project which branch you will ultimately take, but you can plan everything up to that point. Furthermore, as you near that branch, you must begin considering what you will do once the outcome is known. If you don't, you will waste valuable time deciding later. (And you may have no idea what to do next; it isn't a simple thing!)

Figure 8.15 A Project with a Conditional Branch

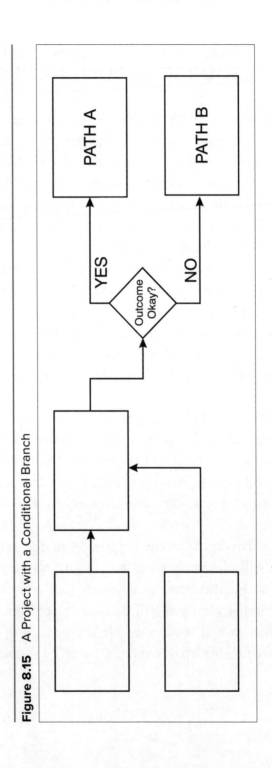

What Is Estimating?

In simple words, estimating is *guessing*! Yes, there are kinder, gentler ways to put it, such as *forecasting* or *predicting*. But the truth is that an estimate is a guess based on something. It is best when it is based on experience. But what if you have no experience—if it's the first time something is to be done?

> Estimating is *guessing!*

In that situation, you must use another approach. There are two primary ones that we will discuss later. However, it should be clear that, no matter how much experience you have, estimating is guessing. Why? Because *all activities are probabilistic, not deterministic!* There is a probability that a task can be completed in a certain time, given a fixed level of effort. If you want to guarantee that the task is finished in a fixed time period, then you must vary effort, reduce scope, or sacrifice quality. You can't have it all. Therefore, "exact estimate" is an oxymoron.

> All activities are probabilistic, not deterministic!

I said that estimating is best done when you have experience, or history, with an activity. Let's see what that means. You have history on an activity that you perform regularly—namely, driving to work. If I ask you how long it takes, you can give me three (or possibly four) numbers. One is the typical driving time. It happens most frequently. Another is the best case. You have never been able to get to work any faster. And finally, there is the worst case, where traffic tie-ups delay you. This worst-case time happens often enough that you are well aware of it.

> "It's a poor sort of memory, that only works backwards," the Queen remarked.
> —Lewis Carroll
> *Alice's Adventures in Wonderland*

There may also be a "worst-worst" case. Just once, you got caught in a traffic tie-up that caused you to take three hours to get to work. However, it happened only once, and you don't expect it to happen again. The "normal" worst-case time does happen fairly often, so it is the one you should use.

When I ask people for their driving times, I usually get numbers like those shown in Table 8.1.

TABLE 8.1   Driving Times Reported by Many People

Typical time	45 minutes
Shortest time	30 minutes
Longest time	60 minutes

Notice that the worst-case time is skewed upward. The driving time is not normally distributed. A normal distribution is shown in Figure 8.16, and a skewed distribution is shown in Figure 8.17.

Figure 8.16   Normal Distribution

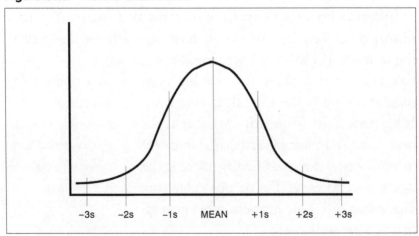

Figure 8.17 Skewed Distribution

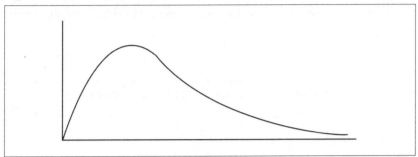

The question is, what do we do with historical data when we have it? To illustrate, write down your own driving times, and then answer this question: If I ask you how long you estimate it will take you to get to work on a random day (you don't know what day of the week it is or what the weather is doing), what will you tell me? Most people give me the typical time. Now, if you have a very skewed distribution, this is probably the modal time. If the distribution is a normal distribution, then the typical time would be an average. For an average, the probability that you could get to work in that time or less would be 50 percent. This is shown in Figure 8.18.

Most people don't feel uncomfortable with a 50 percent probability for the time required to drive to work, but they do feel uneasy if the probability of completing project work is that low. So they tend to pad the number to increase the probability of success. As you can see in Figure 8.18, if you go only one standard deviation above the mean, you increase the probability to 84 percent.

> As the probability of project success goes toward 100 percent, the probability of funding goes to zero.

I often ask people, "If the president of your company wanted to have a meeting with you first thing in the morning, and it was career suicide to be late, how much time would you allow yourself to get to work?" Most of them go to the worst-case time—or higher—and raise their probability to 99.9 percent.

Figure 8.18   Normal Distribution with Probabilities Shown

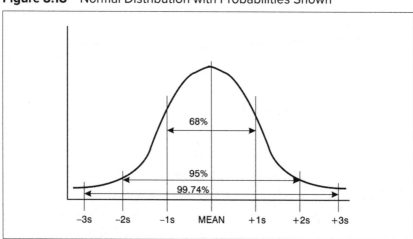

Because there is a significant penalty for being late, they reduce their risk by padding the schedule. They will do the same thing with projects. And when they do, the cost of the project goes sky high, and it most likely will not be funded.

> **PARKINSON'S LAW: Work will expand to take the time allowed.**

I can promise you, however, that if it gets funded, it will cost what we have budgeted, and possibly more. This is based on Parkinson's Law: work will always expand to take as long as has been allowed. The project will never finish early.

Why? Because if you finish early, everyone will think that you padded the schedule, and next time they will cut your time and budget accordingly.

Now this is organizational insanity. A sample of one has created an expectation for all future work!

I am convinced that everyone should have to study statistics, because they would then understand that all processes vary. Your driving time varies. The amount of time you need to get dressed in the morning varies. The time it takes to write a 10-page document varies. Why? Random noise.

All kinds of things affect your driving time, for example. The exact time that you leave home. The weather. Road construction. School buses. You name it. These are factors outside your control, and they must be accepted.

Can we reduce variation? Yes, up to a point. That is what all process improvement is aimed at doing.

Can we eliminate variation altogether?

Absolutely not.

Yet we have two rules in organizations that show that we don't understand this. One is, "Thou shalt not go over budget."

The other is, "Thou shalt not come in under budget."

This is plain stupid. It is insisting that people violate a law of nature—namely, to achieve zero variance in their spending to budget. This is possible only if you finagle, so everyone plays games to achieve the impossible.

The problem is, this is easier to do with a department than with a project. You budget for a department based on head count. You can control spending to a much tighter tolerance than you can on a project, because a project is budgeted based on a bunch of guesses.

We simply must reach a point where everyone understands that variation is a fact of life and must be accepted. We waste millions of dollars every year attempting to make variances approach zero, when it is counterproductive to do so.

Imagine now that you finished a task ahead of schedule and passed it on to the person who is next in line. What would happen? Would she start work on it immediately?

Of course not.

She doesn't have to start until a few days later, according to the schedule, so she won't.

Goldratt (1997) calls this the *student effect*.

Remember when you were in school, and the teacher announced on Monday that there would be a test on Friday? Everyone moaned and groaned. "I already have three tests this week," says one student. "This is going to kill me."

So the teacher relents and says, "Okay, we will have the test Friday of next week, instead of this week."

Everyone sighs with relief.

When will the students start studying for the test?

GOLDRATT'S PRINCIPLE:
A project will accumulate delays but will never accumulate gains

You guessed it. They will start studying on Thursday night the following week! They won't have any more study time than they would have had if the test had been left on this Friday.

Goldratt concludes that, when you combine Parkinson's Law with the student effect, a project will accumulate delays but will never accumulate gains. This means that projects almost always cost more than necessary and take longer than they should. There is plenty of room for improvement.

How do we solve this problem? We must change our thinking. We must accept variation, and in doing so eliminate penalties for being either early or late on a task-by-task basis. As Goldratt argues, it doesn't matter that there is some variation in task completion. What matters is that the project finishes on time. (In the years since I first wrote this, I have realized that I must have had too much wine to drink when I suggested that we change our thinking. There is no way that will ever happen, but it would be nice if it did.)

If you allow task completion dates to vary, some will finish early, some will finish a bit late, and the variations will average out. Otherwise, you will always finish late.

In other words, this means that estimates should be based on that typical driving time, rather than the worst case.

Consensual Estimating

What do you do when you have no history? You could hold a wet string up and see how long it takes to dry, multiply the result by 33, and divide by 6. That is called an estimating algorithm.

Of course, I'm joking.

Some people are using consensual estimating. It works like this: For each of the tasks in your WBS, you ask several individuals who know something about that task to estimate how long it will take, independently of each other. Then you have a meeting in which you compare estimates. Suppose that for a single task you had a result like that shown in Figure 8.19.

Figure 8.19 The Distribution of Several Estimates for a Single Task

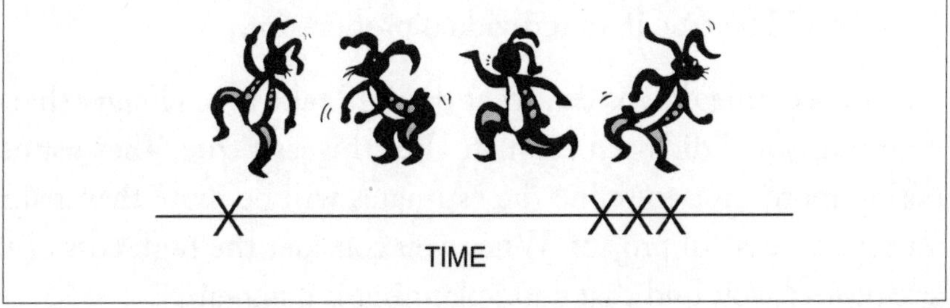

TIME

Notice that there are three individuals in close agreement, and one whose number is considerably lower. It would be tempting to throw out the low number and go with the majority. But that's not a good idea. What you want to do is understand why the difference exists, so you discuss the issues affecting the task. As you do so, the person who estimated low may revise his estimate upward.

Conversely, the majority may realize that they missed something that the other individual thought of, and they may revise their estimates downward.

Whatever the case, they ultimately are asked to choose a number that they can all support. Notice they aren't asked to totally agree with the number. You almost never get total agreement in a group. What you want is that they will all support a single estimate. This is the practical meaning of the word *consensus*.

There are four major advantages of using this approach:

1. No one person is "on the hook" for the estimate. If it turns out to be significantly off, no individual will get chastised for it.
2. Inexperienced members of the team learn from the others, and their ability to estimate improves.
3. Collectively, the team members are more likely to think of all the factors that may affect the time required to do the task than would be true of any individual.
4. You will have higher commitment to the estimate than would be true if an individual produced it.

The seeming downside is that this will take much longer than if an individual did each estimate. But this isn't true. The cost of taking more time to refine the estimates will be more than paid for by a successful project. When you consider the high cost of a late project, you find that good planning is a bargain.

Calendar-Time Estimates

I have suggested that you use working-time estimates to plan a project. However, if you ask a person, "How long will it take you to do a report for me?" the person will most likely tell you, "Oh, I should be able to do that within a week."

She knows it is about two hours of actual work, but because she has a lot of work to do, it will take her a week to get to it. So she gives you a calendar-time estimate.

Do you really care about the actual working time? After all, isn't it the calendar time that is really important?

You need both. You need the actual working time to work out labor costs, and you need the calendar time to predict project completion. In fact, if she tells you that the report will be done in a week, and you need it sooner, you will ask her to give it a higher priority so that she can do it in a couple of days. You are always juggling trade-offs between working time and calendar time, so you have to ask both questions when you ask for estimates.

CLARIFYING ROLES AND RESPONSIBILITIES

I said earlier that you can't estimate task durations unless you begin with the assumption of a resource, either by name or at least by skill level. Once you have assigned resources to all activities, fill out a responsibility chart like the one in Figure 8.20 so that everyone can tell at a glance who is responsible for each task.

Figure 8.20 Responsibility Chart

Linear Responsibility Chart

Project:	Date Issued:	Sheet Number	of
Manager:	Date Revised:	Revision No:	File: LRCFORM.61

Project Contributors

Task Descriptions																	

CODES: 1 = ACTUAL RESPONSIBILITY; 2 = SUPPORT; 3 = MUST BE NOTIFIED; BLANK = NOT INVOLVED

GAINING COMMITMENT FROM RESOURCE PROVIDERS

In many projects, you don't own your resources; they are provided by functional managers on a temporary basis. Once your implementation plan is complete, you should get it authorized (Step 8 of The Lewis Method model). The necessary signatures should be obtained in a project plan sign-off meeting, if possible. Circulating the plan through the interoffice mail to be signed almost always leads to problems—people tend to skim it instead of reading it, and their commitments don't hold up later. They should be clear that their signatures indicate their commitment to provide resources *when* they say, in the *quantities* they say.

I am generally against a lot of red tape in projects. However, there is a principle in psychology called *commitment and consistency*, which says that when a person makes a commitment to something, she generally behaves in a way that is consistent with the commitment. So requiring signatures on a plan is one way to get contributors to commit to the plan. The other way, which was mentioned earlier, is to have them participate in developing the plan. Otherwise, they have no commitment to it and are likely not to support it.

DEVELOPING THE PROJECT BUDGET

Developing a budget is implied in everything that has been discussed up to now. Once you estimate how long tasks will take, you can multiply the amounts of time by labor rates and develop your labor budget. When you need materials, capital equipment, or outside services for some part of the WBS, you can estimate these and include them in your budget. If you start at the lowest level in the WBS and add the costs for each category (labor, capital equipment, and so on), and continue working up toward the top of the WBS, you will eventually have total costs for the project.

Repeating what I said previously, this shows why the WBS is the most important tool of project management. No other tool provides the means for developing a total project budget. Furthermore, if the budget exceeds what you want to spend on the project, you have a convenient way of analyzing the project to identify components that can be eliminated, thus reducing the scope, so that the project can be completed for the desired amount.

Labor Cost Estimates

Labor cost estimates are also known as budgeted cost of work scheduled (BCWS), or *planned value (PV)*. When you start working on the project, you will compare the actual costs of work performed (ACWP, or simply AC) to the planned value to determine spending variances. You can also compare earned value (or budgeted cost of work performed, BCWP, also referred to as EV) to the planned value figures to determine schedule variance. This will be covered in detail in Chapter 12.

Note that the true cost of labor is not simply the salary that you pay an individual. The real cost is the loaded labor rate. This is the labor rate to which has been added the cost per hour of overhead. You have to pay for your facility, equipment used to do work, and so on. Loaded labor rates are often significantly higher than direct salaries.

Contingencies

In addition to labor, materials, capital equipment, and outside service costs that go into a project budget, you may also include some buffer or padding to cover risks. These are called contingencies, and the two kinds of contingencies that are normally placed in project budgets will be discussed in detail in Chapter 11.

Fiscal Budgeting of Projects

Many organizations try to budget projects on a fiscal basis, even though the job spans several years. This creates a host of problems. The main reason is that these same organizations often practice a ridiculous budgeting system in which a department that does not spend all of its budgeted funds in a given fiscal year loses those funds the next year. This practice should have been outlawed years ago, but it persists. The result is that organizations try to find ways to spend every penny they have budgeted so that they won't lose it. This creates huge amounts of waste.

Furthermore, as I mentioned earlier in this chapter, project budgets are based on estimates, whereas department budgets are based on head counts, history, and projections. These estimates can usually be within a few percent. Project budgets typically have tolerances of ±10 to 20 percent, so to expect them not to vary is ludicrous.

Project schedules are dynamic, not static, so as they accelerate or fall behind, spending likewise varies, making the total variance of project spending very large. Cutting the funding of a project because all monies were not spent in the fiscal year demonstrates a lack of understanding of the dynamic nature of projects!

IN SUMMARY

This chapter covers steps 6 through 8 of the Lewis Method®. Primarily it deals with step 6, which is developing a work breakdown structure (WBS) to identify the various tasks that must be performed to deliver desired project results. Once the tasks have been identified, estimates of task durations can be made together with material, labor, and capital equipment requirements (if any). The WBS is an excellent device for showing project scope graphically. It also provides the basis for developing the schedule, so it is important that the WBS be reviewed carefully to ensure that nothing is forgotten.

Guidelines are given for how many levels can practically be used in a WBS. Rules are also suggested for how planning should be done. For example, the people who will do the work should develop the plan. Suggestions are also made for gaining commitment to the plan by important stakeholders.

CHAPTER 9

Project Scheduling

n the first three editions of this book, I demonstrated how to do network computations in the main body of the book. However, with the ready availability of cost-effective scheduling software, almost nobody does such calculations manually anymore. I do believe that you should understand how they are done, or else you won't understand what the software is telling you. For that reason, beginning with the fourth edition of the book, I moved scheduling computations to an appendix, which is where it remains in this edition.

This chapter will concentrate on the practical creation of a schedule using software, and on managing resources, which is the major problem that you will encounter in developing your schedule.

THE BASICS OF SCHEDULING

Before we go any further, let's make sure you are familiar with all the terms and concepts of scheduling. If you are absolutely sure that you know this material, feel free to skip to the next section. Otherwise, read on.

Until about 1960, projects were scheduled using bar charts. Henry Gantt worked out a system of notation for creating such charts and using them to report progress, so they are commonly called Gantt charts. A simple example is shown in Figure 9.1.

Figure 9.1   A Simple Gantt Chart

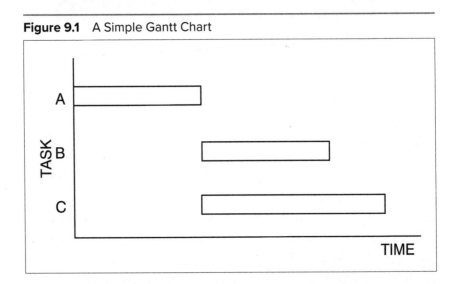

This is the way Gantt charts were drawn before 1960. Notice that the chart gives no indication of whether Tasks B and C depend on the completion of Task A or whether they just coincidentally start when A is completed. This means that if Task A slips, we can't tell what impact it will have on subsequent tasks.

For that reason, a method of showing such dependencies was developed in the late 1950s. The relationships among tasks were shown using arrow diagrams. Two different forms were developed. One was called critical path method (CPM), and

How does a project get to be a year behind schedule? One day at a time.

—Fred Brooks
System 360 Chief Designer, IBM

the other was called program evaluation and review technique (PERT). The difference between the two systems is that PERT makes use of a calculated task duration and allows you to estimate probabilities of completing work, whereas CPM just makes use of estimated task durations with no regard for probabilities.

Both systems allow you to determine which series of activities (or path) in a project will take the longest time to complete. When the project is scheduled to end at the point where the critical path ends, it will have no latitude. Shorter paths, however, will have latitude, which is called either *slack* or *float*. The slack or float provides some protection from unexpected events or from inaccurate estimates. You never want to have a schedule that has no float, as the risk that you won't meet your completion date is extremely high.

CRITICAL PATH: A path that has no float and is the longest path through the project.

FLOAT OR SLACK: Any path shorter than the critical path will have latitude, which is commonly called either float or slack.

In addition to there being two systems, there are two forms of notation. One is called activity-on-arrow (AOA), and the other is called activity-on-node (AON). In AOA notation, the arrow represents the work to be done, and the circle represents an event—either the beginning of another activity or the completion of a previous one. This is shown in Figure 9.2.

Figure 9.2 Activity-on-Arrow Notation

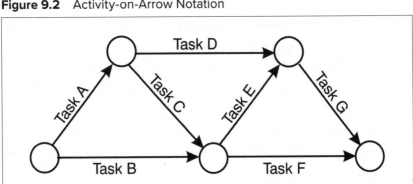

For AON notation, a box (or node) is used to show the task itself, and the arrows simply show the sequence in which work is done. This is shown in Figure 9.3.

Figure 9.3 Activity-on-Node Notation

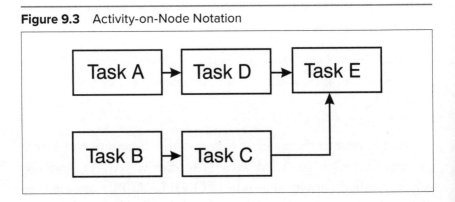

Since both systems get the same schedule results, it makes no difference which one is used. However, most software produces only one of them, and it is usually AON. A few programs, such as Primavera, allow you to choose the system you prefer.

Arrow diagrams allow you to determine whether it is possible for a task to start at a certain time. When you create a large schedule using bar charting, you may inadvertently show tasks starting before a predecessor is finished, and if this isn't possible, then your schedule won't work. This was one of the main reasons why CPM and PERT were created in the first place. So, if you want to create a schedule that will work, you should always work out the interdependencies among all the activities in a project.

> Be careful not to enter too many "must-start-on" and "must-end-on" dates into your schedule, or you will create a schedule that simply won't work.

However, you don't want to give people an arrow diagram to use as a working tool. These diagrams are too hard to read. The bar chart is a much better working tool because it is simple to read. Fortunately, all scheduling software will produce a bar chart for you. Be careful, though. One common error that people make is to tell the software that every task must start on a certain date and end on a certain date, and if these conflict with what is naturally going to happen based on task dependencies, the software will just regurgitate your input, and you will be left with a useless schedule. The software itself is designed to tell you when tasks will start and end, based on their durations, resource allocations, and interdependencies. If you tamper too much with dates, you will have a garbage-in, garbage-out situation.

> You *must* enter dependencies for your software to work out where your critical path and float are.

Furthermore, if you don't enter predecessor or successor information into your software, then it cannot work out your critical path and determine how much slack or float you have on noncritical paths. This approach relegates the software to a presentation tool at best, and only allows you to document your failures.

Although both CPM and PERT find the critical path and float in a project, the emphasis has always been on the critical path. However, in today's world, the objective of project management is universally to complete a project in the minimum possible time, and this is a primary advantage of using arrow diagrams. The shortest possible schedule will be the one in which as many tasks as possible are done in parallel. This can only be calculated using a computer, as the resource allocation problem becomes formidable, and the use of manual methods is nearly impossible for all but the most trivial of networks.

> The real advantage of network diagramming is to help you find all the places where work can be done in parallel, thus creating the shortest possible schedule.

Before You Use the Software

There is a great temptation to create a schedule by entering data into the templates provided by the software. There is a major flaw in this approach. You can see only a small segment of a large project schedule on the screen, and if activities have predecessors or successors that are off the screen, it can be almost impossible to determine what they are.

A better approach is to either sketch the network on paper or use Post-it® notes on a whiteboard to work out the logic. A major advantage of this method is that a group can participate, and members can see possibilities that you may miss if you do the schedule individually. Then, once the logic is worked out to everyone's satisfaction, you

> You should construct the schedule on paper before entering it into your computer.

can have someone transcribe the network into your scheduling software and let the computer generate dates for activities.

In creating a schedule this way, follow this guideline: if two tasks can be done in parallel from a logical standpoint, draw them that way. It is tempting to consider resource limitations while constructing a schedule, but if you do, it will take you forever to work out the network, and you may have tied your hands unnecessarily.

For example, suppose I have assigned Mary to two tasks that can logically be done in parallel. When I start constructing my schedule, I decide that it won't be possible to do the work in parallel, since Mary can't do two things at the same time. So I draw them in series instead.

But who says that Mary *must* do both? Perhaps Jane can do one of them and Mary can do the other. That will produce a shorter schedule than if the two tasks are done in series.

In addition, suppose one task has a 10-day duration and the second has a 5-day duration. They are parallel, but the 10-day task also has 5 days of float. Thus, these two tasks can be done in series without impacting project completion, and Mary can do both of them. This is shown in Figure 9.4.

A little thought reveals that following this rule means that you are adopting a hidden assumption that you have unlimited resources—which, naturally, you don't. So you find that you have double- and triple-scheduled members of your team.

Not a good rule, you say.

Figure 9.4   Schedule with Mary on Both Tasks

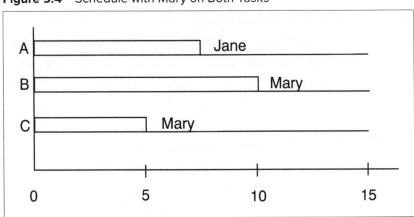

True, but think about it this way. An unlimited-resource schedule will produce the shortest possible schedule. Since most projects are assigned an end date from the beginning, if you create an unlimited-resource schedule and it won't meet the imposed end date, then you are in trouble before you do any work, and you may as well know it. You know it will only get worse when you factor in your limited fund of resources.

The important point is that the software enables everyone to see what possibilities exist for a project and to make informed decisions about trade-offs. Remember, you are always constrained by PCTS, and if you can't meet the required time with the available resources (this equates to cost), then you will have to find more help, reduce scope, or—heaven help you—reduce performance (quality of work). The latter is generally unacceptable, but it is what your team members may do if you don't give them relief from time or scope constraints.

SOFTWARE CAPABILITIES

I have mentioned elsewhere that there are lots of people who think that project management is just scheduling. If they provide you with a software program, they have made you into an instant project manager—or, at the very least, into a scheduler. Of course, this couldn't be further from the truth.

The software can't work out dependencies for you. That is something that you must do yourself. Nor can it tell you how long a task will take. All it can do is computations. It is a tool, and unless you know how to deal with the various issues in a project, all that tool can do is help you document your failures with great precision.

In fact, we have given thousands of individuals powerful scheduling software without training them how to manage. This is like giving someone a fantastic accounting program when the person doesn't know the difference between a debit and a credit and expecting the software to turn him or her into a skilled accountant.

> Giving a person a powerful scheduling software program when he knows nothing about project management just allows him to document his failures with great precision!

One huge advantage of using software is that it will drop out weekends, holidays, and vacation periods for employees, and tell you about the actual dates on which activities should start and finish. Doing calendar computations manually is an onerous task, and the software is worth its weight in gold just for this alone.

Resource Leveling

As I have said earlier, a schedule is initially developed under the assumption of unlimited resources. Once this is done, the software can show you where you have overloaded your resources. If there is enough float in your schedule, it can make use of that float to schedule tasks so that resources are no longer overloaded, and the end date can be met. This is called *time-critical* resource allocation. The software is instructed to level resources without slipping the already determined end date. It will then make use of task float to delay activities until resources become available, but it will delay a task only to the point at which it runs out of float. To delay it any further would cause the end date to be missed.

However, if there is insufficient float in the schedule to level resources completely, the software can be instructed to relieve the overloads, even if it means sliding out the end date. This is called *resource-critical* allocation. Under this condition, you may find that a schedule that was going to end in December 2021 under the unlimited-resource assumption is now going to end in the year 2031 because it is starved for resources.

Clearly, this is an unacceptable solution. Nobody is going to accept a schedule that is going to take so long to complete. So what good is the resource-critical method?

Simple: it creates a *moment of truth.*

It alerts everyone to what is going to happen to a project if something isn't done. More help is needed, scope must be reduced, or performance requirements must be relaxed; otherwise, the project will take forever.

The advantage is partly psychological. In the days before software, when we had this problem, we had no credibility with our managers when we told them about the problem.

"I need more help," you would tell your boss.

"Quit whining and get the job done," the boss would snarl.

And all too often, you pulled it off.

And shot yourself in the foot in the process.

Why?

Because your boss expected you to pull it off the next time. After all, you'd just proved that you didn't need all the help that you claimed you needed. Your boss concluded that you were just whining.

Please don't misunderstand me. I have no objection to pulling off a miracle occasionally. But I don't want it to become the expectation for all time to come. After all, how did I pull it off this time? Through blood, sweat, and tears. Every member of the team put in extraordinary effort to meet the end date. You don't want them to have to do that on every project, because it may not work next time. So if I get shot in the foot, my company may be set up for a fall next time around.

Using software to do a what-if schedule gives you more credibility. We all know that computers simply output garbage when we input garbage, but it is *calculated garbage*, and thus more believable! That is a psychological advantage that you never had in the days before software.

Guidelines for Minor and Major Increments in a Schedule

You may fall into the trap of scheduling work in more detail than you can manage. This is especially tempting when you are using scheduling software. After all, the software can compute virtually any kind of network you create.

Sure, but can you do the work as scheduled?

I know about this trap. I have made most of the mistakes you can make in managing projects. I got carried away and scheduled work in increments of days. The only problem was that we couldn't control the work that accurately, so before I could get the schedule published, it was off, and my boss was on my back because I had already missed a scheduled date. The net result was that I spent all my time managing the schedule rather than letting the schedule help me manage the project.

The first guideline, then, is to never schedule work in more detail than you can control. For some tasks this means that you can schedule to the nearest hour. Projects to overhaul power generators are sometimes scheduled to this level of detail, because they have enough history to know how long each task will take, and also because getting the generator back online as quickly as possible is very important.

For others, scheduling to the nearest day is all that can be controlled, and in some cases, the nearest week is adequate. In large projects that last several years, you may find work being scheduled to the nearest month.

As for major durations, the first rule is that no task should have a duration greater than four to six weeks. Furthermore, you must have a marker that indicates when the task is actually complete, and this can be very difficult with nontangible tasks—that is, those that have no tangible deliverables. When there is no specification or deliverable that indicates task completion, then you must use exit criteria. As an example, the work is examined, and a "pass-fail" judgment is made. This is totally qualitative, but it is the only thing you have where aesthetics are involved.

> **GUIDELINES:** No task should have a duration greater than four to six weeks. For knowledge work, the maximum duration should be one to three weeks.

The rule about four- to six-week increments applies to long-duration tasks. It is especially useful to apply to outside vendor projects, such as long-lead capital equipment. It is a good idea to require your vendors to report progress on their projects in minimum increments of four to six weeks, and the progress report must go beyond an affirmation that the work is on schedule. You must require that they report progress using some method such as earned value tracking (see Chapter 12), or, if this is not possible, then they should use exit criteria to ensure that their progress is really what they say it is.

The next rule applies to engineering, programming, and other knowledge work, in which there may be no tangible deliverables. For such work, the rule is that work should be scheduled in maximum increments of one to three weeks. This is very important to enforce, or you can bet that such work will reach 90 percent completion and stay there forever. The progress report for knowledge work invariably looks like the graph shown in Figure 9.5.

Figure 9.5   Progress Graph for Knowledge Work

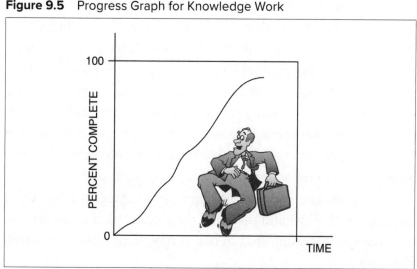

This is a universal graph. Here's how it is generated. Suppose the work is supposed to take 10 weeks to complete. This is by agreement with the person doing the work. At the end of the first week, you check on progress.

"How's your project work going?" you ask.

"Fine," says the person.

"I can't plot 'fine,'" you say. "I need to know what percent complete the job is."

Now what do you think she will tell you?

You guessed it. It's the end of the first week on a 10-week job, so she must be 10 percent complete.

And at the end of the second week?

Right again. She will be 20 percent complete.

This is called *reverse-inferential* progress reporting, and it is a method that people use when they can't tell exactly how much they have done.

Now you notice that when the work reaches around 80 or 90 percent complete, the graph turns horizontal. One of two things has happened. Either the person has had an existential crisis, which means that she discovers the part of the iceberg that's underneath the water (that is, all the work she has to do that she has forgotten), or she is in the debugging phase of her design work. If it is an iceberg problem, she will have to show that she is really only perhaps 50 percent complete—which means that she will have to report negative progress. This is shown in Figure 9.6.

However, we know that we can't report negative progress because senior managers get very agitated if we do this. The best alternative is to report only that progress is stalled.

In the situation where debugging has started, it is common to pass the deadline and then find the solution to the problem, so that the work is completed in one simple step. This is shown in Figure 9.7.

Figure 9.6 Graph Showing Negative Progress

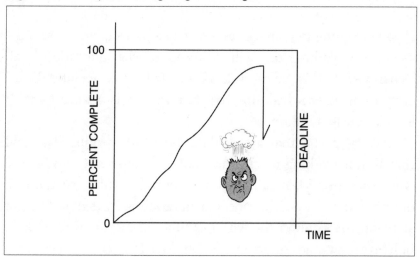

Figure 9.7 Graph Showing Progress Being Completed in One Step

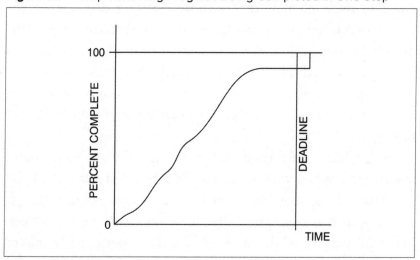

RESOURCE ALLOCATION

If you are going to manage resources in a project, you must specify who is working on each task and at what allocation level. When you do this, be careful. Microsoft Project operates differently from other scheduling software in how it treats allocation level and task duration.

If you specify that a task duration is 10 working days and that Ron is working on the task half-time (50 percent would be what you specify), most software programs will leave the task duration at 10 days. The calendar duration is treated as *fixed*, or as being the same as the working time minus any weekends or holidays that may intervene. With MS Project, however, you get a different result. Project will change the duration to 20 calendar days. The assumption is that the duration of the task is *variable*, meaning that the calendar duration depends on the rate at which the person works on the task. You can change the default so that Project works like other programs, treating task durations as fixed. However, there is a certain logic to the Project default. Ideally, you should always estimate working time and convert to calendar time in exactly the way that Project does it.

In any case, be careful that you assign the correct resource availability, or you will get an invalid result. For example, I had a fellow tell me that his company had always assigned people to tasks on the assumption that they were working on projects about 80 percent of the time. When they continuously missed project deadlines, the company did a time study to determine what was really happening. To do this, they had people log their time once an hour for two weeks and then analyzed the logs. To the company's surprise, they found that people were working on projects only 25 percent of the time, not the 80 percent that had been assumed! This meant that schedules were off by a factor of 3 because of the incorrect allocation assumption.

This is a common cause of problems. The only time you ever get 80 percent availability from people is when they are tied to their workstations, and the only people for whom this is true are factory workers. You may get close to 80 percent availability from them, but for knowledge workers—who aren't tied to their workstations—you'll never get such a high level. It is more likely to be around 50 or 60 percent.

The thing is, you must know what that number is if you are going to schedule work correctly. So it helps to do a time study, as was described above, to determine that level. Have people log their time once an hour—it need not be more often—to discover their true availability. If the number seems too low, then you must remove the causes.

Major Causes of Reduced Availability

There are two major causes of reduced resource availability. One is having people work on too many projects at the same time, and the other is overallocation of people to their work. When people have to work on more than one project at the same time, they constantly have to shift back and forth between them. This is called multitasking. The trouble is, every time a person "shifts gears," to use the normal expression, it takes time for that person to remember where he or she was, get the work in place, and so on. This added time is called *setup time* in manufacturing, and remember, we learned years ago that setup time is total waste. Setup time adds no value to the product. So, in manufacturing, an effort has been made to reduce setup time as much as possible or to eliminate it altogether by running a process continuously.

Think about it this way. Suppose you are sitting at your desk working and the phone rings. You answer it. The person says, "Sorry, I have the wrong number," and you hang up.

"Now where was I?" you think.

You have completely lost your train of thought. Time management experts say that you will typically lose 10 to 15 minutes every time you get interrupted, so if you get four phone calls in an hour, you may easily lose the entire hour!

So let's assume that each time you switch from one project to another, you add 15 minutes of setup time to each task. As an example, suppose you had planned to work on a single project task all day. You could finish the task in that single eight-hour day if you could just work on it continuously.

However, if you are working on several projects, you will be expected to share your time among them, and if you get no more than one hour of uninterrupted work at a time, your eight-hour task will take at least nine hours and forty-five minutes. This is shown in Figure 9.8.

Figure 9.8   Eight-Hour Task Performed in One-Hour Increments

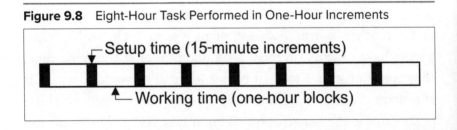

We assume that all tasks have some setup time built in, so we add 15 minutes for each time the task is stopped and restarted. That is seven increments above the single eight-hour block, so it adds one hour and forty-five minutes of setup time, rather than two hours.

I can almost guarantee you that this task will take 10 to 12 hours to complete, rather than the original 8 hours. The 15 minutes of setup time is a very conservative number.

Queuing and Resource Availability

The second major cause of reduced availability is overallocation of people to their work. To understand this, we need to understand the basics of queuing theory. You may never have studied queuing theory, but I can assure you that you have experienced it. Every time you try to get onto a busy highway at rush hour, you experience the effects of queuing.

As an example, Raleigh, North Carolina, has a beltway around the city. At rush hour, you can bet that the beltway is packed with cars, all doing 60 to 70 miles an hour. In fact, let's assume that the cars are packed so tightly that you couldn't put another car on the road if your life depended on it.

No problem. Everyone is happy.

How can this be?

No one wants onto the beltway, and no one wants off.

Of course, you realize that this is a fictitious condition that could exist only in a steady-state universe—one that may have been approximated about 1800, when people weren't in as much of a hurry as they are today.

Today, we live in a turbulent universe. Everyone wants to be where they are going 10 minutes ago.

So suppose someone wants onto this bumper-to-bumper beltway. If no one gets off, how long will it take this interloper to get onto the beltway?

You guessed it. It will take forever!

Queuing theory shows how long you must wait to get access to a system as a function of how fully it is already loaded. The curves look something like the one in Figure 9.9. Notice that, by definition, a system can't be loaded beyond 100 percent. It doesn't matter. At 100 percent, you have to wait forever to get access to the system, just as our driver has to wait to get onto the beltway.

Figure 9.9   Waiting Time as a Function of System Loading

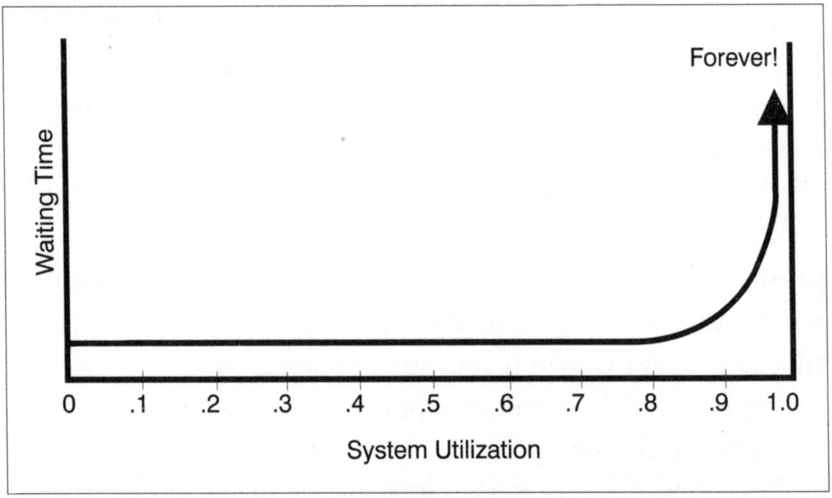

Okay, what does this have to do with projects?

First, let's think about a practical application of queuing theory. Manufacturing people have known for a long time that you shouldn't load a factory more than about 85 percent on the average. You may exceed that level occasionally, but if you consistently stay higher than 85 percent, you are asking for big trouble, because if anything out of the ordinary happens—a machine breaks down, or someone calls in sick, or a supplier is late delivering materials—you are already so high on the curve that your waiting time goes to forever in a heartbeat.

However, we don't load people to 85 percent. We load them to 120 percent. We know that if we loaded them to only 85 percent, they would sit around and do nothing during that 15 percent of free time, and that would be costly, so we make certain that they have no free time. This is commonly called "being lean and mean"—a biological metaphor. The question is, do you want to get rid of all your body fat? No way. You want some for reserve energy. The same is true of an organization. Carrying lean and mean too far is shortsighted.

When you have no reserve capacity, you can't respond to surprises, glitches, or even opportunities. And since Murphy's Law guarantees that there will be some glitches in every project, you can also be sure that there will be delays caused by queuing and that the result will be a late project.

Every organization should have some reserve capacity if it is to be able to respond to turbulence. But tell that to senior managers who believe that *lean and mean* is the correct way to fly!

> No system should be loaded beyond 85 percent capacity for very long.

Beginning around 1995, a few people had begun to realize that the lean-and-mean paradigm had gone too far. Alan Downs was a downsizing consultant until he realized this. His book *Corporate Executions* (Downs, 1996) goes into far greater detail about the pitfalls of going too far with cutting fat from an organization than is possible to cover in this chapter.

And what do you do about setup time?

You reduce it by prioritizing projects.

As a rule, no one should be working on more than three projects. Ideally, a person would work on a single project until it is completed and then shift to the next job.

Can this really be justified?

You bet.

When I first realized this, I was working with a company that was having difficulty getting new products released. They would go along for most of the year, and nothing would be released. Then headquarters would call and ask why no new products had come out the back door.

"We're working on them," would be the response.

"Well, we want to see something get to market by the end of the year," headquarters would say.

> You can do *anything*, but you can't do everything!
>
> —From the cover of *Fast Company*, May 2000

So there would be a big push to release all the products that were in various states of completion, and the company would turn out 10 or 12 new products near the end of the year.

Do you know what happens when you release that many products in December?

Absolutely nothing.

Manufacturing can't get set up to make them, and even if it could be done, the salespeople couldn't sell them.

But let's pretend that they could both make them and sell them, and let's assume that they were able to sell all those new products during the entire month of December. If that happened, you would have a sales graph like the one in Figure 9.10.

I said to the managers at this company, "You need to prioritize your projects. Work on them one at a time and get them out the back door so that they start selling sooner."

It took nearly three years to make it happen, but by that time, the company was releasing a new product every month or so. That is, they had a steady stream of new products entering the market.

Figure 9.10   Sales for All Products in December

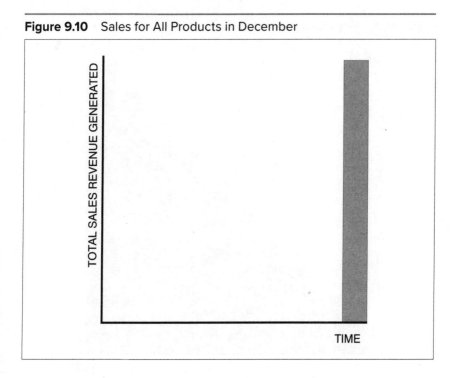

The result can be shown in another graph, superimposed on the one from Figure 9.10. As you can see, if a new product comes out at the beginning of the year, and we assume flat sales, you get the rectangle labeled Product 1. The next month, Product 2 is released, again with flat sales throughout the year. Then Product 3 comes out, and so on. This is shown in Figure 9.11.

As the graph indicates, the sales for the year approximate a triangle. The area under the triangle shows the units of money multiplied by time. This is called the *time value of money* or interest or cost of capital. So which figure has the greatest area, the rectangle for the month of December or the triangle for the entire year? It's a no-brainer. The triangle has considerably greater value to the company than the rectangle.

Figure 9.11   Sales for a Constant Stream of New Products

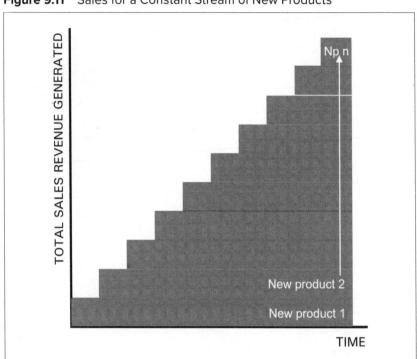

This demonstrates that the only economically viable approach that a company can take is to prioritize its projects. To have "all the balls in the air" at once is to confuse activity with progress. When you ask a manager what must be done first, and she tells you, "It all has to be done," she is overlooking the time value of money and its impact on the organization.

Think of this in reverse: when you are late to market with a new product, you have lost both the revenue that would have been generated by sales during that period and the cost of capital associated with it. That is why it is so important to complete projects on time.

CONCLUSION

In closing, let me say that if you follow the guidelines in this chapter, your schedules will be more workable. The only thing you must worry about is whether your estimates of task durations are realistic, and these can usually be improved through consensual estimating. Whatever approach you take, the schedule should be used to help you manage the project, not make you a slave to software.

 IN SUMMARY

This chapter is consistent with the idea of managing project communications. It does not cover interpersonal communication, which would require a book in itself.

It is important that project stakeholders be kept informed of project status throughout the various stages of the job. To that end, a plan should be developed that identifies various stakeholders and their information needs, which will include content requirements and update frequency.

Distribution methods and channels will also be identified. As technology changes these will also change.

CHAPTER 10

Managing Project Communications

According to the *PMBOK® GUIDE*, "project communications management is the Knowledge Area that employs the processes required to ensure timely and appropriate generation, collection, distribution, storage, retrieval, and ultimate disposition of project information" (2008, p. 23). Communications management has to do with determining who needs information, when they need it, and how it will be transmitted. It does not include the act of communicating itself, although this is certainly an important area with which every project manager should be familiar. The art of communication is not specific to project management, and it deals with such things as how to write effectively; whether to communicate orally or in writing; sender-receiver models, such as barriers to communication; and so on.*

Every project plan should include a communications plan that addresses these issues. The importance of such a plan cannot be overstated. Projects live or die by the flow of information, and

---

* This chapter is largely taken from Lewis and Dudley, 2005.

many problems occur simply because various stakeholders are not kept informed. John Cashman, who flew the first 777 airplane, told me that the team developed a communications plan early in the program. The result was people saying, "Oh, that's why they're doing that. I wondered about that." Furthermore, they referred to the big jet as "our airplane." Being kept constantly informed gave them a sense of belonging to the entire team and a sense of ownership.

COMMUNICATIONS MANAGEMENT PROCESSES

There are four primary processes for communications management listed in the *PMBOK® GUIDE*:

1. **Communications planning.** As stated earlier, this is determining the information needs of all stakeholders: who needs what information, how frequently they need it, and how it will be given to them.
2. **Information distribution.** This is the process of making needed information available to those who need it in a timely manner.
3. **Performance reporting.** This involves collecting and distributing information on progress. It includes measuring progress, reporting status, and forecasting future results.
4. **Administrative closure.** This includes gathering information and generating and disseminating information about the closeout of a phase or the final project.

Communications Planning

Not all stakeholders to a project have the same needs for information. The first step in communications planning is to identify all stakeholders and then survey them to determine their information needs. This will be discussed later in this chapter. Communications planning is often tied to organizational planning, since the organizational structure of the project will affect how information is disseminated. In addition, while this is not specifically covered by the *PMBOK® GUIDE*, as the size of a project team grows, so does the overhead cost of communication. This overhead can, in fact, be very substantial and can tax the project manager to keep everyone informed of what is going on. This is because the number of channels of communications is given by the following equation:

$$C = N(N - 1)/2$$

Inputs to Communications Planning

Communications Requirements

There is often a temptation to communicate everything to everyone (or nothing to anyone), but this can quickly become a significant burden. As was shown earlier, as the number of participants in a project grows, so does the number of channels over which information flows, and if the amount of information also increases, it can overwhelm the communications network. People then begin to suffer from information overload. It is therefore important that only information that is necessary for the correct functioning of the project be disseminated, and only to those stakeholders who actually need it. Another way to think of this is that the only information that should be communicated is information that contributes to success, or that could lead to failure if it is not communicated. To determine communications requirements, you should consider the following:

- The project organization and stakeholder responsibilities
- Disciplines, departments, and specialties involved in the project
- The number of individuals involved in a project and at what locations
- External parties that want information, such as the media

Communications Technology

The methods used to convey information among all project stakeholders can vary considerably, from brief, face-to-face encounters in the hallways, to formal meetings, to e-mail, Internet-accessible databases, and videoconferencing. Some factors that may affect the communications plan include:

- **Immediacy needs of stakeholders.** That is, do some individuals need almost real-time information about the project, or can they use simple, periodic reports?
- **Availability of technology.** Are the systems already in place, or would they have to be developed?
- **Skills of project team members.** Will team members already have the skills required to operate the required technology, or must some training be provided?
- **Project duration.** Will technology change over the life of the project, and if so, must these changes be incorporated into the project?

Constraints

Constraints are factors that will limit a project team's options for communicating. For example, projects in which work is contracted out will require different communications from those in which all work is done internally.

Assumptions

We discussed assumptions in Chapter 8, so these will not be considered in this chapter other than to say that all projects involve assumptions, which must be clarified to avoid later problems.

Tools and Techniques for Communications Planning

Stakeholder Analysis

It is important to understand the information needs of all stakeholders and ensure that they receive that information in a timely manner, using the appropriate technology. Discussion of stakeholders is covered in Chapter 6.

Outputs from Communications Planning

Communications Management Plan

The purpose of communications management planning is to produce documents that prescribe how communications in the project are to be handled. This document will, of course, be a communications management plan. It should specify the following:

- How information will be collected and filed, and in what format. What procedure will be used to update documents and ensure that everyone has the latest revision? This is very important, as failure to control revisions can lead to some members of the project team working with obsolete schedules, and other such problems. Usually a revision number is attached to a document, together with a date so that you can quickly determine whether the document is the most recent version.

- The information to be collected and the format in which it will be distributed. What level of detail will be provided? Are there specific terms to be used in specific ways? If so, these should be identified.

- Who receives what information, and how it will be distributed. Not all stakeholders need all information. There must be a distribution matrix that specifies this. Examples of how information is distributed include written reports, meetings, and face-to-face verbal communication. In the case of widely dispersed teams, these may be supplemented by e-mail, teleconferencing, and so on. Documents may also be distributed electronically, using either PDF files or native files (doc, xls, msp, and so on).

- A production and distribution schedule. How often will each kind of information be collected and distributed? In some projects, project status data is collected and distributed weekly. Others may use a monthly schedule.

- A method of accessing information in between scheduled distributions.

- A procedure for revising the communications plan itself as the need arises. An example would be that when stakeholders change, the distribution list must change.

The communications plan may be very formal or informal, highly structured or not, as the needs of the project dictate.

Information Distribution

Perhaps this is obvious, but information has no value unless it reaches the appropriate individuals involved in the project. Furthermore, that information must be in the proper format and must be timely. Often, because of flaws in the communications system, information reaches a person too late for him to act on it in the required manner. Also, even though the *PMBOK® GUIDE* does not discuss this, people in today's world tend to suffer from information overload, which can result in project communications being overlooked or ignored by the intended recipients. Information distribution involves implementing the communications plan and responding to nonplanned requests for information.

Again, the *PMBOK® GUIDE* does not discuss distributing anything but information about work results. Nevertheless, stakeholders are concerned about events that may affect the work, organizational changes, and other events that could impact the project either positively or negatively.

Tools and Techniques
for Information Distribution

Communications Skills

Communication is a two-way street. It involves not only the dissemination of information, but the receiving of it as well. The *PMBOK® GUIDE* says that the sender is responsible for ensuring that information is clear, unambiguous, and complete, and that the receiver is responsible for making sure that information is received in its entirety and is understood correctly. I disagree with this, but if it is asked on the exam, give the *PMBOK® GUIDE* answer.

Here is the problem. The receiver cannot be held responsible for communication. Only the sender has that responsibility. The sender must ensure that the intended message was received and understood. An example of this is seen in air traffic control. I was flying into Chicago's O'Hare airport on a United flight, and at the time United had an audio channel on which you could listen to air traffic. The controller told a pilot to descend to a certain altitude and fly 300 knots exactly. The pilot responded, "Roger. Descend to 6,000 and fly 300 or better." The controller replied, "Negative. Three hundred exactly!"

This is a system in which the receiver of the communication is expected to repeat back what he has heard, so that the sender can ensure that it was received correctly, and in this example the message was misunderstood. Had the controller not detected the misunderstanding, the plane would have been flying too fast, overtaking traffic ahead of it, and this could have led to a disaster.

To make the point a little more strongly, how can the recipient of a communication know that she has misunderstood it? Clearly, she cannot. So the basic premise that we must remember as project managers is that responsibility for communication rests with the communicator, not with the recipient!

There are several dimensions to communications, and all of them can affect the ultimate outcome. These include:

- Written and oral, listening and speaking
- Internal (that is, within the project) and external—to the customer, the media, the public, and so on
- Formal (written reports, briefings, review meetings) and informal (casual memos, conversations in the hallway, and so on)
- Vertical (up and down the organization hierarchy) and horizontal (with peers)
- Information retrieval systems

Many of us share the problem of trying to find information that we have filed away somewhere. Information can be shared in projects through several methods, including manual and electronic filing systems, databases, project management software, and other information systems. Some of the information that project stakeholders may need includes technical drawings, design specifications, test plans, and personnel data. An information retrieval system should be designed so that people can access such information in a timely manner.

Marvin Patterson, in his book *Accelerating Innovation* (1993), has argued that a reference librarian can be a big help to a project team that relies on processing information to develop new products. Such an individual can provide that information in a just-in-time (JIT) manner, thus improving the performance of the project team.

Information Distribution Methods

The ways in which project information can be distributed are almost unlimited. Though not used (much) anymore, smoke signals, carrier pigeons, and telegraphy are all possibilities. On a serious note, the conventional methods include formal meetings, the grapevine, document distribution in either electronic or hard-copy format, e-mail, the project intranet, and so on.

Outputs from Information Distribution

Outputs from information distribution include project records, project reports, and project presentations.

Project records include memos; progress and status reports; purchase requisitions; correspondence; various documents describing the project, including revisions to the plan; and so on.

These must be maintained in some organized fashion. A project notebook (which may comprise a number of binders for large projects) is one way to do this. The advantage of a notebook is that you have everything in one place, and it can serve as a convenient resource when doing lessons-learned reviews later on.

Project reports are, of course, formal documents that detail project status and/or issues that need attention or have been dealt with.

Project managers are often asked to make project presentations to various stakeholders to keep them up to date on what is happening with the project. In fact, research has shown that projects are often judged negatively when stakeholders are not kept informed and when the project is not presented in a good light. It is therefore useful to "sell" your project—that is, present it to key stakeholders in the best possible light. The downside is that stakeholders can make heavy demands on project managers to keep them informed. I remember a project manager on a very large government project telling me that he spent about 60 percent of his time doing such presentations to members of Congress and several other stakeholders, so that, if he had not had a project administrator who handled the day-to-day management of the job, it would have gotten into serious trouble.

Performance Reporting

Performance reporting involves the development and dissemination of documents and exhibits that show the status of the project at a given point in time. Typically, these are used to measure schedule and cost, but any number of other indicators—such as training, testing, or other project objectives—can be included.

The process of performance reporting generally includes:

- **Status reporting.** Where does the project currently stand?
- **Progress reporting.** What has been accomplished since the last status report?
- **Forecasting.** What is expected to be accomplished in the next period?

Tools for performance reporting include:

- **Performance reviews.** These are typically meetings that are set up so that you can present the current status of the project. They can be formal or informal, and the depth of the content will depend on the audience. Senior management reviews can be more general than those for the engineering manager, although my experience is that senior managers cannot resist getting into the details, so be prepared.
- **Variance analysis.** This involves comparing the actual value of an item to what that value should be at this time. The list of items to be measured should have been developed during project plan development (covered in Chapter 8).
- **Trend analysis.** This is tracking performance over time to see if things are improving or deteriorating. An example might be the number of bricks laid in a shift. Trend analysis could point out problems with the supply or quality of materials. Note that trend analysis extends over time, while variance analysis focuses upon a given point. You can, of course, track the variance over time.
- **Earned value analysis.** Earned value analysis (also called earned value management in the *PMBOK® GUIDE*) is a method of tracking schedule and cost variances together. (I cover earned value analysis in great detail in Chapter 12, so I will not go into it here.)

The result of performance reporting is the actual documentation that will be distributed and archived for future use. Other outcomes might include:

- Change requests. A change in direction or emphasis might result from your review. Perhaps more staff will be needed. This will improve the schedule at the expense of the budget. On the other hand, maybe things are going too well, and companion parts of the project will not be ready when you are finished.
- Budget adjustments.
- Scope additions or deletions.
- Firing the project manager.

Performance reporting should be done routinely and should continue through administrative closure.

Administrative Closure

This is the process of documenting the results of your work to ensure that you have met all requirements and specifications. It should be done whenever a phase of the project is complete, and at the end of the project as well. This is valuable, since near the end of a project, team members are often reassigned and thus are not available to participate. Some items to be considered during administrative closure include:

- Collecting and archiving all project documents, including final cost and schedule information.
- Updating records and specifications to reflect what actually happened on the project.

- Revising employee databases to reflect current skills and anticipate future training needs.
- Developing the final project report, which will assess just how the project went and review the results of the project as it relates to the resulting product. Remember, well-run projects can produce lousy products!
- Performing a lessons-learned review that includes all stakeholders and team members.

IN SUMMARY

We have discussed the need for communication planning in projects so that the information needs of all stakeholders will be met. Some parties will require more detailed information than others, and timeliness requirements will also differ. It is necessary to identify all stakeholders and assess the kind of information needed, the frequency, level of detail, and mode (verbal or written) needed. As for work status reporting, this will be covered in detail in the chapter on status reporting.

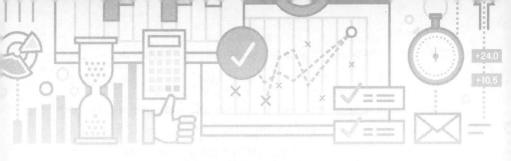

CHAPTER 11

Managing Risks

When I first started teaching seminars in 1981, there were many managers who objected to discussions of risks because they considered this to be "negative thinking." They believed that people should always think positively. What they didn't understand is that there is a difference between being *realistic* and being either overly positive or overly negative. I don't believe there are so many managers today who avoid discussing risks, because risk management is much more prevalent than it was in 1981. Furthermore, risk management is conducted in a positive way. You ask what might go wrong and what do we do about it? That is a positive response.

One of the single most important things you can do to ensure a successful project is *manage* risks. A risk is anything that could adversely affect your schedule, costs, quality, or scope. That is, a risk may impact your PCTS targets. Simply put, either you manage risks, or they will manage you.

A supermacho mentality that doesn't understand this still exists. "Damn the torpedoes, full speed ahead!" is an approach

> There is a greater probability that things will accidentally go wrong than that they will accidentally go right.
>
> —Murphy's Law

that sounds glamorous, but it can wreck your project. It may be appropriate in a military setting, but not in projects. In fact, there was a time when the airlines hired a lot of former military pilots, who proceeded to scare the daylights out of passengers by flying the airplane like a fighter aircraft. The airlines had to retrain them to consider the fear factor in their passengers.

> **Damn the torpedoes—full speed ahead!**
>
> —Admiral David Farragut

I previously mentioned the manager who told me that he didn't want me to suggest to his people that they pad their schedules. "I want them to be aggressive," he said. As I have remarked, there is a difference between an aggressive schedule and a foolish one. To reiterate a previous example, if you are doing construction work and are certain that weather could delay your project, you would be derelict in your duty as a project manager by not addressing potential delays. You'd do so by allowing a bit longer for work to be completed than it would take if there were no weather delays. This is called padding the schedule and is proper risk management in construction.

> **What we anticipate seldom occurs. What we least expect generally happens.**
>
> —Benjamin Disraeli

In Step 4 of The Lewis Method, you are asked if SWOT and risks are okay. This was discussed briefly in Chapter 7. You will note that Step 6 also asks if risks are okay. So, there are two specific places in a project where risk management is important—in planning strategy and in implementation planning. It is important that you constantly ask, "What might go wrong?" so that you can anticipate and deal with risks, even in the execution phase of the project.

Also in Chapter 7, I pointed out that there is a difference between threats and risks. A risk is something that you can do yourself, such as having an accident, or that can happen to you in an impersonal way, such as bad weather. A threat, on the other hand, is something that will usually be done to you by some entity, whether a person or an organization. As an example, a threat to project success is that a competitor beats you to market with a new product. In practice, it is okay to lump the two together for the purpose of analysis and contingency planning.

THE RISK MANAGEMENT PROCESS

There are three steps in the risk management process:

1. Identify risks and threats by asking, "What could go wrong?" or, "What kind of threats exist?"
2. Quantify threats and risks by assigning them a risk priority number (RPN).
3. Develop contingency plans to deal with risks that cannot be ignored.

Risk Identification

As I said earlier, you need to identify risks that may impact your strategy and your implementation plan. To revisit another example, if you are developing a new product using cutting-edge technology, the possibility exists that you won't be able to get the technology to work. The more unproven the technology, the higher the probability that you will have difficulty. One way to manage such risk is to do a feasibility study to see if you can make the new technology work before you launch a full-scale development effort. If you can't get the results you want, you can fall back on more proven technology.

If you launch a development program using unproven technology and can't make it work, the consequences are far more serious than if you do a feasibility study and reject the new approach. For one thing, it is more obvious to everyone that a feasibility study is a success regardless of the outcome. If you say yes, we can make it work, that is a success; but so is the negative result, because it will save you a lot of grief trying to make something work that can't be done.

When you get to the implementation planning stage of your project, you again want to identify potential implementation problems. In this case, the WBS can be used to guide your thinking.

I previously used a yard project as an example of developing a WBS. That WBS is repeated in Figure 11.1.

Now, suppose I want to do risk management. For each task in the WBS, I ask, "What could go wrong?" Here are some examples for each task:

1. **Cleanup.** The dump may be closed when we get there, so we have wasted time driving over there. The contingency would be to call and see if the dump is open.

2. **Cut grass.** It might rain while we are cutting the grass. The contingency would be to check the weather forecast and schedule the activity on a day when good weather is forecast.

3. **Trim work.** You run out of string for your string trimmer. The contingency would be to keep a supply of string on hand.

4. **Prepare equipment.** Your mower runs out of gas. The contingency would be to make sure you have plenty of gas before you start.

5. **Trim hedge.** You might trim unevenly, and the yard would look bad. The contingency would be to have someone who is more skilled at it do the trimming.

Figure 11.1 WBS for a Yard Project

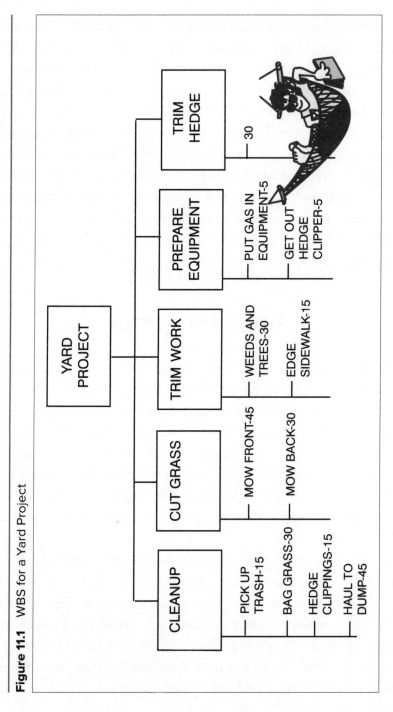

I have listed only one risk for each task. Clearly, more than one thing could go wrong on complex tasks, so you list all of them, then quantify them and deal with the more serious ones.

At this stage in planning, be careful that people don't go into "analysis paralysis." You will probably identify the most likely risks quickly. Trying to find every single thing that could go wrong is unproductive. However, you should be careful not to reject a risk simply because you consider it highly unlikely to occur. As you will see in a subsequent section of this chapter, there are low-probability events that will have a very severe impact on the project if they do occur. These should never be ignored.

RISK QUANTIFICATION

We know that risks are not all equal in their impact on a project. The question is, how do you decide which ones you can ignore and which ones you should manage? The desired approach would be to find some way to prioritize the risks. This can be done by calculating risk priority numbers (RPNs) for them. Three factors contribute to the RPN. First is the *probability* that the risk may occur. Second is the *severity* of the effect on the project if the risk should occur. And third is the question of whether you can *detect* the risk before it hits you.

This risk management methodology was worked out in an engineering discipline called failure mode effects analysis (FMEA). When designing a product, an engineer is supposed to identify possible modes of failure for various components and then ask what the severity of each failure may be and whether it can be detected. As an example, the dome light in your car may burn out, and you could have your transmission seize up. The probability of both occurrences may be very low. However, the severity of a dome light burning out is far lower than that of the transmission seizing up. Furthermore, you will know immediately if your transmission seizes up, but you may not know until you open your door at night that your dome light has burned out, since you may not notice it during the daylight.

To calculate RPNs, we use three tables. The first assigns a rank of 1 to 10 to probability, based on a logarithmic probability scale. The second table assigns a similar rank to severity, and the third does the same for detection.

In the original FMEA approach, detection means that you may or may not be able to tell that a failure has occurred in a product. For example, if you have manufactured a car that has a crack inside the engine block, you may not be able to detect that crack before the car leaves the factory. On the other hand, if a tire goes flat, that is easy to spot and correct before the car is shipped. If a fault can be detected with certainty, the number assigned is 1. If it absolutely can't be detected, it gets a rank of 10.

The problem with this approach to detection is that it usually yields a 1 when it is used in project risk analysis, and so it loses its utility. I think a more helpful way to consider detection is to ask whether a failure mode can be detected *before* it happens.

Table 11.1 is used to quantify risk probability.

Table 11.2 is used to quantify the severity of the failure. Finally, Table 11.3 is used to quantify detection capability.

TABLE 11.1   Probability of Occurrence

Probability of occurrence	Possible occurrence rates	Rank
Very high: occurrence is almost certain	≥ 1 in 2	10
	1 in 3	9
High: repeated occurrences possible	1 in 8	8
	1 in 20	7
Moderate: occasional occurrences	1 in 80	6
	1 in 400	5
	1 in 2,000	4
Low: relatively few occurrences	1 in 15,000	3
	1 in 150,000	2
Remote: occurrence is unlikely	≤ 1 in 1,500,000	1

TABLE 11.2   Severity of the Effect

Effect	Criteria: severity of effect	Rank
Hazardous— without warning	Project severely impacted, possible cancellation, with no warning.	10
Hazardous— with warning	Project severely impacted, possible cancellation, with warning.	9
Very high	Major impact on project schedule, budget, or performance; may cause severe delays, overruns, or degradation of performance.	8
High	Project schedule, budget, or performance impacted significantly; job can be completed, but customer will be very dissatisfied.	7
Moderate	Project schedule, budget, or performance impacted somewhat; customer will be dissatisfied.	6
Low	Project schedule, budget, or performance impacted slightly; customer will be mildly dissatisfied.	5
Very low	Some impact to project; customer will be aware of impact.	4
Minor	Small impact to project; average customer will be aware of impact.	3
Very minor	Impact so small that it would be noticed only by a very discriminating customer.	2
None	No effect.	1

TABLE 11.3 Detection Capability

Detection	Rank
Absolute uncertainty	10
Very remote	9
Remote	8
Very low	7
Low	6
Moderate	5
Moderately high	4
High	3
Very high	2
Almost certain	1

Examples of RPN Calculation

An example that I find helpful for illustrating risk management is to assume that you are riding a bicycle from the East Coast to the West Coast of the United States. You identify several risks that could affect your trip and estimate the numbers shown in Table 11.4.

TABLE 11.4 RPNs for a Bike Trip

Identified risk	P	S	D	RPN
Flat tire	10	2	10	200
Get hit by a car	2	10	10	200
Bad weather	10	2	2	40

You will see that having a flat tire and being hit by a car both have RPNs of 200 points, which would imply that they are equal in importance. However, they are *qualitatively* very different. The RPN for having a flat tire is 200 points because the probability is high and detection capability is poor. Getting hit by a car has a very low probability, but high severity and poor detection. These two risks demand very different responses. This is why we talk about risk *management*, not just risk *identification*.

As a rule, *any time severity is in the range of 8 to 10 points*, you should require that some action be taken to deal with the risk. This is especially important to consider when probability is low. People tend to ignore risks when they think that there is a very low likelihood of their occurrence.

The *Challenger* space shuttle disaster is a good example of this. Many of the members of the team responsible for the launch believed that the probability of failure of the O-ring seals was very low. Perhaps it was. Nevertheless, the severity of failure was a 10, as demonstrated by the fact that the explosion killed all the astronauts aboard. Had the team considered severity and followed the rule, they would have delayed the launch until the temperature rose.

Of course, we now also have the *Columbia* shuttle disaster. According to Wikipedia: "The loss of *Columbia* was a result of damage sustained during launch when a piece of foam insulation the size of a small briefcase broke off the Space Shuttle external tank (the main propellant tank) under the aerodynamic forces of launch. The debris struck the leading edge of the left wing, damaging the Shuttle's thermal protection system (TPS), which protects it from heat generated with the atmosphere during reentry. While *Columbia* was still in orbit, some engineers suspected damage, but NASA managers limited the investigation, on the grounds that little could be done even if problems were found."

This is certainly no forum for discussing whether this contention was true, but it highlights the issue of severity in managing risks. It would seem that under the circumstances, it would have been prudent to keep *Columbia* in orbit longer to determine if another solution could be found, such as sending another shuttle up to make repairs.

For a complete discussion of how risks were managed in this situation, go to the following web page: http://en.wikipedia.org/wiki/Space_Shuttle_Columbia_disaster.

The *Challenger* disaster is also a good example of groupthink, and CRM Learning and YouTube have videos that discuss this. Groups are particularly prone to ignore risks when they are under pressure to get a job done, as was the case with *Challenger.* If you don't remember the history, Christa McAuliffe was supposed to address Congress from space. This was a big political event, so the team felt pressured to launch on schedule. For more on groupthink and how to avoid it, see Chapter 15.

> Regardless of the value of the RPN, when severity is high, you must do something to manage the associated risk.

Develop Contingency Plans

As I stated earlier, it is not enough to identify and quantify risks. The idea is to manage them. There are several responses to risk:

1. Risk avoidance
2. Mitigation (reduction, such as using air bags)
3. Transfer (as in loss prevention through insurance)
4. Accommodate: accept and live with the risk
5. Ignore the risk (very dangerous)

Risk Avoidance

As my colleague Harvey Levine has said, it is better to avoid a risk than to have to manage it. Delaying the *Challenger* launch would have been risk avoidance. This is a trap for the obsessive "can-do" manager. He drives on in the face of a risk and pays the consequences later.

Risk *prevention* is a special case of risk avoidance. Japanese manufacturing has for many years employed "foolproofing" as a risk avoidance strategy. The idea is to set up the assembly process so that it cannot be done incorrectly. One example was the auto plant that, when installing a gas tank in a car, would on occasion find that one of the four mounting brackets had not been welded onto the tank. The solution was to set up a fixture to hold the tank while the brackets were being welded onto it. Feelers were attached to detect the presence of the brackets. If any of the four brackets was not in place, the welding machine would not weld any of them.

> The mouse that hath but one hole is quickly taken.
> —George Herbert

In construction projects, we pad the schedule with rain-delay days, based on the weather history for the area and the time of year. This way, we avoid the risk that we will be delayed by bad weather. In engineering design, I mentioned the use of parallel design strategies to avoid the possibility that the deadline might be missed because one strategy proves difficult to implement. In any project, risk aversion or avoidance might be the most preferable strategy to follow.

Mitigation or Severity Reduction

If we can think of contingencies in the event that a risk takes place, we may be able to mitigate its effect. Placing air bags in cars is an attempt to reduce the severity of an accident, should one occur. Stafford Beer (1981) has argued that seat belts and air bags in cars give drivers a false sense of security, so that they take chances they might otherwise not take. We have defined the problem as protecting the driver from being harmed if she is in an accident. Beer argues that it would perhaps be better to redefine the problem as how to keep a driver from having an accident in the first place (risk avoidance). He suggests that if we lined the dashboard of the car with spikes, making it very clear that an accident has serious consequences, we might give drivers incentive to be more careful. His suggestion is not without merit, though the exact implementation would have to be some other mechanism than a spike-lined dashboard.

In projects that involve procurement, sole-sourcing is a risk to consider. The alternative is to second-source all procured parts or equipment. That way, if a supplier can't deliver on time or at the specified price, the second supplier might be able to step in. This can be thought of as either risk avoidance or risk mitigation.

Temporary workers are used as backups for critical personnel who become ill or are injured. Overtime is used as a contingency when tasks take longer than estimated. This is one reason why overtime should not be planned into a project to meet the original targets, if possible. Rather, it should be kept in reserve as a contingency.

Another possible contingency is to reduce scope to permit the team to meet the original target date and then come back later and incorporate the deferred work to finish the job.

Having a fire evacuation plan in a building can be thought of as both a contingency and a loss-prevention plan.

Transfer or Loss Prevention
Insurance is one way of protecting against loss in the event that a risk manifests itself. Having alternative sites available into which

a group can move in the event of a disaster is a loss-prevention strategy. Backup personnel can also be thought of as loss avoidance. When a key person falls ill, if someone else can do the work, there will be no loss to the project. Of course, this is difficult to do with highly skilled personnel.

Cost Contingency

Cost contingency is also called management reserve. Unfortunately, it is misunderstood. Too often it is believed that management reserve is there to cover poor performance. This is incorrect. Management reserve is a fund that is part of a project budget to cover the cost of unidentified work. All projects should have a work budget that covers the cost of identified work, and a management reserve to cover work that has not yet been identified. In addition, on projects that are paid for by a customer, there will be a component of the total job cost called *margin*. This is the intended profit for the job. Poor performance eats into margin, not into management reserve.

The management reserve account is not touched unless we identify new work that needs to be done. This is a change in scope, of course. At that point, money is transferred from the management reserve account into the work budget, and performance is subsequently tracked against the revised budget. A log should be maintained of all scope changes and their effect on the work budget, management reserve, and margin (if the change has such an effect). In customer-funded projects, the customer may be required to pay for scope changes, and in that case, there is no impact on the management reserve account.

Accommodate

Sometimes we just accept the fact that risk is present, and we take our chances. All of us do this when we drive a car or fly in an airplane. We know that there is a chance of an accident, but if we refused to accept that possibility, we would never get into a vehicle or a plane. This is not the same as ignoring a risk, which is covered next.

Ignore

This is different from accommodating a known risk. It is like putting your head in a hole in the ground and pretending that the risk does not exist. People do this when they practice unprotected sex with partners whose past sexual histories they do not know.

IN SUMMARY

Risk management makes good business sense. Failing to account for factors that may sink a project is not aggressive management; it is being derelict in one's duty as a project manager. Banks won't finance homes or cars unless the buyer carries insurance to protect against loss from fires or accidents. Risk management is an important aspect of effective project management.

EXECUTION AND CONTROL

CHAPTER 12

Project Control

T he primary reason for doing a project plan (including the schedule) is to achieve control of the project. Remember the definition of control? If you have no plan, you can't possibly have control, by definition!

I also think it is important to understand that we are not implying the use of personal power to control a project. The kind of control we are talking about is that of guidance, as in the example of piloting an airplane. You establish a destination and put together a flight plan on how to reach it, and as you fly, you keep track of how well you are following your flight plan. And as the wind blows you off course, you correct for those deviations to bring the plane back on track.

It is also useful to remember that there is usually more than one individual working to deliver project results, and each of them must have a personal plan to guide his or her work, so that collectively the team will steer the project to hit the target. One way to think of this is that, to achieve macrocontrol, you must do it through microcontrol, and as I pointed out elsewhere, this does not mean micromanaging. Every individual contributor must be exercising self-control, or your project will eventually be out of control.

MEASURING PROGRESS

If you are going to control a project, you need to know two things: where you are supposed to be, and where you are. The plan tells you where you are supposed to be. As for where you are, that comes from your project information system—which in many organizations is nonexistent.

This system must provide information on all four project constraints. Remember, the relationship between them is given by the formula

$$C = f(P, T, S)$$

where P is performance, T is time, S is scope, and C is cost. (And f means *function*.)

So, if you want to know the true status of the project, you must know what costs have been incurred to date, whether the work meets the functional and technical requirements (that is, performance), whether the work is on schedule, and whether the scope of work done is at the right level.

Again, remember that in this equation, the cost is for labor only. As I have said before, you care about the cost of materials, capital equipment, and other project requirements (such as travel or insurance), but they do not belong in this equation; they are tracked separately.

The easiest of the four variables to ascertain is cost. You may not have a system in place to provide that information, but if you wanted to get it, you could do so by having everyone record the hours spent on the project, multiply those hours by the hourly labor rate that they are paid, and then add them up.

> To measure progress, you must know the value of all four constraints.

It is harder to obtain data on the right-hand side of the equation. To illustrate, let's begin with a simple example. Say you are building a brick wall. It is supposed to be a foot thick, 10 feet high, and 100 feet long by today's date. When it is finished, it will be a foot thick, 20 feet high, and 200 feet long.

The nice thing about brick walls is that you can measure them. So you take a scale out to the wall and determine that it is indeed 1 foot thick and 100 feet long. You inspect the mortar between the bricks, and it looks nice and clean and uniform. In addition, you check to see if the wall is perfectly vertical, and it is. This tells you that the quality of work done (functional and technical performance requirements) is okay. Next, you measure the height of the wall and find that it is only eight feet high. This tells you that the scope is not correct—the workers have accomplished only 80 percent of what they were scheduled to do up to now. (Note that we are not measuring the percentage of total work that will eventually be done. We are measuring whether the status of the work is correct as of today, so we compare actual performance to what the plan says should have been completed by today.)

That being the case, we also know that the workers are behind schedule. How far behind? Well, if you assume that work is linear over time (which it isn't, but we will assume that it is for now), and they have been working on the job for 10 days, then they have accomplished what they should have done by day 8. Therefore, they are about two days behind schedule.

This isn't totally correct because work is almost never linear. But it is a fair approximation for a wall of this height. This is tangible work, which is much easier to measure than knowledge work.

Writing software is knowledge work, and if you were checking progress on a software task and the programmer had estimated that she would have written about 10,000 lines of code by today's date, but she has only written 8,000 lines, we might assume she is 80 percent complete. But is she?

Who knows? She may find that the code she has written won't work and she'll have to start over. Or she may actually be finished because she found a way to write the code using fewer lines than she originally anticipated.

In addition, knowledge work usually proceeds along a progress curve like the one shown in Figure 12.1. Note that very little progress is made for a long period, then the work accelerates quickly, and then near the end it slows down again. We call these S-curves, because they have a shape similar to an italicized letter S.

Figure 12.1   Progress Curve for Knowledge Work

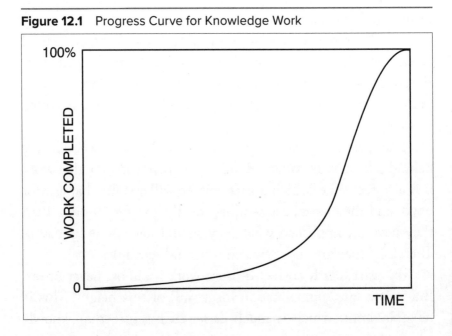

This is sometimes a source of great anxiety for senior managers who do not understand the nature of this progress curve.

They expect work to be more linear, so when a knowledge worker seems to be "going nowhere" for a long time, managers may get very concerned and start putting pressure on the person to get the job done. The net result of this pressure may very well be to slow the person down. As one of my engineers told me once, when our manager was putting pressure on him to speed up, "Putting two jockeys on one horse won't make him run faster."

So how do we measure the progress of knowledge work?

With difficulty.

If you remember the guidelines that I presented in the scheduling chapter (Chapter 9), they establish that knowledge tasks should have durations no greater than one to three weeks. Furthermore, I said that the increments must have markers that tell you they have been completed. These markers are called exit criteria. For software or engineering design, the exit criteria may be that the design has been reviewed by one's peers, who have reached consensus that it should perform correctly once it is completed. Of course, this is a judgment on their part, and they could collectively be wrong, but it is the best we can do with work of this nature.

If the task is to conduct a test, the exit criteria may be raw data that verifies that the part meets the technical and functional specifications. Or, in an environmental cleanup project, we may have a situation where oil has seeped into the ground, and at this stage of the project, the oil in a certain area has all been removed. That makes it binary. The oil has or has not been removed. As you can imagine, though, we don't know how far into the ground the oil has seeped, so the ultimate time it will take to complete the cleanup may be difficult to estimate.

In some cases, the exit criteria take the form of a checklist (such as pilots use to ensure that all of their instruments and controls are functioning correctly before they take off). In others, it is a judgment by someone in the organization, as when a marketing vice president approves the aesthetics of a design.

It is hard to know if P and S are correct, and if these cannot be determined, then you don't know how you are doing schedulewise. For that reason, I have been told that there is no point in trying to measure progress in knowledge work.

I can't agree with that. If you don't know where you are, you can't have control. My suggestion is that we simply must recognize the limitations of our ability to measure exactly where we are. If we are building a brick wall, we may hold tolerances of ±5 percent.

For knowledge work, the tolerances are more typically ±20 to 25 percent, and if there is a lot of research involved, we could have a situation where the tolerance may be −100 to +20 percent on schedule. In other words, we must accept very large tolerances on poorly defined or intangible work.

THE PITFALLS OF REPORTING SCHEDULE ONLY

Estimates are that several million individuals have purchased some form of scheduling software. So far as I know, all the major programs allow you to report progress using a bar chart schedule. The reports typically look like the one in Figure 12.2. Small bars are run through the larger schedule bars to show how far along the work has progressed. For noncritical tasks, the smaller bars are black, and for the critical path, which is usually shown with a solid black bar, the progress bar will be white. (Some programs allow you to print the critical path in red, so it stands out.)

In Figure 12.2, weekends are shown by vertically shaded areas indicating that no work is done on these days. (The shading

Figure 12.2 Schedule Showing Progress

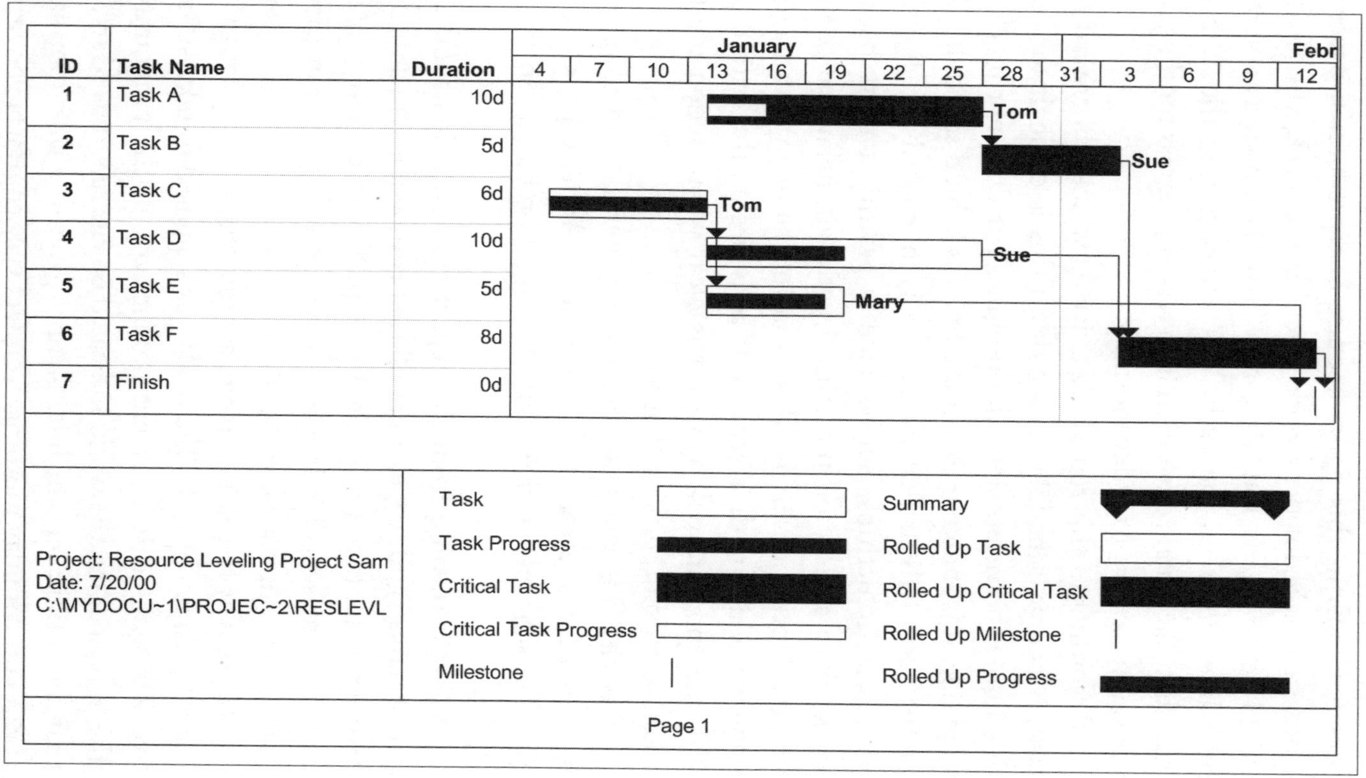

ID
Task Name
Duration
January
Febr
4
7
10
13
16
19
22
25
28
31
3
6
9
12
1
Task A
10d
Tom
2
Task B
5d
Sue
3
Task C
6d
Tom
4
Task D
10d
Sue
5
Task E
5d
Mary
6
Task F
8d
7
Finish
0d
Project: Resource Leveling Project Sam
Date: 7/20/00
C:\MYDOCU~1\PROJEC~2\RESLEVL
Task
Task Progress
Critical Task
Critical Task Progress
Milestone
Summary
Rolled Up Task
Rolled Up Critical Task
Rolled Up Milestone
Rolled Up Progress
Page 1

does not show in this figure because of reproduction issues.) If a project is scheduled to work seven days a week, the shading would be removed. The "time-now" date is shown as a vertical solid line shown on the 19th. You will note that the 19th is a Monday. The usual convention is to report progress for the previous seven days on Monday morning.

According to this report, Activity A, which is a critical path task, is behind schedule by one day. (This is difficult to see on this figure; however, since the progress bar does not touch the solid line, it is showing that the activity is behind schedule.) This immediately tells us that the project is in jeopardy of slipping a day unless something can be done to get this activity back on track, since a delay on the critical path will delay the completion date correspondingly. This is one of the main advantages of knowing which path is critical. If activities on the critical path slip, the end date will slip so it is clear where action must be taken to prevent missing that date.

Activity B is scheduled to start at a later date, so no progress is shown for it. Activity C is complete, Activity D is one day ahead of schedule, and Activity E is right on target. So says the report.

What is missing from this report is information about cost, performance, and scope. Since all that is shown is schedule progress, we must take for granted that performance and scope are correct if the schedule is where it is reported to be. But there is nothing we can infer about cost.

To see why this is a problem, assume that Activity D is a software development task. The work was supposed to take 40 hours (we will assume 100 percent productivity of the programmer). The person doing the work, indicated on the report as Mary, says that she is right on schedule. She has given you this information at 8:30 on Monday morning. You feel very comfortable with her work. You are concerned only about that critical path activity. Something must be done about it.

At 8:45 a.m., Tom comes by and has a brief conversation with you. "I really felt sorry for Mary last week," he confides.

"How so?" you ask.

"Oh, didn't you know? She had a terrible time with the code she was writing. Instead of the 40 hours she expected the work would take, she actually put in nearly 80 hours to get the job done."

"Really?" you say, pondering the situation. "Well, I'm sorry to hear that she had so much trouble, but she's salaried, so it doesn't affect my budget. Everything is fine."

Wait a minute! Is that true?

No way!

If Mary missed her estimate by 100 percent last week, perhaps her estimates for subsequent weeks are off in a similar way. If so, how many 80-hour weeks can she work before she burns out and starts making errors and missing deadlines? This is a sure sign of potential trouble, and you must do something about it right away. (In fact, how many errors did she make last week? If she worked 80 hours instead of 40, there is a good likelihood that she made a lot of errors. That means that the progress she reported is not correct, as she will have to correct those errors in the future, so the scope of work actually done is less than reported.)

So, you go talk to Mary.

"I understand that you had problems with your code last week," you say.

Mary seems a bit surprised that you know about this, but she agrees. "Yes. It turned out to be a lot harder than I expected."

"Well, do you think this will continue to be true?" you ask.

There are two possibilities—yes or no.

If she says yes, then you must do something right away. There are only a few possibilities. You can get some help for her if that is possible. You can reduce the scope of the remaining code that must be written. Or you can accept that the task is going to take a lot longer to complete than the original estimate, in which case it may use up all its float and end up on the critical path. You may also decide between you that Mary is not the right person for this job and replace her.

If she says no, it was a one-time occurrence and she is confident that the remaining work will go according to plan, then you tell her to keep you posted. If the work does turn out to be as difficult this week as it was last week, you want to do something before Mary gets herself—and your project—into serious trouble.

Notice what has happened here. Without knowing how much effort (cost) Mary put into the work, you have no indication that there is a problem. This leads to an immutable law of tracking progress: unless you have an integrated cost-schedule tracking system, you don't have a clue where your project is! *It is simply not enough to let people report schedule progress alone.*

Knowing cost allows you to figure out what is going on. If the work is on schedule and fewer hours were required than estimated, then people are working more efficiently than you expected. If work is on schedule and more hours have been expended than planned, this is a sign of trouble. If work is behind schedule and total hours worked are less than planned, then people are not doing what they are supposed to, and you need to find out why. And so on.

We still have no good way to measure scope or quality, so these will have to be estimated or evaluated using the best approach possible for the work in question. This means that the accuracy of our control system will not be very good, but we must have some way of tracking progress, and this is the best we can do.

TRACKING PROGRESS USING EARNED VALUE ANALYSIS

The earned value system is derived from standard cost systems that are used to measure performance in manufacturing. An industrial engineer determines (estimates) how long a manufacturing procedure should take and multiplies the time by the labor rate for that operation. This becomes the *standard cost* for that operation. Work is then tracked, and the time required to do the step is multiplied by the existing labor rate at the time the step is done. This is the actual cost of the operation, also called *actual cost of work performed*, or ACWP (or simply AC). Note that the labor rate could change between the time the standard cost is established and when the operation is performed, so you could have a variance caused by a change in labor rate. You can also have a variance because the actual time required for the step is different from what was determined by the industrial engineer in the beginning. Thus, it is a composite variance. Finally, we measure what proportion of the work is completed in the standard time. If it is exactly what should have been done, the operation is 100 percent efficient. If the time taken is less, then efficiency is greater than 100 percent, and the converse is true as well.

The earned value system was adopted by project management practitioners as a way of measuring progress, and it is considered to be the best system designed to date. However, the earned value system for tracking projects has detractors. The most common complaint is that you can't measure knowledge work, and I wholeheartedly agree. You can't; however, you must pretend you can or else you can't possibly achieve control of knowledge projects, and this category probably is the largest in the world at present. As I have said previously, we simply must accept that the precision of our measures will be much less than is possible for well-defined or tangible work, but at least we have some indication of how we are doing before a disaster occurs.

As I just stated, the earned value system provides three measures that allow us to determine project status. These are measures of what is supposed to be done, or planned value (PV); what has been done, or earned value (EV); and the amount of effort or cost that has been expended to do the work, or actual cost (AC). (I should say at this point that the original system used four-letter acronyms for these measures—as I did above—but the system was simplified by changing them to two letters, as I've used here. Unfortunately, numerous books and articles use the four-letter versions, so you may find it hard to follow these other sources unless you know how to translate. So, as I continue this discussion, I will provide translations for you.)

To see how earned value works, we will start with a very simple example.

Assume for a moment that you have guests coming to stay with you for a few days, and you want to make a good impression by having a spotless house. You don't have time to do all the cleaning yourself, so you call a cleaning service and ask what they will charge to clean the house from top to bottom. An agent of the service comes out to your house and gives you a quote.

"We should be able to thoroughly clean your house with one worker in 40 hours," the agent tells you. (The numbers in this example are not meant to be realistic, only to illustrate the procedure. Thus, 40 hours are too many, and the labor rate quoted next may be too high.)

"How much will that cost?" you ask.

"Our billing rate is $20 per hour," says the agent, "so it will cost you approximately $800."

"Is that a fixed price?"

"No, we charge by the hour. If it takes a little less, you will pay less, and conversely."

"Okay, let's do it," you say.

The agent agrees to have someone at your house by eight o'clock Monday morning. You make a note that the job will cost about $800. This number is called the budgeted cost of work scheduled (BCWS) to be done—or, to use the new term, this is planned value (PV).

On Monday morning, around 7:00, the phone rings. It is the agent.

"I have a problem," she tells you. "The guy we were going to send over to clean your house had an accident this weekend and can't make it. However, I have another person available, but we bill him at $22 an hour. Is that okay?"

"You have me at a disadvantage," you say. "I have to get the house cleaned, so go ahead and send him over."

So the alternative worker comes out to your house and starts the job. You must leave town on business, so you don't talk with the worker until you return on Friday. He is just wrapping up for the week.

"How did it go?" you ask.

"I'm afraid I didn't quite finish," he says.

"Well, how much did you get done?" you ask.

He thinks for a moment. "As near as I can tell, I got about 80 percent of it done," he says.

Notice those words. *As near as I can tell.*

In other words, he is *estimating* where he is!

As former president George H. W. Bush used to like to say, estimating is one of those kind, gentle words that really substitutes for the fact that you are guessing. That's right, an estimate is a guess.

Let's think about this. Control is exercised by comparing where you are (which you know only by guessing) to where you are supposed to be (which is another guess) and then taking action to correct for differences between the two. Does this sound like witchcraft and magic to you? It does to me. Does it give you a good sense of truly being in control? Probably not.

Nevertheless, as I've said earlier, even though this is not precise, it's better than doing absolutely nothing.

Most important, the example shows the difficulty of measuring progress even on tangible work. How do you know how much of the house has been cleaned? Can you measure it on a square-foot basis? What about cleaning walls or dusting furniture? The truth is, you have no choice but to estimate progress, compare it to the scheduled work (also estimated), and do your best to correct for deviations.

Fine. How do we assign a value to what has been done?

Well, if we compare what has been done to the original target, how much should it have cost you to do 80 percent of the total job? The BCWS (PV) was $800 worth of work. If the worker has done only 80 percent of that, it *should* have cost me $640, calculated as follows:

$$BCWP = 0.80 \times BCWS = 0.80 \times 800 = \$640$$

Or using two-letter codes, we have:

$$EV = 0.80 \times PV = 0.80 \times 800 = \$640$$

The term earned value (BCWP, or EV) means that the worker has contributed $640 of value to cleaning the house. Of course, he was supposed to have done $800 worth of work, so he did not perform according to plan.

The fact that the worker did less than was supposed to be done is bad enough, but then it occurs to you that he has worked

40 hours at a higher labor rate ($22 per hour) than you originally budgeted for, so the actual cost of the work performed (ACWP, or AC) is $880.

This is not good. Not only did you get less than you were supposed to get, but you have paid more for it as well.

The status of this task is determined using the following equations:

Schedule variance (SV) = BCWP − BCWS (or EV − PV)

Cost variance (CV) = BCWP − ACWP (or EV − AC)

Budget variance (BV) = BCWS − ACWP (or PV − AC)

Using these formulas, we arrive at the following variances:

Schedule variance = 640 − 800 = −$160 worth of work

Cost variance = 640 − 880 = −$240

Budget variance = 800 − 880 = −$80

In conventional accounting practice, a negative variance is *always* unfavorable, so this means that the job is behind schedule by $160 worth of work. To convert that to time, you divide by the original $20 per hour labor rate, and you see that the person is eight hours behind schedule. That makes sense. If he only did 80 percent of the work and it was supposed to take five days, he has done what should have been done in four days, so he is one day (or eight hours) behind.

But notice the cost variance. Why is it $240? Because you have spent $80 more for the work than originally budgeted, and you have gotten $160 less work done than you were supposed to get. So your cost variance in this case is the sum of the budget

$$SV = BCWP − BCWS = EV − PV$$
$$CV = BCWP − ACWP = EV − AC$$
$$BV = BCWS − ACWP = PV − AC$$

and schedule variances, and since the number is negative, you are overspent by $240.

Here is an important point. We have already seen that if you look only at the schedule, without knowing the cost, you have no warning that a project may be heading for trouble. In the same manner, if you were tracking only your budget variance, you would know that you were spending too much, but that alone does not show the true picture. Not only are you spending too much, but you are getting much less than you should for what you are spending. This also confirms the need to know both cost and schedule to form a true picture of project status.

It is also instructive to notice how this job got into trouble. You failed to check on progress during the week. Rather, you waited until Friday afternoon to find out that the worker was not on target. Had you checked progress around midweek and found that the work was already falling behind, you might have been able to get the worker to spend some overtime to get it finished by Friday afternoon. Now all you can do is pay for work on Saturday or have the person come back next week to finish the job.

This suggests a guideline: the rate at which you monitor progress must be proportionate to the total time the work will take. A task that is supposed to take a week should probably be monitored daily. That doesn't mean that the project manager should do this—the individual(s) doing the work should monitor their own progress and should be told how much leeway they have before they must take steps to get back on track.

Budget Variance and Spending Variance

It may sound trivial, but it is important to differentiate between budget and spending variance. In the housekeeping example, you are behind schedule and spending more than originally budgeted, so you have a composite of budget and schedule variances that add up to spending variance. In the end, this project will most likely be late and overspent.

RESPONDING TO DEVIATIONS

In tracking a project, you must always ask three questions:

1. What is the status?
2. When there is a deviation, what caused it?
3. What should be done about any deviations that exist?

If we apply these questions to the housecleaning example, the answer to the first question is that you are behind schedule and overspent. When it comes to the second question, however, is it clear that you don't know the cause of the deviations? It could be that this person is not as efficient as he should be, or it could be that the estimate was wrong in the first place.

How would you figure it out?

Suppose you bring back this same worker week after week to clean the house, and he can never get it all done in 40 hours. Does this prove that it is the person?

No. It could be impossible for anyone to do the work in 40 hours.

Then suppose we alternate between two workers. If neither of them can clean the house in 40 hours, we are convinced that the estimate was optimistic. However, if one of them can clean the house in 40 hours and the other cannot, then it is clearly the person.

Or is it?

MONITORING PROGRESS

When you monitor progress, you ask three questions, as follows:

1. What is the actual status of the work?

2. When there is a deviation, what caused it?

3. What should be done to correct for any deviation that exists?

To answer question 3, note that there are only four responses you can make to a deviation.

They are:

1. Ignore the deviation.

2. Take steps to get back on track.

3. Revise the plan to show that the deviation cannot be recovered.

4. Cancel the project.

Well, clearly, one person can work faster than the other, but it is important to remember what we said about estimating back in Chapter 8. All estimates are person specific. It makes no difference what someone else can do. If you want to know when a project will end, you must estimate for the individuals doing the tasks.

Simply put, there are a very few runners who can run a mile in less than four minutes. So it would be totally unreasonable for you to expect an average person to run the mile in four minutes just because somewhere there is *someone* who can do it.

Given these facts, you can't answer the second question now. All you can do is move on to the third one, which asks what you want to do about deviations. To answer this question, you have to look at your options: ignore the deviation, take corrective action to get back on track, or change the plan to accept the deviation.

In the housecleaning situation, you have only a limited number of choices—have the person work overtime on Saturday at premium pay or return on Monday to finish the job at regular pay. If you can wait until Monday, that will be the cheaper option.

Otherwise, you may have no choice but to pay premium wages. Of course, there is a third option, which is to leave the 20 percent as is, but that isn't a very attractive choice. None of the preferred options fits with the second choice. Both are examples of changing the plan. And of course, it is too late to ignore the deviation.

When would it be okay to ignore a deviation? When it is smaller than the tolerances you can hold and does not show a trend that will eventually take it out of bounds. Consider the deviation chart in Figure 12.3. This chart is showing a project in which tolerances of ±20 percent are the best that can be maintained. During the first few weeks of the project, the deviations vary randomly within those boundaries. Then there is a definite trend that suggests that the project will break the 20 percent boundary if nothing is done to get it back on track. Corrective action must be taken, or, if nothing can be done to get back on track, the plan may have to be revised.

In examining deviations, you must always go back to the equation that relates the constraints to each other, namely,

$$C = f(P, T, S)$$

If you are trying to get back on schedule, you can increase costs (add labor), reduce scope, or reduce performance requirements. All of these can be considered a change to the original plan, except that you may not formally revise the published

Figure 12.3   Deviation Graph for a Project

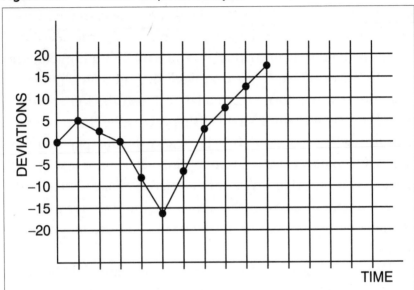

plan. In the case of reducing scope or performance, you probably have no choice but to revise the plan. If you can increase resources without going over budget, you may be able to leave the plan alone.

Let me reiterate, just so no one misses it. There are *only* four responses you can make when a project is off track. You can ignore the deviation. You can take corrective action to get back on target. You can change the plan. And you can cancel the job altogether. Cancellations happen when the project has slipped so much that it is no longer viable—it will be too late, too expensive, or nonfunctional.

Now, before we continue to the next section, to recap, here are the two-letter and four-letter acronyms:

$$BCWS = PV$$

$$BCWP = EV$$

$$ACWP = AC$$

Because the two-letter versions are now used by PMI® on their PMP exam, we will use these throughout the remainder of this chapter.

USING GRAPHS TO TRACK PROGRESS AND FORECAST TRENDS

To get an overall assessment of project status, we can plot earned value data graphically. These graphs will also allow us to forecast where the project will end up in terms of both schedule and spending.

Consider the bar chart in Figure 12.4. There are only three activities. As you can see, Task A spends $800 a week for labor, Task B spends $3,000 per week, and Task C spends $2,400 a week. On the first line below the bar chart, you see the weekly spending figures, which are obtained by summing the spending on each bar for the week. The final line shows the cumulative spending for this project to be $28,800 at the end of the job. Note that these figures represent the PV for the project. If these are plotted, we simply transform the bar graph into a line graph, which shows the dollar value of the cumulative work to be done over time. Since the bar graph is a major component of the project plan, the line graph is also, and is, in fact, called a *baseline plan*. This plot is shown in Figure 12.5.

Figure 12.4   Bar Graph for a Small Project

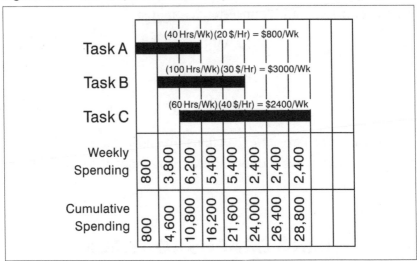

Figure 12.5   Cumulative Spending for the Three-Task Project

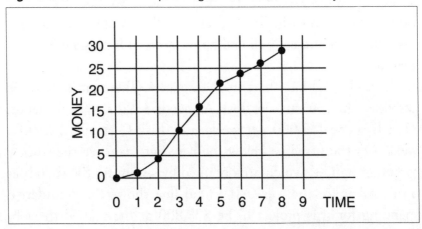

Once this curve has been plotted, we can compare progress to it so that deviations from plan can be spotted. To show this, I am going to use a new curve, one for a larger project than the simple three-task example.

First Case: Behind Schedule and Overspent

For this project, I have total cumulative spending of about $90,000. To show progress, I need to find out how much has been accomplished and how much it has cost. To do this, I go around and find out from each contributor how much work he or she has done, expressed as EV, and I add up the total value of everyone's work. As you can see from the graph in Figure 12.6, people were supposed to have done $50,000 worth of work by the date in question. This was supposed to be 1,000 hours of work at a loaded labor rate of $50 per hour. When I total what they have actually accomplished, I find that they have only done $40,000 worth of work. In addition, when I collect their time reports, they have put in 1,200 hours of labor at a loaded labor rate of $50 per hour. Thus, the AC for the project work is $60,000.

Returning to our progress questions, we first ask, what is the status of the project? We saw previously that the schedule variance is given by

$$SV = EV - PV$$

I suggest that you begin with schedule variance, because cost variance doesn't always make sense until you know what has happened to your schedule.

For this project, the schedule variance is −$10,000 worth of work. This is calculated as follows:

$$SV = 40,000 - 50,000 = -\$10,000$$

Figure 12.6 Plot Showing Project behind Schedule and Overspent

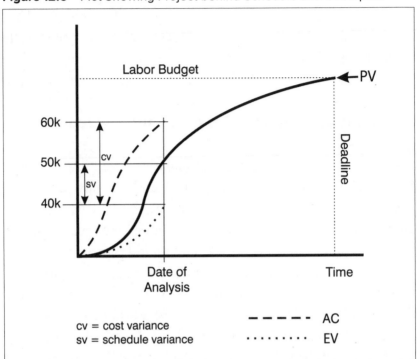

cv = cost variance
sv = schedule variance

– – – – AC
· · · · · · · · · EV

If you divide $10,000 by $50 per hour, you find that the project is 200 hours' worth of work behind schedule. What this means in calendar time depends on the number of hours per day that are scheduled to be worked. However, you can tell the schedule variance by looking at the horizontal axis. This is shown in Figure 12.7.

Figure 12.7 Schedule Variance Shown on Horizontal Axis

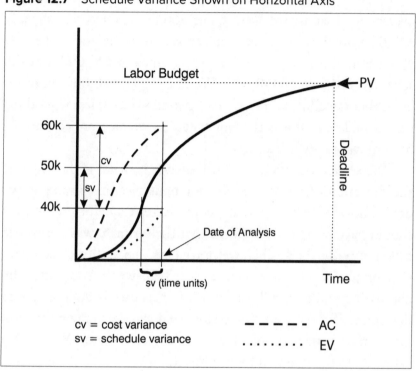

Notice that the schedule variance is shown both as a –$10,000 deviation on the vertical axis and as a time deviation on the horizontal axis. We have done $10,000 less work than was scheduled. We have also spent $60,000 to do the work, so the cost variance is $20,000. This is calculated as

$$CV = EV - AC$$

$$CV = 40,000 - 60,000 = -\$20,000$$

Since a negative variance is unfavorable, we are $20,000 overspent. That is, we have spent $60,000 to accomplish only $40,000 worth of work. As you can see from the graph, the cost variance is the sum of the budget variance of $10,000 and the schedule variance of $10,000. We have spent $10,000 more for labor than scheduled, and we have gotten $10,000 less work done than scheduled. This is the worst state in which a project can be, but unfortunately it happens.

The second question we must answer is, what is the cause of the deviation? As was true for our housecleaning example, we don't know. It could be that people weren't as efficient as they should have been, or it could be that the estimate was optimistic to begin with. And, since we don't have the ability to compare this project to another one, we can't answer the question by comparing workers. All we can do in this case is do a review to determine if there were any factors that caused the work to take longer than expected, then try to project from there. We can also ask what to do based on those projections.

This is the third question—what should we do about the deviation? To answer that question, we need to have some idea of what is going to happen to the project. That is, where will it end up? If we had some way to extrapolate the EV and AC curves in Figure 12.7, we might be able to determine the end state.

You might do a linear regression to extrapolate these curves, but if you are on the very steep part of the PV curve, fitting a linear projection to the EV and AC curves can be very misleading. It would be better if you reestimated where the curves are heading, but I am going to pretend that we can fit a nonlinear projection to each curve, which would give the result shown in Figure 12.8.

Figure 12.8 Project with EV and AC Extrapolated

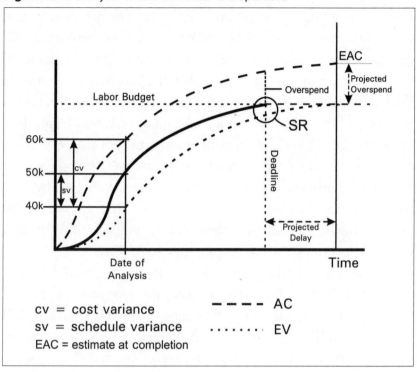

To extrapolate these curves, assume that if all the work is to be completed, the EV curve must eventually hit the BAC line (budget at completion). As you can see from the figure, it will do so later than originally targeted, so the project will be late. Second, the AC curve must hit the finish point for the project, so extrapolating it gives a new estimate at completion (EAC), as shown in the figure. Note that the difference between this new EAC and the original BAC indicates how much the project will go over budget.

Based on these projections, the project is going to be *seriously* late and overspent unless something can be done to get it back on target. What to do?

First, consider the worst case—that the project can't be salvaged. It is going to be late and overspent. The question in this case is whether it is still viable. If it is product or software development and we estimate lost sales (because it is late) and increased development costs, we may find that the return on investment (ROI) is no longer at an acceptable level. If that is the case, unless something can be done to get it back on target, it may be prudent to cancel the job and get on with another project that will bring an acceptable return. If the ROI is unacceptable, the only reason we would continue the project would be if it is mandated by contract. If the product were a loss leader or one that was needed for position in the marketplace, then ROI wouldn't be a factor and we might continue the job despite the projections.

But is there anything that can be done to recover? Perhaps. Notice that if the scope were reduced, the project could be finished by the original completion date, although it would still be overspent. This is shown as SR in Figure 12.8. If that is an acceptable trade-off, we would agree on a scope reduction, meaning that the plan would be revised, and we would continue.

Suppose, however, that you are told that it's unacceptable to reduce scope, and it is not permissible to be late. You must bring this project in on time.

This means that you must somehow make the EV curve turn upward so that it intersects the PV curve at the deadline. This is shown in Figure 12.9. Also note that you will most likely incur even greater cost to make this happen, because you'll probably have to throw resources at the project to complete it on time.

Of course, you can finish the project on time and on budget if you are dealing with salaried people who don't get paid overtime. That is, you can *appear* to do so. But is that true? Is nonpaid overtime really free?

Figure 12.9   Project Ending on Time but Overspent

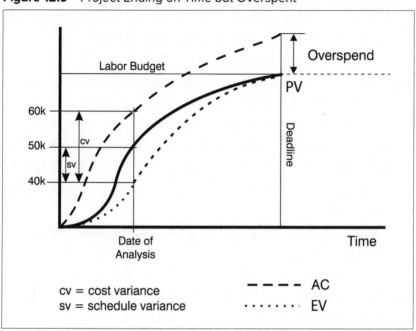

cv = cost variance

sv = schedule variance

– – – – AC

· · · · · · · · EV

You can be sure it is not. You will pay in terms of lost productivity, increased rework, field failures, employee absenteeism, stress-related illness, or turnover. In a job market in which unemployment is only a few percent, people can find new jobs easily and may very well leave if unpaid overtime hours mount. And the cost to replace professionals in the United States today is in the range of $100,000 to $200,000. So your unpaid overtime can turn out to be very expensive!

As a final question, you may ask if there isn't something that can be done to get the project completely back on track without going way over budget.

> If you are 15 percent into a project on the horizontal timeline and you are in trouble, you are going to stay in trouble!

I can assure you that it would take a miracle.

I'll cite the 15 percent rule: if you are 15 percent of the way into a project on the horizontal timeline and you are in trouble, you are going to stay in trouble. This means that if a project is supposed to take 100 weeks to complete, and you are in trouble at the end of week 15, you are going to stay there. Period!

How can I be so confident of this? Aren't there any exceptions?

To answer these questions, consider a study that found that of 800 defense contract projects that were in trouble at the 15 percent mark, not a single one ever recovered (Fleming and Koppelman, 1996).

I know, I know. You're thinking that this is typical of defense contracting.

But I can assure you that it applies to your projects as well, even if you aren't in defense contracting.

How can I be sure?

Easy. Where did the PV curve come from?

The bar chart schedule.

Where did the schedule come from?

Forecasts—which are estimates. And we all know that if the weather forecast for *tomorrow* can't be trusted, there is no need to believe the forecast for six weeks out. In other words, if the near-term forecast (just 15 percent into the project) isn't right, why would it be any better at the end of the job?

This is a good-news, bad-news story. The good news is that you can forecast a losing project very early so that you can perhaps cancel it and cut your losses early on. The bad news is that even if it is doing well at the 15 percent point, it won't necessarily continue to do so.

Second Case: Ahead of Schedule
and Spending Correctly

To illustrate another combination, consider the situation shown in Figure 12.10. This time the EV curve shows that $60,000 worth of work has been done and that the AC is also $60,000. The PV target on this date was $50,000. The status is ahead of schedule, and the cost variance is zero.

Figure 12.10   Project Ahead of Schedule and Spending Correctly

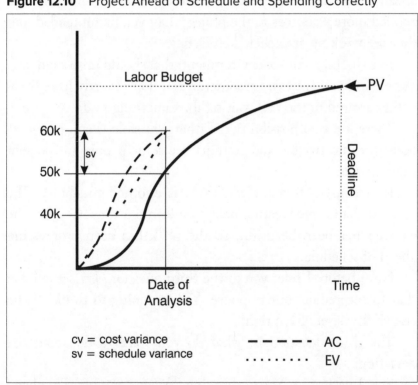

Be careful to distinguish between *budget* variance and *cost* variance, as I cautioned earlier. The project is above budget by

$10,000, but that is because it's ahead of schedule. In words, the workers have done $60,000 worth of work (EV) and spent $60,000 (AC) to do it. A simple way to keep this in mind is that when EV is larger than PV, you have done more than scheduled, so you are ahead of schedule. If you have done less, you are behind.

The second question we must answer is, what is the most likely cause of this variance? Unlike the first one, where the project was behind schedule and overspent, this variance has a generic cause. Remember, this is labor cost. When you are ahead of schedule and spending correctly, it means that you have applied more resources to the project than you had intended, but they are working at expected efficiency.

In a shared-resource environment, that should raise a red flag. Where did you get extra resources? You don't exactly have them sitting around in the hall waiting for something to do.

There are two possibilities. Either you stole them, or somebody got into trouble and couldn't use some people and so sent them to you.

In a construction project, there is another possibility. The schedule had some weather delays built into it for safety, but the weather has been beautiful, so the work has been progressing ahead of schedule.

Now, before I refer you to the third question, I must tell you that I can predict your response. You are going to think, "Is he crazy?" Let's see if I'm right.

The third question is, what do you want to do about the deviation?

See, I was right. You're thinking, "Wait a minute. I'm ahead of schedule and spending correctly, and he wants to know what I'm going to do about it? Like nothing, man! Hide it maybe. I'm sure not going to slow down."

Before you go too far with that thinking, you have to ask if being ahead of schedule can cause problems later on. And the answer is yes.

Suppose you deliver a product before the customer is ready for it. You may have to pay to warehouse it. You may also have to wait to get paid for it.

Speaking of pay, suppose the project is a construction job. Contractors usually want progress payments for their work, so they send you bills totaling $60,000. Your controller may kill you. Your plan said that you were going to do $50,000 worth of work, but the contractors have done $60,000. Although the difference may be small, the controller may have cash flow problems and tell you to slow down.

Darn. What a thankless job! Just when you thought you were doing something good, everyone starts trashing you.

It's a matter of degree, you understand. If you are a little bit ahead, nobody will get excited. In fact, we all know that it is always better to be ahead than to be behind. But there are definitely situations where being ahead can be a problem. I know of a company that finished some equipment ahead of time and shipped it. It was delivered to a new facility—where the customer hadn't finished building the loading dock. The manufacturer had to warehouse it temporarily and pay the rental charges.

Third Case: Behind Schedule and Spending Correctly

The next scenario is shown in Figure 12.11. In this case, EV is at $40,000, and so is AC. The target PV is still $50,000. What is the status? The project is behind schedule, but it has no cost variance. What is the most likely cause? Lack of resources. You may be waiting for supplies, or too little labor may be being applied to the project.

Figure 12.11 Project behind Schedule and Spending Correctly

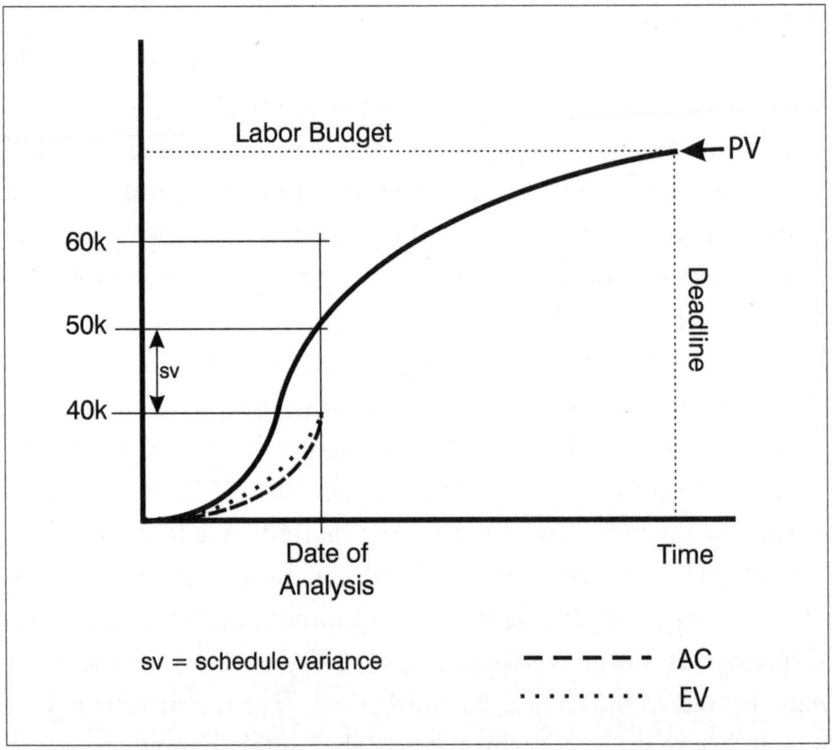

What do you want to do about it? Usually, you want to catch up. However, you can almost be sure that to catch up, you will have to blow your budget. It is usually better to stay on schedule than to try to recover once you get behind.

Final Scenario

Examine Figure 12.12. What is the status?

Figure 12.12   Project Ahead of Schedule and Underspent

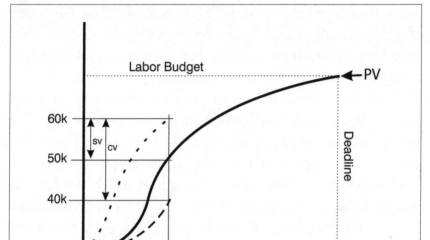

The project is ahead of schedule and underspent. How much? The work is $10,000 ahead (EV is at $60,000), and spending is $20,000 less than expected. In other words, you have spent only $40,000 to accomplish $60,000 worth of work. Sounds great, doesn't it?

Not so fast.

What is the most likely cause of this variance? There are two possibilities. One is that the estimate was very conservative—to the point of sandbagging. The other is that you had a very lucky break. You can bet that sandbagging is far more likely than a lucky break.

Question three asks you what to do about it. I know what you're thinking: Leave it alone. Hide it maybe. You sure aren't going to slow down, and if you were to give the money back, they would expect you to do the same thing next time. Nobody in his right mind would do either—or would he?

I submit that you should give some of the money back and reschedule the project. If you don't, the organization will lose the opportunity to make good use of the money until the project ends, and that opportunity cost can be significant.

Remember our first project scenario in which the job was behind schedule and overspent? We said that the project could be canceled if it is no longer viable, but it could be viable but still be canceled simply because there is no money to fund it. However, there would be money to fund that project if we freed it up from this one, which is under budget.

Notice that I said you should give *some* of the money back. As I have explained elsewhere, all work varies. There is some tolerance that we must accept as normal variation. If it is plus or minus 15 percent, then give all but 15 percent of the money back. Keep some in reserve to cover the variation. This is proper control of variance.

Again, I know what you're thinking. If you give it back and then hit a rock later on, you won't be able to get it back. This is true in many organizations. What I am advocating is that the organization must change the way it treats project budgets. They must all be examined once a quarter, with adjustments made in either direction. That way people will be willing to give back extra money, as they know that they will be able to get it back later if they need it.

In more companies than I care to count, the solution to this problem is simply to tell members of the overspent project to quit charging time to it. They are told to charge to the underspent project instead. That way, both projects will come in on budget.

In defense contracting, if you get caught doing this, you could go to jail. It is illegal, because earned value is used to determine when progress payments should be made to a contractor, and if you charge for work you haven't done, you are lying, and this is illegal.

Most seriously, this tactic destroys our ability to detect a troubled project and do something to help it. Or, if the project is too far gone to be saved, we could cancel it. But we can't tell that it is bad off if no one charges time to it.

> Cross-charging contaminates databases. The proper approach is to be above-board about rebudgeting.

In addition, this practice, called *cross-charging*, contaminates both history databases. Next time you do similar projects, you will underestimate one and overestimate the other. And you will be in trouble again.

Instead, an aboveboard adjustment to both project budgets should be made. The funds should be transferred from one to the other. This does not contaminate your databases and is acceptable.

USING SPREADSHEETS TO TRACK PROGRESS

The graphical method of tracking progress is effective at showing trends and visually presenting an overview of a project, but it is not very effective at determining the true state of the job.

The reason is that the graph presents composite data for the project, and that data is not good for seeing problems that exist with individual tasks.

Consider the situation shown in Figure 12.13. There are three tasks going on in parallel. One is $100 overspent, the second is right on target, and the third is $100 underspent. What you see on the bottom line will be a zero variance in spending, because one deviation cancels the other. This would tell you that the project is fine when it is not. To really track progress, you need to look at every task, and the best way to do that is with a spreadsheet.

Figure 12.13   Three Tasks in Parallel

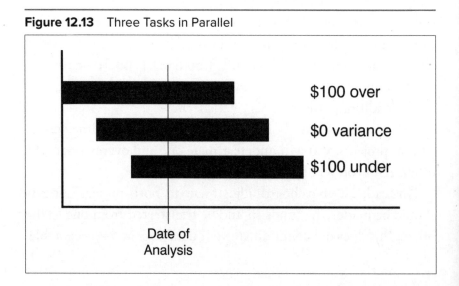

Most scheduling programs today allow you to report progress using earned value analysis and present it in spreadsheet format. However, not all of them have one feature that I find very useful, and that is the critical ratio. This is a performance index that is the product of two individual ratios. One is the schedule performance index (SPI), and the other is the cost performance index (CPI). These are shown as follows:

$$SPI = \frac{EV}{PV}$$

$$CPI = \frac{EV}{AC}$$

Before continuing, I think it is helpful to review the meaning of these equations. First of all, EV, or earned value, is a measure of *what you got*. The amount of work you were *supposed* to get is PV. SPI is simply *work efficiency*, or the fraction of work done. Finally, AC is the actual cost of work performed, so the CPI can be thought of as *spending efficiency*.

If the two ratios are multiplied together, you get a combined index called the critical ratio (CR):

$$CR = SPI \times CPI$$

Like all ratios that indicate performance, the SPI and the CPI will have a value of 1.0 if the work is going exactly as planned. If the work is going better than planned, the ratios will be greater than 1.0, and if it is going worse than planned, they will have values of less than 1.0. When you multiply the two together, one of them may be slightly above 1.0 and the other slightly below 1.0, and the CPI can still be 1.0. As an example

$$CR = SPI \times CPI$$

$$= 0.9 \times 1.11$$

$$= 1.0$$

A spreadsheet that uses the critical ratio to indicate progress and suggest actions to be taken is shown in Figure 12.14. Note that the critical ratio is calculated in the next-to-last column, and

Figure 12.14 Spreadsheet for Tracking Progress

Earned Value Report

Project No.:   Date: FILE:

Description: Page _____ of _____

Prepared by: Signed:

WBS # or Name	Cumulative-to-Date			Variance		At Completion			Critical Ratio	Action Required
	PV	EV	AC	Sched.	Cost	Budgeted (BAC)	Latest Est. (EAC)	Variance		
				0	0			0	NA	NA
				0	0			0	NA	NA
				0	0			0	NA	NA
				0	0			0	NA	NA
				0	0			0	NA	NA
				0	0			0	NA	NA
				0	0			0	NA	NA
				0	0			0	NA	NA
				0	0			0	NA	NA
TOTALS:	0	0	0	0	0	0	0	0	NA	NA

NOTE: Negative variance is unfavorable || If Critical Ratio < 0.6, INFORM MANAGEMENT!

( ) = NEGATIVE VALUES

that the last column is headed "Action Required," which has the following meaning (this spreadsheet can be downloaded from my website free of charge).

A manufacturing process can be monitored by measuring the process outputs and plotting those measures on a deviation graph. If those measures fall randomly around the centerline, the process is in control. When the deviations cease to be random, there is a probability that the process is either out of control or about to go out of control. The tests for nonrandomness are beyond the scope of this book; a good reference is Walpole (1974).

Critical Ratio Greater than 1.0

A similar idea has been developed for keeping track of the critical ratio over time. The control limits are shown in Figure 12.15. If the critical ratio is between 0.8 and 1.2, we consider the deviation to be acceptable. If it falls between 1.2 and 1.3, we are told to check the task (or project), and if the ratio goes above 1.3, we are told to "red flag" it. This means that the ratio is seriously out of line.

However, I said earlier that ratios greater than 1.0 mean that work is going better than planned. So why would a critical ratio above 1.3 be cause for concern?

Have you heard the saying, if something seems to be too good to be true, it probably is? The first concern is whether the data is actually valid, or people are deceiving themselves. If the data is valid, then what is going on?

In all likelihood, the project is way ahead of schedule and underspent when the critical ratio goes this high. Wonderful, you say!

Well, maybe.

Figure 12.15   A Critical Ratio Control Chart

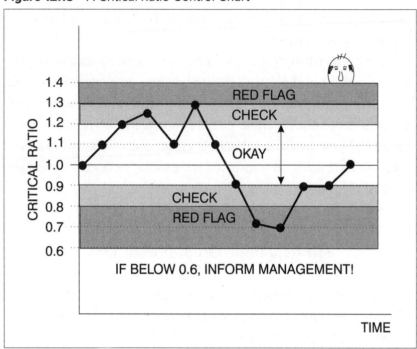

IF BELOW 0.6, INFORM MANAGEMENT!

But this is the last situation we examined in the section on tracking progress graphically, and we said that the project should be rescheduled and some of the money given back. So the critical ratio is flagging you that something should be done about the project.

Critical Ratio Less than 1.0

When the CR is between 0.8 and 0.9, it is in the check range. If it is below 0.8, it becomes a red flag, and if it drops below 0.6, we are told to inform management. The reason is that this project is really sick, nigh unto death. For a critical ratio to be around

0.6, the project is most likely far behind schedule and seriously overspent. It is a good candidate to be canceled (if that is an option), and cancellation decisions are usually made by senior management—so we are being told to inform them so that they can decide what to do.

Of course, this applies only to the overall project critical ratio. If a single task has a critical ratio of around 0.6, you wouldn't tell senior management about it. It is you, the project manager, who should be alarmed and act. Chances are that if this task had any float, it probably doesn't have much left; if it becomes critical and slips any more, it will impact the finish date for the project. You need to act immediately.

The spreadsheet shown in Figure 12.14 has an "if" formula in the Action Required cell to test the critical ratio against the specified limits, and it displays the words Okay, Check, or Red Flag in the cell so that you can scan the right-hand column and see your trouble spots immediately. In addition, you can set up conditional formatting of the cell to highlight it in red, yellow, or green to correspond to Red Flag, Check, or Okay, respectively. You can then distribute color printouts that make it very easy for people to spot problems.

Forecasting Final Cost and Schedule Results

There are a couple of ways to forecast results for a project. One is to replan based on what has been learned to date. Another is to calculate forecast results using earned value data. Perhaps the best would be to do both.

The most common and most accepted of the statistical forecasting methods is to use the cumulative CPI estimate at completion (previously labeled EAC on the projection graphs). The formula for making this projection is

$$SPI = \frac{BAC - EV}{cummulative\ CPI} + AC$$

If we go back to the first project status example we used, in which the project was behind schedule and overspent, and ask what the EAC will be, we would get the following. The original BAC (budget at completion) is about $90,000. The current EV is $40,000 and the AC is $60,000, so the CPI is therefore 0.533 (the numbers in the equation are expressed in thousands):

$$\$EAC = \frac{90 - 40}{0.533} + 60$$

This calculates to an EAC of $153,800. If nothing is done to bring spending in line, the project is going to be overspent severely! The only problem with this formula is that it is a more or less linear projection that depends on the slope of the curve at the present time for its forecast. It is better to reestimate each task and forecast from those estimates, but this is a quick way to find out how much trouble you are in.

ALTERNATIVES TO EARNED VALUE

As far as I am concerned, there is no completely adequate alternative to earned value tracking. I showed at the beginning of the chapter that unless you know both how much effort has gone into a project and where the schedule is, you can't tell whether you have problems. However, there are some approaches that can be used in lieu of earned value if you simply can't find a way to measure EV, for example.

Using Run Charts

One of these is the run chart. You can plot any four of the project variables (P, C, T, S) using this approach. The chart in Figure 12.16 shows a plot of a fraction of work completed each week for a hypothetical project called "Echo." To plot the fraction of work completed, you divide the amount of work completed to date by the amount of work scheduled to be completed. This could be called percent of scheduled work actually completed and is equivalent to the ratio EV/PV. From this chart, you can see that there is a downward trend starting in week 3. People are clearly having trouble. Then they somehow begin to recover, and there is an upward trend that peaks in week 15, then falls back a bit. Since the work following week 12 is being performed at a faster rate than scheduled, it is likely that the project will finish early, possibly by week 21, rather than as scheduled in week 23. This chart is highly unlikely to occur in reality, because the team is in a lot of trouble early on, but it illustrates the approach.

There are two guidelines for interpreting run charts to detect meaningful systemic changes:

1. Since it is expected that there would be approximately the same number of points above the *average* line as there are below it, a good rule of thumb is that if there is a run of seven consecutive points on one side of the average, something significant may be happening, and it would probably be a good idea to call "time out."

2. A second test is to see whether a run of seven or more intervals is steadily increasing or decreasing without reversals in direction. As such a pattern is not likely to occur by chance, thereby indicating something needs to be investigated (Kiemele & Schmidt, 1993, pp. 2–25).

Figure 12.16   A Run Chart for Project Echo

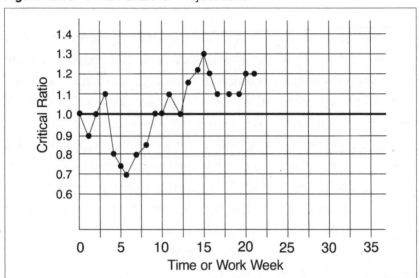

To track quality, you might want to record rework hours. It is likely that most projects will incur from 5 to 40 percent rework. If you are improving your project management process, you should see a decline in rework. A run chart that tracks hours spent on rework is shown in Figure 12.17.

If you compare Figure 12.16 with Figure 12.17, you will notice that the curve showing rework hours is almost a mirror image of the progress curve. This suggests that one reason that the team was not making good progress prior to week 10 is that they were making numerous errors, which had to be corrected. After week 10, the team had reduced the rework significantly, and their progress reflects this. These figures would be for a very small team.

Other indicators of project quality might be documentation changes, engineering changes, design revisions, customer complaints, test failures, number of software bugs, and so on.

Figure 12.17 A Run Chart for Project Echo Showing Rework

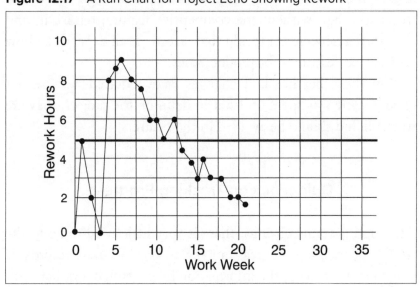

It is also useful to track the number of scope changes in a project, but you need to capture the impact of a scope change for this to be meaningful. You might be able to absorb a dozen small scope changes with almost no impact on the project, while a single larger change in scope might nearly sink the project. Since scope changes result in additional work, you can track their impact by looking at the dollar value of the extra work required (or the number of working hours if you don't have dollar figures). You can also show impact by any resulting slip in schedule.

The other issue that should be addressed is the cause of the scope change. If the cause was, say, new environmental regulations that no one could foresee, then the scope changes are probably legitimate. On longer-duration projects, the world is going to move around before you can finish the project. Competitors may bring out products that necessitate changes in your design if you are going to continue to compete. This is understandable, although sometimes you should go ahead and freeze a design without the competitive feature, release it, and then start a new project to add that feature. It all depends on how critical that feature is for product sales.

On the other hand, if changes were required because not enough time was spent up front in defining the project, they are wasteful and should be avoided in the future.

Guidelines on Tracking Progress

Although it seems obvious, there is very little need to go to the trouble of tracking progress unless you keep accurate records. If you don't want to use the information for control, but rather want to make your project look good, then why bother to collect data? Just write down what you want people to see and save yourself a lot of effort.

There are two major sins committed in tracking progress. One is to let people record their time once a week. I know. I did this 40 years ago when I didn't know any better. We had to record time to the nearest quarter-hour, and we turned in the reports on Monday morning.

Even when I was younger, I could never remember what I had done the previous Monday. Now I can't remember what I did yesterday. So when my time report was due, I guessed at it the best I could, but you can be sure that it was highly inaccurate. That means that the database was a fiction—one that would subsequently be used to estimate future projects. It was useless!

The only reasonable way to record work is to do it daily. It doesn't take that long. If it takes longer than five minutes, you are being obsessive. I don't think it makes sense to record time in increments much less than a half-hour. If you work an eight-hour day, that is 16 entries into your time log. It should take less than 15 seconds to write each one down, so that is about four minutes. (Okay, you're slow; allow yourself 10 minutes, but that's it.)

The second deadly sin is to not track unpaid overtime. In some organizations, salaried personnel are allowed to report only 40 hours a week, because that's all they are paid for. That is a payroll issue, not a project one. For project purposes, you need to know exactly how many total hours are spent on a task so that your database will reflect actual hours for use in future estimating. In addition, if you strip off the overtime, you can't tell that you have problems, as was shown at the beginning of this chapter.

PROJECT CHANGE CONTROL

One major cause of project time and cost overruns is scope creep. Stakeholders ask for "small" changes. They aren't very significant, so you absorb them. The problem is, five-cent changes add up to dollars, and the next thing you know, the project has grown considerably larger than it started out to be. Feature creep is also a cause of scope creep. The interesting thing is that the very people who ask for all the changes develop very convenient amnesia at the end of the project. To protect yourself and everyone else, you must control changes to the project.

This is done through a formal project change approval process. When someone asks for a change to the project, you should let that person know the impact if the change is made. What will it do to schedule, cost, or performance? Then ask if the individual really wants to accept the impact. If she says yes, then you initiate a formal change procedure.

This procedure requires that a change be approved by more than just the person who asked for it. The change may impact the inventory of parts that have already been purchased for the project. It may affect market introduction of a new hardware or software product, which could have a severe impact on sales. It may affect tooling. So a formal change process requires that an approval board review all of these possible effects and sign off on them.

The form shown in Figure 12.18 can be used to control changes to a project. Note that tick boxes are placed in front of signatories so that, unless the box is checked, that person does not have to approve the change. The rule is that only those individuals who have a need to review the change should sign the form. That way, you cut down on the endless rounds of approvals that can delay the process.

IN SUMMARY

This chapter defines control as comparing current status to planned status and taking action to correct for significant deviations from plan. Determining status is relatively straightforward for well-defined work that can be measured but can be very "iffy" when measuring cannot be done with precision. Nevertheless, it is not acceptable to dismiss control simply because of measuring difficulty. Rather, it is a matter of recognizing accuracy limitations.

Earned value is suggested as a robust way of measuring status of work, and a graphical approach is presented for tracking status over time and projecting eventual outcomes.

Figure 12.18 Project Change Approval Form

Project Change Approval

Project Name:	Project Number:	Date:
Project Manager: Requested by:	Department:	Change in: ☐ Scope ☐ Schedule ☐ Budget ☐ Performance

Deviation Information

Description of change being requested:

Reason for change:

Effect on schedule:

Effect on cost (budget):

Effect on performance (quality):

Effect on scope:

Justification:

Class	Distribution of estimated cost deviation	The requested change is:	
Capital		☐ Absolutely necessary to achieve desired results	☐ Scope reduction that will not impact original targets
Noncapital		☐ Discretionary—provides benefits beyond the original target	☐ Scope reduction that will impact original targets

Required Approvals ☐

☐ Project Leader/Manager (type name)	Sign:	Date:
☐ General Manager (type name)	Sign:	Date:
☐ Concerned Dept. Manager (type name)	Sign:	Date:
☐ Controller (type name)	Sign:	Date:
☐ Concerned Vice President (type name)	Sign:	Date:
☐ President (type name)	Sign:	Date:
☐ Other (type name)	Sign:	Date:

CHAPTER 13

Conducting
Project Reviews

There are three kinds of project reviews that can be conducted: status, design, and process. Each has a different purpose. A status review concentrates on whether the P, C, T, and S targets are being met. Are we on schedule and on budget? Is scope correct? Are performance requirements okay?*

A design review applies only to those projects in which something is being designed, such as a product, service, or software. Some of the questions asked during such a review are these: Does it meet specifications? Is it user-friendly? Can we manufacture it? Is the market still looking for what we are developing? Are return on investment and other product justifications still in line?

A process review focuses on *how* we are doing our work. Two questions are asked: What are we doing well? What do we want to improve? This is also commonly called a lessons-learned review. We will discuss how this review is conducted later in this chapter.

---

* Some of the material on project reviews has been adapted from my book *The Project Manager's Desk Reference*, Third Edition.

During status and design reviews, a project may also be evaluated. An evaluation is usually focused on software or hardware development projects and tries to determine if the total end result that is supposed to be achieved will be accomplished. Will the return-on-investment target be met? Will the product be manufacturable? Can we sell it? The answer to these questions determines whether the project will be continued or canceled. Table 13.1 shows a summary of the three types of project reviews.

TABLE 13.1   The Three Kinds of Project Reviews

Project Reviews and Their Nature	
Status	Looks at the status of cost, performance, schedule, and scope
Design	Examines a product, service, or software design to see if it meets requirements
Process (lessons learned)	Reviews project processes and asks if they can be improved

Following are some of the general reasons for conducting periodic project reviews:

- Improve project performance together with project management.
- Ensure that the quality of project work does not take a back seat to schedule and cost concerns.
- Reveal developing problems early so that action can be taken to deal with them.
- Identify areas where other projects (current or future) should be managed differently.
- Keep client(s) informed of project status (this can also help ensure that the completed project will meet the client's needs).

- Reaffirm the organization's commitment to the project for the benefit of project team members.

REVIEWS

Stories abound of projects that are supposed to be within days of completion and are suddenly "discovered" to be weeks behind schedule. This usually happens because people have been lying to themselves, and to everyone else. When technical problems exist in a project, the experts (e.g., engineers, programmers, or life scientists) are inclined to be overly optimistic about how long it will take to resolve the problem. If you ask them how long it will be before they have solved the problem, they are likely to say, "We hope to have it solved momentarily." I'm sorry, that answer is inadequate. There is a book entitled *Hope Is Not a Strategy* (Page, 2003), and this should be the response to those technical people who are *hopeful*. What approach are they going to use to resolve the problem? What are all the issues surrounding the problem? Do they need outside expertise? And so on.

I'm not advocating beating up people who have problems. Our approach to problems should be helpful. But I am intolerant of people who won't admit the severity of their problems and keep plodding along without asking for help. This is usually caused by egos that won't admit that they can have problems like ordinary mortals.

AT&T found years ago that one of the things that differentiated the most successful engineers from the less successful ones was their willingness to ask for help after they had tried unsuccessfully to solve a problem (I no longer remember the source of this finding). The old saying, "If at first you don't succeed, try, try again," should be amended to, "If after a reasonable number of attempts you can't make it work, ask for help!"

DISPLAYING PROGRESS

We saw in Chapter 12 that the most common method of displaying progress, using a Gantt or bar chart, can lead to serious problems (see Figure 13.1). This is because the chart shows schedule progress only. It tells you nothing about the amount of effort that was expended to achieve those schedule results. We saw that if a person has worked twice as many hours as originally planned in order to stay on schedule, this is a sign of trouble to come. Our conclusion was that you must have an integrated cost/schedule tracking system in order to know your true progress on a project. We also saw that you must actually know the value of all four PCTS targets in order to determine true progress, because even if schedule and cost are okay, you may not reach full scope, or the work may have been performed poorly, resulting in problems later on.

The preferred system for showing progress is earned value analysis, using spreadsheets, as shown in Chapter 12 (see Figure 13.2). However, many managers don't want to wade through all the numbers, so the spreadsheet also performs a critical ratio calculation, compares the index to prescribed control limits, and displays the result in stoplight format—that is, if everything is okay, you get a green box; if there are reasons for concern, you get yellow; and if you see red, there is a definite problem! (The phrase "stoplight format" derives from the colors used on a standard traffic light—red to mean *stop*, green to mean *go*, and yellow to indicate *caution*.)

Figure 13.1 Gantt Chart Showing Progress (from Chapter 12)

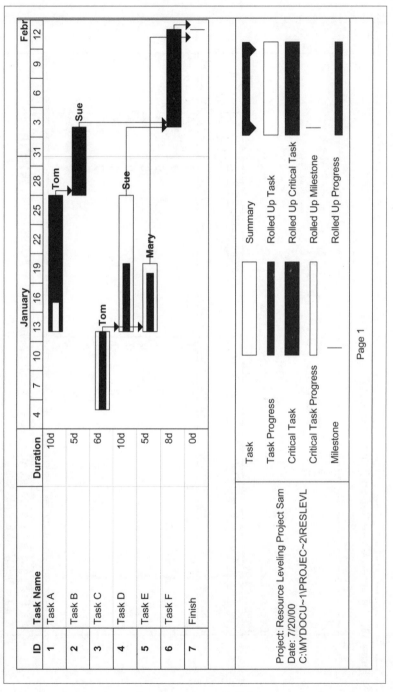

Figure 13.2 Earned Value Report (from Chapter 12)

Earned Value Report

Project No.:   Date: FILE:

Description: Page _____ of _____

Prepared by: Signed:

WBS # or Name	Cumulative-to-Date			Variance		At Completion			Critical Ratio	Action Required
	PV	EV	AC	Sched.	Cost	Budgeted (BAC)	Latest Est. (EAC)	Variance		
				0	0			0	NA	NA
				0	0			0	NA	NA
				0	0			0	NA	NA
				0	0			0	NA	NA
				0	0			0	NA	NA
				0	0			0	NA	NA
				0	0			0	NA	NA
				0	0			0	NA	NA
				0	0			0	NA	NA
TOTALS:	0	0	0	0	0	0	0	0	NA	NA

NOTE: Negative variance is unfavorable || If Critical Ratio < 0.6, INFORM MANAGEMENT!
( ) = NEGATIVE VALUES

We also learned in Chapter 12 that you can't just display summary data for the entire project because you may have two tasks that have almost equal and opposite variances that cancel each other out, so that the summary gives a misleading result. Stoplight reporting is okay if it occurs at the task level and is backed up by earned value data, so that a person can dig in and analyze that data.

A stoplight report for a project is shown in Figure 13.3. Note that this approach allows you to see what has happened between the previous reporting period and the current one. For example, if the status has gone from yellow to red, we know that the task was getting into trouble previously and is now worse off. Conversely, a change from yellow to green shows that the situation has improved.

Figure 13.3   A Simple Stoplight Report

Activity	Last Period	This Period
Perform activity one.	Yellow	Red
Perform activity two.	Yellow	Green
Perform activity three	Green	Green
Perform activity four	NSTS	NSTS

NSTS = Not Scheduled to Start

PROCESS REVIEWS

The objective or purpose of a process review is to improve the performance of the team. In reviewing performance, note that we do not ask, "What have we done wrong?" Asking that question simply raises defenses in team members, and they will try to hide anything that they think is wrong because they assume that they will be trashed for any mistakes that they have made. The purpose of a process review is to learn from experience, so that we can avoid those things that were not done so well and continue doing those things that have been done well. It is not a witch hunt. If you go about it in a retributive way, people will hide their faults.

> The purpose of a process review is to learn how to improve performance. If you go on a witch hunt, you will create witches where none existed before.

The other reason for not asking what has been done wrong is that the answer may be "nothing," and thus everyone may come to believe that reviews are unnecessary. This is not true. The best-performing team must always attempt to get even better, as their competitors are not sitting idly by, maintaining the status quo. They too are improving, and if you stand still for very long, they will pass you.

It is also a fact that the most dangerous thing a team can be is successful. That may sound wrong, maybe even a bit depressing, but it is true. A successful team can easily get complacent. Coaches of sports teams know this. When you have won every game of the season, your very next game is risky because you may get cocky and careless. For that reason, you can never be satisfied with the status quo.

> The ability to learn faster than your competitors may be the only sustainable competitive advantage.
>
> —Arie P. de Geus

One favorite expression of some managers is "no excuses." When something goes wrong, they regard any explanation of what happened as an excuse. I find this attitude very dangerous and totally counter to being able to learn. There is a big difference between an excuse and an explanation. Comedian Flip Wilson used to have a wonderful excuse when he did something he shouldn't have: "The devil made me do it," he would quip. That is an excuse.

Saying that El Niño caused so much rain in California one summer that the construction of a new plant fell far behind schedule is an explanation, not an excuse. To say that there has been a fire in an auto parts plant and that parts are not available for production, is an explanation, not an excuse.

You cannot learn from problems or failures if you behave like an ostrich and stick your head in the sand, or if you hold your hands over your ears and refuse to listen to the facts. And those who refuse to learn from history are doomed to repeat their mistakes.

Process Always Affects Task

It is very important to understand that process will always affect task outcomes! That is, the *way* you do something will always affect the results you get. As the old saying goes, "If you always do what you've always done, you'll always get what you always got." And the corollary is, "Insanity is continuing to do what you've always done and hoping for a different result." In terms of process, these statements mean, "If you aren't getting the results you want, change your process!"

In any project team, the processes that we care about include those shown in the "Team Processes" box. One of the most important of these is meetings. Projects cannot succeed without periodic meetings. However, as we all know, the majority of meetings are badly run, leaving participants drained, frustrated, and wishing that

> **Process will *always* affect task!**
> —Marvin Weisbord

they would never have to attend another one. In his video "Meetings, Bloody Meetings," John Cleese makes a profound comment about meetings: "The essence of management is in how we run meetings." (This video can be purchased from Video Arts, www .videoarts.com.)

TEAM PROCESSES

- Leadership
- Decision making
- Problem solving
- Communications

- Meetings
- Planning
- Giving feedback to team members
- Conflict management

Now if that doesn't depress you, you haven't thought about the implications. Meetings typically lose focus, have no clear direction to begin with, go on ad nauseam, and don't accomplish anything. If you can't manage a meeting, how can you manage an organization?

CONDUCTING PROCESS OR LESSONS-LEARNED REVIEWS

As I have already said, lessons-learned reviews focus on processes; that is, how is work being done, and can those processes be improved? There are some problems or pitfalls in conducting lessons-learned reviews, so here are suggestions on how to make them effective.

First, it tends to be hard to get people to open up when you initially do these reviews, especially when issues that might seem critical of people are involved. You must work on building trust by teaching people how to phrase their comments. For example, if I were a team member, I might say something like, "Communication in this team sucks." Now, all that comment will do is make some people defensive. Furthermore, it is very vague. What kind of communication? All, or just some? As a group facilitator, I would first explain to everyone that such comments are not helpful. Rather, the comment would be much better if it were rephrased to be specific, such as, "I did not receive information about slippage in tasks that feed my work until several days after the slip was identified. Because of that, I was unable to react in time to keep my own work on track."

> Lessons-learned reviews focus on processes. If you want to get better results, you have to improve the way you do your work.

The more specific the comments are, the better. Also, the more impersonal they are, the better. One rule is to describe everything in terms that others can verify by direct observation—they can see, hear, or feel it. The second rule is to express your comments in nonjudgmental terms; avoid remarks that can be interpreted by others as attacking them in some way.

I use two flipcharts in such reviews. On one I list things that were done well. The other is used to list things that we want to do better. These are the words I write at the top of the two charts: "Done Well" and "Do Better." Note: I do not like the system of placing a plus sign (+) at the top of one page and a minus sign (–) at the top of the other. This still designates good and bad, and as I mentioned earlier, saying that something was done badly makes people defensive, and they quit participating. Clearly you can't capture information about problems if people won't tell you about them, so you want to frame the entire process as a way of

> You can't solve problems with processes unless you know exactly what the problem is.

improving, not of ascribing guilt so that you can place blame and punishment.

I have two scribes available, who are (preferably) not members of the team, to record entries on the charts. When a person makes a comment (these can be in any order), it is recorded. If I am not clear about the meaning or if the person has framed the comment in violation of the rule, I ask for a reframing before it is written down. I also suggest that each person write notes to himself as the process goes along, so that he doesn't forget a thought.

I also make a flipchart page that contains all the processes and issues to be examined and post it in the room to jog people to think about everything. (See the Team Processes sidebar.) One issue that can be a problem is leadership. Team members can be very reluctant to say anything negative about their leader, so it may be necessary for the leader to leave the room so that the group can talk openly about any leadership concerns without fear of reprisal. In that case, a stand-in facilitator should be available who understands the process and can help the group members frame their comments properly. Rather than saying, "Doug is a sorry leader," the person would be coached to say, "I sometimes feel that Doug isn't listening to me when I tell him about a problem." That would help the leader change his behavior, perhaps by practicing active listening.

Once all comments have been captured, I give each person 10 votes to cast for what he or she believes are the top items. Team members can cast all 10 votes for one item, or distribute them. They do this by simply placing a checkmark on the page beside the item they are voting for. Two checkmarks means two votes, and so on. (This is called *multivoting.*)

Votes for each item are then counted. The items with the most votes are selected for resolution. I suggest that no more than four items be addressed at one time. Furthermore, someone on the team should accept an action assignment to deal with each issue. A target date for resolution should be established. I would ask for a progress report before the target date is reached, and a final report (verbal is fine) on the target date.

I strongly suggest that you publish the findings of the review and circulate them to all team members, and to parties outside the team, so that everyone can benefit from what has been learned. If you have an intranet on which the review can be posted, that is good, too. You can now proceed down through the list that was initially generated to solve the next-ranked items, so that eventually you resolve them all.

There is one suggestion: if problems fall into the following categories, they should be resolved in the order shown, regardless of the number of votes they receive.

1. Goals
2. Roles and responsibilities
3. Procedures
4. Relationships

The rationale for this is that if team goals are not clear, you are headed for disaster no matter how other procedures are going. Furthermore, it is possible that other processes are being affected because people aren't clear on goals. Next, people must be clear about and agree on their roles and responsibilities, or there will be significant problems within your team. Once these are clear, you should then agree on procedures—how things will be done. Some of the items generated in the lessons-learned review will point to ineffective procedures that can be taken up for resolution.

> Conflict among team members is sometimes caused by lack of goal clarity, uncertain roles and responsibilities, or conflicting procedures.

Finally, if there are relationship problems within the team, you can work on resolving these. However, working on these matters when there are problems with any of the first three categories can be a waste of time, because the first three categories can themselves cause relationship problems.

THE PROCESS REVIEW REPORT

When a project is reviewed, the lessons learned should be shared with other teams so that they can avoid the mistakes that the team being reviewed made and can take advantage of the things that the team did well. The lessons-learned report should contain, at a minimum, the following:

1. **Current project status.** This is best shown using earned value analysis. However, when earned value analysis is not used, status should still be reported with as much accuracy as possible.
2. **Future status.** This is a forecast of what is expected to happen in the project. Are significant deviations in schedule, cost, performance, or scope expected? If so, the nature of such changes should be specified.
3. **Status of critical tasks.** The status of critical tasks, particularly those on the critical path, should be reported. Tasks that have high levels of technical risk should be given special attention, as should those being performed by outside vendors or subcontractors over which the project manager may have limited control.
4. **Risk assessment.** Have any risks been identified that highlight the potential for monetary loss, project failure, or other liabilities?

5. **Information relevant to other projects.** What has been learned from this review that can or should be applied to other projects, whether those projects are presently in progress or about to start?

6. **Limitations of the review.** What factors might limit the validity of the review? Are any assumptions suspect? Is any data missing or suspected of being contaminated? Was anyone uncooperative in providing information for the review?

As a general comment, the simpler and more straightforward a project review report, the better. The information should be organized so that planned versus actual results can be compared easily. Significant deviations should be highlighted and explained. Figure 13.4 is a form intended to be used for a milestone process review. Note that this form will be inadequate to capture all the data generated for an end-of-project review, but it can be used as a guide for questions to be asked.

DESIGN REVIEWS

A design review is conducted to determine whether the product being developed is going to perform according to requirements and whether the company will be able to manufacture it at the intended price. If the answer to either of these questions is negative, then a decision could be made to terminate the project. The answers to these questions become more certain as the project progresses and approaches completion. Unfortunately, by the time the answer is certain, significant expenditures have already been made, making cancellation less helpful than it would have

Figure 13.4   Process Review Form

Project Lessons-Learned Review

Project Name:	Project Number:	Date:
Project Manager:	Department:	Type of review: □ Major milestone □ Periodic
Project Status: Attach current status report.	Comments:	
Top three things done well to date: 1. 2. 3.	Comments:	
Top three things to be done better: 1. 2. 3.	Comments:	
Actions to be taken to develop improvements: 1. 2. 3.	Assigned to:	Due date:
Comments:		

been earlier in the project life cycle. However, canceling a project early based on limited information may be unwarranted.

Since decisions to cancel projects are usually made not by project managers but by business managers, I will not go into detail about the process. A good reference is Patterson (1993).

IN SUMMARY

This chapter suggests the various kinds of reviews that are appropriate for projects and provides guidelines for conducting them. In a status review, for example, problems identified should not be addressed for solution in the status meeting.

In lessons-learned reviews, it is good practice to use terminology *done well* and *do better.* Avoid asking what was done badly, as this makes people defensive. Also, the purpose of lessons-learned reviews is to avoid similar situations in the future. They are not for the purpose of ascribing guilt and administering punishment. That behavior belongs in a fact-finding meeting, which is not discussed in this chapter.

OTHER ISSUES IN PROJECT MANAGEMENT

CHAPTER 14

Managing the Enterprise Using Project Management Methods

I pointed out earlier that the tools of project management were developed to manage manufacturing operations and were adapted for use in managing projects. I would like to go further and suggest that the methods of project management are equally suitable for managing the entire enterprise.

When I met Alan Mulally, when he was president of Boeing Commercial Airplanes, he told me that Boeing made very little distinction between project and general management. For that reason, I want to refer you again to my model. It is repeated in Figure 14.1 for easy reference. I am not including the expanded Step 6, as it is not needed for this chapter.

Figure 14.1   The Lewis Method

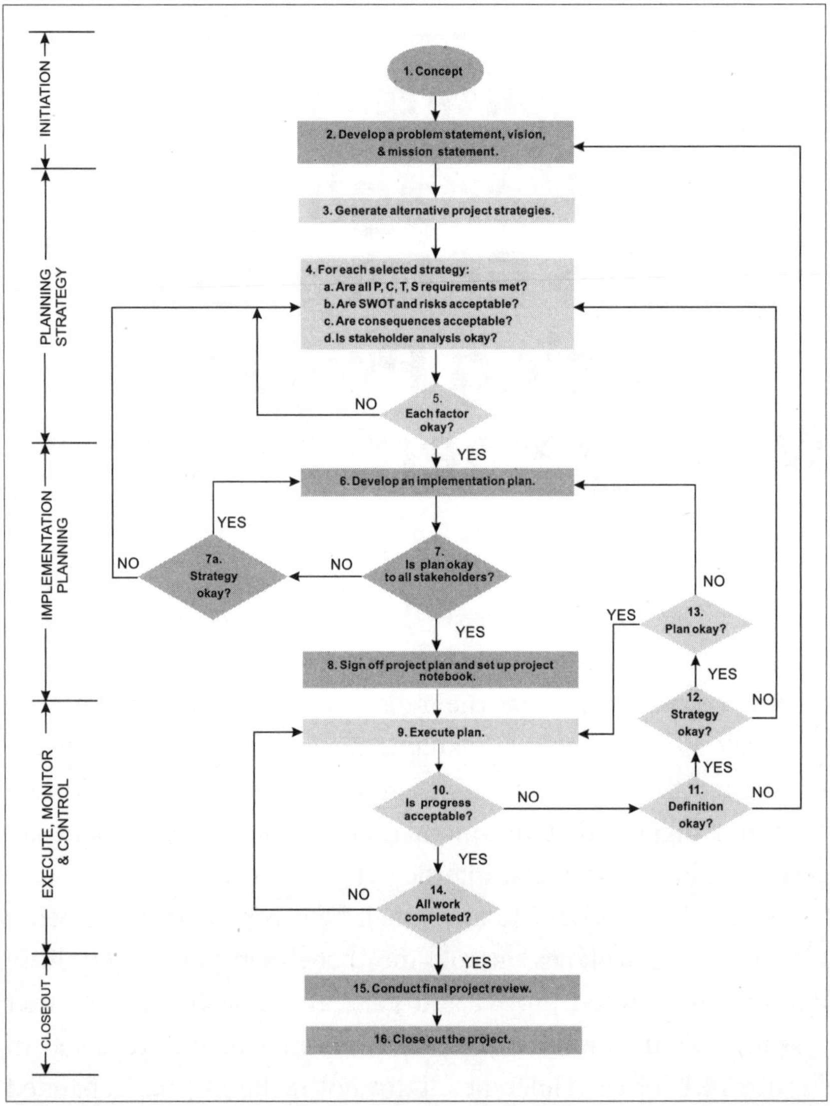

STRUCTURE

First of all, a project office is like any other functional department in any company. Accounting, Human Resources, Marketing, Engineering, and Manufacturing are all functional departments, in that each provides a specific *function* for the organization. For that reason, it seems logical to me to have a Project Management functional department. In a very small company, this may be only one or more project managers. In a large company, it would probably have a department head who supervises a number of project managers, a scheduler, and various administrative individuals.

Such a department would gather project status information weekly and publish status reports that would be sent to appropriate stakeholders, both within and outside the business. They would also conduct project reviews, which include status and lessons learned. Design reviews would be managed by the engineering department, with members of the Project Management Office present as needed.

Let's now think about applications of project management methods to various business activities.

STRATEGIC INITIATIVES

I want to begin with strategic initiatives, which are ordinarily the purview of senior managers or executives. These are projects, in every sense of the word, and certainly lend themselves to being managed as such. They also can be quite large, encompassing almost all departments in an organization.

Let's think about some of the critical or key factors for success of a project (also referred to as KFS). I would list them as follows:

- A clearly designated project leader
- A clear vision and mission
- A well-thought-out strategy
- An implementation plan that details how the strategy will be executed and includes communications, risk management, and logistics
- Responsibility charting, delineating levels of responsibility and accountability for all major tasks that must be performed
- Exit criteria for all major tasks
- Estimates of time and costs for all major tasks
- A stage-gate model for tracking the initiative, and for establishing go/no-go criteria at each gate.

Depending on the complexity of the initiative, you may need a detailed schedule, but regardless of size, a work breakdown structure (WBS) will be invaluable. It makes the responsibility charting possible, as well as enables an estimation of costs, times, and logistics requirements.

Signoffs

If you follow The Lewis Method, in Step 7, you get all major stakeholders to the strategic initiative to review the plan and sign off, signifying their commitment to the plan. Remember that a commitment is not a guarantee, but signifies that the individual will do their best to deliver what they are responsible for to the best of their ability. This, of course, is barring unforeseen circumstances that render execution of the plan difficult or impossible.

If anyone is unwilling or hesitant to sign, you must ask what it will take to get them to sign without reservation. This ensures that there are unlikely to be any factors that would doom the initiative before it even launches.

Monitoring and Control

If you apply the Stagegate process advocated by Cooper (1999), you will have progress reviews on a periodic basis, and you will establish at each major milestone a gate that calls for a decision on how to proceed. There are essentially three possibilities:

1. Continue as originally planned
2. Continue with revisions to budget, schedule, or planned activities
3. Cancel the initiative

The first needs no comment. The second could indicate a change of direction, an increase or reduction to funding, a change of timing, or a combination of any and all of these. The third option is to cancel the project and get on with something else. This could be because the project has gone hopelessly off track or is not expected to deliver the intended results. This option is sometimes considered unacceptable because of the money already spent, commonly referred to as sunk costs. This is not a good viewpoint: you can't recover sunk costs by going down with a sinking ship.

OPERATIONS MANAGEMENT

Ordinarily, operations involve repetitive processes, and while these don't lend themselves to project management in its entirety, it certainly makes sense to have a standard operating procedure

(SOP) for such activities. These can be developed around a WBS and a schedule that simply loops back on itself as each SOP is executed and completed.

Certainly, the WBS has application to any kind of work. As I have said in previous chapters, it was originally developed to help plan manufacturing operations, so it is applicable to any kind of function in an organization. It is the best tool for showing scope of work, for estimating time, cost, and accountability, and for developing the schedule if there is one.

OTHER TOOLS APPROPRIATE FOR GENERAL MANAGEMENT

I have said that organizations should follow the lead of sports teams and practice continuous improvement. As Dr. Edwards Deming once said, "you are either improving or dying," because if you're standing still, it is only a matter of time until your competition passes you.

To improve, however, you need to know those areas in which improvement is needed. One of the best ways to determine these is to periodically conduct lessons-learned reviews, as covered in Chapter 13.

SOME SPECIFIC APPLICATIONS

There are a lot of areas in an organization besides standard operations or strategic initiatives that represent projects. Among these are quality improvement programs, marketing campaigns, mergers and acquisitions, restructuring, moving facilities, and installation of new systems.

In the two decades beginning in 1980, there were many quality improvement projects conducted. However, many of them failed, simply because they were not managed using formal project management methods. Seat-of-the-pants approaches frequently fail to get results. You cannot define failure as missing schedule targets when there are no schedule targets. But even unstructured approaches generally have some outcomes that are important, and failing to achieve these is certainly a project failure.

Another cause of failures is not having official project managers, or having an individual supposedly responsible for managing a project, yet that person has no authority, no budget, and often has responsibility for work other than the project work. In these cases, that other work will usually take priority over project work.

SHOULD YOU HAVE A PROJECT OFFICE?

Managing projects should be considered a function exactly as is Accounting, Procurement, Human Resources, or Manufacturing. For that reason, I strongly believe that a department typically called a PMO, or Project Management Office, is the proper structure for an organization. The people in that office can then specialize in the skills needed for proper management of projects. Furthermore, you can designate one individual as the scheduler, optimizing their knowledge of how to get the most from scheduling software and relieve project managers from the day-to-day work of keeping their schedules up to date.

This does not relieve some individuals in other departments of the need to manage projects, but it does provide a cadre of experts on whom those individuals can rely for advice on how to handle their projects, and the scheduler in the PMO can be tasked with keeping up their schedules. As an example, engineers, senior scientists, and other specialists may have to manage projects in their everyday work, but they need not be required to do the administrative work.

In several instances I have worked with biotech companies in which we set up a PMO to do all the administrative work of projects, freeing the scientists to concentrate on the work of science. They can get a bit testy when the project manager starts asking questions that the scientist interprets as meddling, but role clarification should take care of that. In this case, the project manager has responsibility for ensuring that plans are followed, while the scientist is primarily responsible for technology and only secondarily for the administrative work. See Chapter 16 for more information on how such an office should be structured.

IN SUMMARY

Project management methods are applicable to almost any management function in an organization and should be considered a necessary skill set for all managers. The approach should be to pick and choose those tools that are appropriate for each application. One size may not fit all, but it can be adapted to work in almost every situation.

CHAPTER 15

The Leadership Imperative

I n 1980, I taught my first seminar on project leadership. It was titled *Leadership Skills for Project Managers*. It was held in San Jose, California, and had 23 participants enrolled, almost all from Silicon Valley.

It was a fun class and ended with very positive reviews. Furthermore, I greatly enjoyed teaching it. I had recently completed all the coursework for my doctorate in organizational psychology and was working on my dissertation. I had done a master's thesis on leadership, and my dissertation was to be on an aspect of leadership as well. For the previous four years, I had been managing various departments in ITT Mackay Marine, and at that time I had 63 people in a Quality Control department. This had allowed me to translate the leadership theories that I studied into practice, and it was a delight to share the practical methods to these eager students, all of whom were managing groups at work.

I had also just attended a symposium in New Orleans on a new discipline called neuro-linguistic programming (NLP), led by the developers themselves—Richard Bandler, Leslie Cameron Bandler, and John Grinder. I went directly from New Orleans to

San Jose, so there was no time to redo the syllabus for the course, but I just inserted some new tools into the course, and the audience loved them.

One of those tools was a method for finding what specifically motivates an individual; we divided the class into triads and had them practice the method on each other. In that way, each person got to do the interviewing and processing and also learned their own motivation pattern as they rotated through the group. The exercise requires 45 minutes to an hour to process all three individuals, and it is extremely powerful. When the exercise was finished, I had one fellow say, "This is amazing. I always kind of knew this, but this exercise confirmed it for me. It's right on target." See Chapters 5 and 20 for more on motivation patterns.

RECESSIONS AND TRAINING

We conducted this class three times with good results, and the agency I was working with decided to go ahead with the program on a regular basis. It takes about six months' lead time to promote seminars, so in May 1981 I left my management job at ITT and became a full-time seminar instructor, on a contract basis with the agency in New York.

Unfortunately, a recession hit, and enrollments in the new seminar dropped like they were afraid of the plague. I learned that businesses uniformly have one response to a recession, and that is to cut all *unnecessary* expenses. For businesses, that means any expense that does not positively affect their bottom line, and that means that one of the first cuts made is to training, and especially to programs that they refer to as *soft skills*, like leadership.

SOFT SKILLS—REALLY?

This definition of leadership as a soft skill has always been a mystery to me. The first thing we need to do is define leadership and understand the way it is different from management. They are not the same. The word *manage* means to handle, and in terms of projects means the administrative work—planning, scheduling, and controlling the work to be done. To *lead* means to get people to go along with you—to literally *follow* you. Leading is explicitly dealing with people, and managing is dealing with things. I like the definition Vance Packard gave: *Leadership is the art of getting others to want to do something you think should be done.* The operative word is *want.* Coercion or authoritarianism may get people to do something, but it shouldn't be called leadership.

> Leadership is the art of getting others to *want* to do something you believe should be done.
>
> —Vance Packard

Now, managing is considered a *hard skill.* But ask yourself, how much money will planning, scheduling, and controlling things make for you? None, right? How much money will people make for you if you lead them to do the work itself? More than managing, but we can't place a number on it. However, the basic truth is that your capital equipment, facilities, and other assets won't make a penny for you *unless your people engage with them properly.* This is why I have trademarked the expression *Projects are People*®. It is clear that leadership is really the most relevant bottom-line skill you have.

> Leadership is the most relevant bottom-line skill you have. Management itself won't make any money for you.

LEADERSHIP IS IMPERATIVE

This leads to an inescapable conclusion: leadership, rather than management, is imperative. Leaders inspire people, whereas management activities don't. Peter Drucker made a point about the role of managers in his 1973 book, *Management: Tasks, Responsibilities, Practices*. He said that the job of a manager is to get people to go beyond the minimal performance level. The minimal level is survival level, and you cannot run a business at survival level very long. That's not the motive for a business. A business's motive is to make money by achieving its mission, which is to provide goods or services that meet the needs of customers.

This again reinforces the need for managers to exercise leadership, and to be very candid, there are many managers who got the job because they were good at the work they were doing, but who have absolutely no skill for dealing with people. In fact, one of the key reasons for turnover in organizations is the employees can't tolerate working for their supervisor.

THE BIGGEST SIN

I personally believe the biggest sin committed in businesses is to promote individuals to management positions just because they were good at doing work, without also giving them training in leadership and, for that matter, in management as well. Leadership and management require a different skill set than the work did. As a scientist told me once, "Nobody told me when I was working on my doctorate that I would have to supervise people. I have no clue what I'm doing."

I had the same experience as a young engineer. It is a default requirement that you supervise technicians and other engineers in technical projects. In 1965, when I became an engineer, I had received no training in management or leadership in college, nor did the company give me any. I was on my own. I wasn't totally clueless, but very nearly so when it came to certain aspects of the role.

I began reading management books—principal among them those of Peter Drucker—and I learned what I could from them. The trouble is, leadership is *behavior*, and you don't learn behavior by reading or even attending lectures on the subject. You learn these by practicing and rehearsal. That is why, when I teach my seminar Practical Leadership Skills, there are a number of skill-practice exercises. (A lot of people call them role-playing; I don't like the term, even though it is technically correct. I think it is important to call it skill-building or skill-practice, so it is clear what the objective is.)

IMPORTANCE TO PROJECT MANAGERS

Not only is leadership important to managers in general, but it is especially important to project managers. The reason is that most project managers don't *own* their own team members. Rather, the team members come from functional groups and are assigned to work on the project until it is complete, but they may have functional department duties simultaneously. We say that the project manager has dotted-line authority over them, which really means no authority at all. The net result of that is the project manager must exercise leadership (influence) to get the best performance from those people. In addition, he/she should have input to the individual's performance appraisal—not about his or her technical work, but about responsiveness, collaboration, and other behavioral aspects of how the person worked in the project team. In addition, a project manager may not be able to terminate a team member from the company, but should be able to terminate him or her from the project. Otherwise, it may be nearly impossible to get satisfactory work from that individual.

PMP CERTIFICATION

One of the criticisms I have of the PMP certification is that it is knowledge-based only; there is no skills assessment. There is a requirement that the person should have 2,000 or more hours of work experience *leading projects*. The reality is that many do not have that experience, yet their supervisors sign off that they do. They need the person to be certified because some contracts—especially government ones—require that a PMP lead the project, so in order to get the contract, the supervisor signs off on the requirement. I believe this is a level of fraud that should be prosecuted; I have no patience with this practice, because it undermines the integrity of the PMP certification, and companies are going to get burned badly by unqualified PMPs.

My advice to companies looking to hire a person who has PMP certification is to practice caveat emptor—let the buyer beware. Interview carefully. The best questions are framed as *what would you do if . . . ?* or *how would you handle this . . . ?* You can also ask interviewees to describe the teams they have led, and have them tell you about various problems they encountered and how they handled them. In this way, you can separate the qualified from the imposters.

IN SUMMARY

Although management of projects is certainly necessary, so is leadership. The reason is that management deals with things and leadership deals with people. Furthermore, it is important to realize that the things won't get the job done unless people make it happen. Leadership is defined as the art of getting others to *want* to do what must be done, with *want* being stressed strongly. This means that the real job of a project manager is to lead team members in a way that gains willing compliance with the tasks that must be done to achieve the project outcome.

CHAPTER 16

The Digital Project Office

I have already suggested in Chapter 14 that I believe the Project Management Office is useful and encouraged companies to consider creating one. I also realize that in today's world, the PMO will be heavily digital. Not only do all members of the project team have mobile phones, desktop computers, tablets, and GPS devices, but there are numerous software programs designed to assist in managing projects. In this chapter, I am going to discuss digital products generally, but not in much specific detail.

The reason is twofold. One is that it is nearly impossible for anyone but a software evaluator in a company like Capterra to have the time or resources to fully check out the multitude of programs available. Second, the landscape changes so constantly and dramatically that by the time we can get a book into print, any specific writeups will be useless. In the late 1990s and early 2000s, there were around a hundred project scheduling programs on the market, among them Project Workbench, Primavera, and Microsoft Project. Project Workbench is now Open Workbench, but Primavera is still available, as is Microsoft Project.

When you go to the Capterra.com website, you can search for project management software. The site offers you a shortlist of the top 10 and also an option for those programs that are aimed at not-for-profit organizations. The top 10 are then itemized with a general review of each one. Since these are updated periodically, it will be useless for me to list them in detain at this time because by the time this book is published, the list may be obsolete. Following, however, is Capterra's top 10 list of programs as of May 2022: Jira, ClickUp, Monday.com, Wrike, Zoho Projects, Asana, Kintone, Hive, Autodesk Construction Cloud, and Backlog. You can read their reviews yourself, and I suggest you keep Capterra on your list of resources.

A Word of Caution
about Scheduling Software

Scheduling software can be complicated to use properly, especially as it gains more power or capability. As we all know, the risk you have is garbage in, garbage out, and this is definitely true of scheduling software. Unless you have entered predecessor-successor relationships correctly, you will get a misleading critical path, and that can be worse than not knowing where the critical path is at all.

The big difficulty with scheduling is resource allocation. As I have pointed out in Chapter 9, you should never allocate a person to work on a project more than 80 percent of their time, and in many cases it should be lower. Furthermore, if you put individual names on resources, and you are in an environment where people are shared across projects, you need to have all schedules in a computer program so that resources can be leveled across projects.

The best solution is to let a skill category represent the resource; for example, use *technician*, instead of Joe, Henry, or Susan. Then let the functional manager who owns Joe, Henry, and Susan decide which of them is right for each job.

Mathematically, the software can level resources so no one is overloaded. Practically speaking, however, this seldom works well. Schedules are often so dynamic that the computer solution is invalid almost as soon as it is issued. Another consideration is that people don't necessarily work linearly for the duration of a task. They may work on the project for the first day, or they may work at a variable rate along the total task length. If you need solutions that accommodate this, then choose your software wisely. One thing I believe is going to revolutionize scheduling is the application of AI. It's an exciting prospect that continues to evolve.

COMMUNICATING BETWEEN PROGRAMS

There are many instances when you will want to pass information between programs, rather than having to manually enter it. The solution may lie with Zapier, which provides programs that will pass data between nonconnected applications. For example, I use a program called Kartra, which is for creating marketing pages. I also have an online learning site that is a Moodle-based learning management system (LMS). I can use Kartra to promote one of my courses and pass the registrations to my LMS using Zapier. I also have a Zap (produced by Zapier) that connects purchases to Stripe, so I can take credit cards through Stripe.

I checked with Zapier and found that MindManager, which is a great program for creating work breakdown structures, can be connected to Excel, Outlook, and Trello, useful for creating task boards for teams. And while it unfortunately does not connect to Microsoft Project, it does connect to Zoho and several other project software programs.

WORK FACILITATION PROGRAMS

If you hadn't heard of Zoom prior to 2020, the COVID-19 pandemic and the subsequent boom in remote work likely changed that. This video-capable meeting program is affordable by almost anyone (in fact, there is a free version with limited functionality). You can hold meetings, conferences, webinars, and more with the program. For webinars or online live seminars, there are many programs available, such as GoToWebinar, LiveWebinar, WebinarJam, and Teams. There are also some phone-based programs that are useful for group meetings.

As for coordinating work in a project team, one of my favorite programs is Basecamp. As of this writing, it costs nearly $100 monthly, but it can handle unlimited projects and unlimited users, and it allows you to distribute documents to all members of the team with minimal hassle. You can do the same thing using Outlook, but Basecamp has additional features and may be easier to handle.

TEAM MANAGEMENT

I have one beef with Zoom, Teams, and other video-conferencing tools: I hate when people won't turn on their camera. Many tools allow you to hide the room background, so if you're concerned that people will see your messy room, that problem is solved.

Remote working is here to stay, so video conferencing and online learning require that we adapt to that mode of working. I will address managing remote teams in the final chapter of this book.

PATENT AND TECHNOLOGY EVALUATION SOFTWARE

If you are managing product development projects, you frequently need to complete searches to determine if patents already exist, or you may want to find technology you can license. My associate Dr. Alan Letton recommends Innography and PatSnap.

 **IN SUMMARY**

As I mentioned at the beginning of the chapter, by the time this book goes to press, some of the programs may already be dead in the market or the company bought, resulting in changes in pricing, availability, and so on. All I can say is that the Digital Project Office goes hand in hand with the Project Management Office, and I feel it is certain to endure, despite the changes in the mix of programs you need.

CHAPTER 17

Using Stagegate® to Select, Evaluate, and Control Projects

Companies sometimes undertake projects that should never have been started, or continue jobs that should have been canceled. Stagegate is a method developed by Dr. Robert G. Cooper (1987) that can be used to prevent these errors. This concern about errors was explained by Marvin Patterson in *Accelerating Innovation* (1973): If you cancel too many projects, you are taking on projects that should never have been selected to begin with. And if you never cancel any projects, you are sure to be continuing projects that should have been shut down because they will never deliver the intended results. How many is too many? Consider the normal distribution; 68 percent of the projects you do will fall at ±1 standard deviation around the mean, 95 percent at ±2 standard deviations, and 99.74 percent at ±3 deviations. That means that 0.26 percent will fall outside the 3 standard deviation limits, or 0.13 percent in each tail. If you assume that the tails are outside the limits, you should not have selected 0.13 percent of the projects you undertake, and another 0.13 percent should be canceled because they turned out to be losers. To be harsh about it, nobody is so good that 100 percent of their projects are viable.

THE ESSENCE OF STAGEGATE

Stagegate was developed by Cooper in response to this problem. We can assume for any project that there are a series of stages in its life cycle. Initially is conception, followed by formulating the concrete vision for what the project should deliver. Next is screening to determine if a project should be started, and then developing plans for how to achieve that vision (which we call the mission). Finally, we reach the execution stage, which may involve several additional stages—prototyping, assessment, refinement, rollout, and closeout of the job. These might be simplified as follows:

Concept 1> Selection 2> Planning 3> Prototyping 4> Refinement 5> Production 6> Delivery 7

Each of the right-pointing > symbols is a gate. To pass that gate and proceed with the next stage, certain criteria must be met. These include meeting such criteria as return on investment (ROI), performance specifications, production cost targets and production capability, and market acceptance. They also include fit with the business itself; in other words, a project to make a wheelbarrow would not fit with a bicycle company's product line, or *the business we're in*, even if it could be very profitable to make one. The bike company knows nothing about the wheelbarrow market, would have logistics problems with manufacturing and shipping the units, and likely has the wrong distribution network.

Let's use the example of the wheelbarrow and a bicycle company to go through the model. Often, a marketer will conceive of a new product that they believe their company should produce. Wheelbarrows have wheels, just like bikes. They have frames. They transport things. And spring and summer are coming. The wheelbarrow is easy to design and build. We should be able to make millions on one, says the marketer.

So, the concept is presented to a business development panel at gate 1>. The head of the panel comes to the meeting loaded for bears. "What business are we in?" she says.

"Bicycles," comes a weak reply.

"Does a wheelbarrow fit with our mission?" she asks. "Let me remind you that our mission is to produce affordable bicycles for children aged 4 to 18. We don't make racing bikes that cost $10,000 and up. Just inexpensive bikes for kids."

The marketing guy who came up with the idea withdraws the suggestion.

The next product concept to be offered is a child's bicycle fabricated using a beryllium-aluminum alloy, which is nearly indestructible, weighs 50 percent of a standard kid's bike, and can be produced at 75 percent of the cost of the regular one. After much discussion, the panel agrees that this concept fits their business, the forecasted ROI is above their minimal acceptable level, materials are readily available, manufacturing agrees that it should be easy to make, among other considerations that also pass muster. The panel gives it a green light. It has passed gate 1.

For simplicity, let's say that the project proceeds to the design stage. The engineers design it, they produce a prototype, and they discover a small problem. There are a couple of parts that must be drilled, and they find that this alloy has a nasty reaction to being drilled—it produces jagged holes that are structurally sound but look bad. The marketing manager is concerned that customers will notice the jagged holes and be concerned for child safety. This also bothers the legal team, whose job is to keep the company out of trouble.

"Unless you can solve this problem," they say, "we'll have to drop it."

The engineering and manufacturing folks work on the problem for several weeks but cannot find an acceptable solution. At the next gate meeting, the panel votes to drop this product idea.

Let's try another scenario: that the engineering group develops a solution, and the gate review gives it another green light. It now goes to refinement. However, they have invested several weeks working on the jagged-hole problem, which has added to the development cost, thus reducing the projected ROI.

In the next stage, they develop manufacturing tooling, so they can mass-produce the bike in the thousands of units. Once again, they encounter issues; the tooling company reports that they cannot make the required tooling perform a single step and must perform the operation in two steps. This is going to add at least 15 percent to the manufacturing cost of every unit, reducing profits per unit and cutting the ROI even further.

At the gate review, the panel looks at the costs incurred to date and compares that to the forecasted sales and profits. It is going to take longer to reach breakeven and they will miss the targeted date at which profitability should begin; this is not acceptable in their business model. They are concerned about the sunk costs but agree that to continue will be just pouring good money after bad, and they vote to cancel the project, to the disappointment of all concerned.

You get the idea: each gate has the possibility to go ahead as planned, go ahead with caution, go with increased or decreased funding, or cancel the program altogether. This allows the company to deal with market changes, funding issues, technical problems, production issues, and so on. I once observed a situation where the marketing department discovered that a competitor had just introduced a bike almost exactly like the one they were working on, except without any alloy problems. By being first to market, they will probably capture 80 percent of the market. For these reasons, there was no point in continuing with their bike project.

PORTFOLIO MANAGEMENT

Along with the gate process, the business development team should have a portfolio of products under development—a mix of both high-risk, high-profit products and low-risk, low-profit products, with perhaps a few low-risk, high-profit ones as well. It is the job of the portfolio manager to balance the mix, to keep the company profitable and viable in the marketplace. The CFO at Merck Pharmaceuticals once pointed out that standard ROI justification can't be used in their business, because only 1 in 10,000 compounds examined for a new drug pans out.

The job of portfolio management is to prevent a company from starting work on a project that does not fit with the company's business, unless senior management decides there is a reason to deviate, and even then, this generally is a bad idea. Tom Peters once commented that excellent companies *stick to their knitting*, meaning that they don't try to make wheelbarrows when they are a bicycle company.

Companies sometimes violate this rule because they want to diversify. The idea behind diversifying is that if your regular product market declines, the market for some other product will be stable or grow, minimizing the impact of the downturn. That is all well and good, but if you are going to diversify, you should do it by entering a market that you have capability to service. As an example, if you make baby clothes, and the market tanks, you may find that the market for teen clothing is stable—diversifying into that market makes sense, because you have the capability to make teen clothes with minimal issues.

IN SUMMARY

It is very costly to develop products for which the market is soft or even nonexistent, or for which the development cost is so high that the ROI is unacceptable. Stagegate is a process that, if applied properly, can prevent these errors. Combined with portfolio management, Stagegate offers a winning system for optimizing your development of products.

CHAPTER 18

Dealing with Stakeholders

When the fourth edition of this book was current, I was in China, and a new translation had just been published. Project management was a hot topic, and I had been invited to speak in five locations throughout mainland China. In each location, I had a translator, who did sequential translation. I would say a sentence or two and she would repeat it in Chinese.

In one province, my translator had received a master's in project management from a British university and her English was first-rate. We had a book signing while I was there and they sold a bunch of books. In fact, there were around 300 attendees in each of the locations. During a break in my presentation, I was talking with the translator and she said, "Dr. Lewis, do you know how your book refers to 'stakeholders'?"

I had to laugh. I had tried to learn Mandarin before I went to China and found it to be nearly impossible. I've learned both Spanish and German and a little Japanese through Pimsleur language programs, but the tonal nature of Chinese was just too

411

much. I would listen to a phrase and then be asked, "Did you hear how that word would rise and then fall?" My answer was a resounding "no." I couldn't hear it, so there was no way I could reproduce it. With my lack of Chinese-language skills, of course, I had no way of knowing how this phrase was translated.

She explained. "The translator expressed stakeholders as people walking around carrying stakes."

I was almost overcome with laughter. I hadn't given any thought to how the jargon word "stakeholders" in the context of a management book would be translated. I could see that in my imagination. It reminded me of vampire movies.

We both had a good laugh, and I assured her that there were no stake-driving vampire hunters intended in my project management book.

WHAT IS A STAKEHOLDER?

I suppose if there were a project to find and kill a vampire, then people tasked with driving a stake through the vampire's heart would truly be stakeholders. The word defines itself: when someone has ownership, interest, or participation in something, we say they have or hold a *stake* in it, thus, *stakeholder*. People affected by a project have an interest in it, so they are stakeholders.

"Interest" here can be defined very broadly. For example, when the Pentagon was being renovated before 9/11 took place, the community around the Pentagon became concerned because there were construction vehicles using neighborhood roads to get in and out of the construction area, creating noise, road damage, and potential danger on the now busy roads.

In that way, people who were simply affected by the project developed a strong interest in the operation—they became stakeholders. And the colonel in charge of the project, in addition to dealing with the bigwigs on Capitol Hill and the various military brass who were having their lives disrupted while the contractors moved them to temporary quarters in order to update their offices, now also had to take steps to address the concerns of a new set of stakeholders, the community, as well.

THE IMPORTANCE OF MANAGING STAKEHOLDERS

The stakeholder issue is important enough that PMI established a new process group on it. I have previously mentioned a study on project success that determined that stakeholder satisfaction with the outcome of a project was a key factor in how the project was judged. Even when the job failed to meet some of the PCTS targets, if key stakeholders were happy with the result, then it was deemed a successful project; conversely, if the targets were all met but key stakeholders were unhappy with it, then it was called a failure, or at least an unsatisfactory job.

I once worked with a fellow who used many contractors to do work on a university campus. John had ensured that his project managers were trained in project management skills, including team management, but one of them seemed to have one skill that was causing major problems. He had a way of interacting with contractors that made them angry, and my associate then had to spend unnecessary time on damage control. John tried to coach his PM on how to deal with contractors, but to no avail. Finally, he had to pull the plug, removing the fellow from the PM job.

There is a kind of SOP that can be applied to dealing with stakeholders:

1. Keep them informed of status and various events in the project that may affect them—beforehand if possible.
2. Treat them with respect.
3. If they voice a complaint, *actively listen* to them. That means that you listen so you can repeat to them—in your own words—what you heard them say. This means you listen to the intent of their words, rather than just the words themselves.

   Suppose a neighborhood woman says, "I'm concerned about the safety of my children with these big trucks coming by our house all the time." When you reflect what you heard back to her, it might sound like this: "You're afraid a child might be hurt by one of the trucks?" "Concerned" really means "afraid." You convey to her that you understand that when you rephrase it. If you simply parrot back her exact words, she knows you heard her, but did you *understand* her? That's what she really wants to know.
4. Ask what you can do to reassure the person or to satisfy their concerns. If you can't do it, don't bluntly say that you can't. Instead, say, "I may not be able to do exactly what you're asking, but I could do *this*. Would that be satisfactory?"
5. Make notes. Write down what you agreed to, so you don't forget, and also read it back to the person so you're sure you understood exactly what was said.
6. Follow up. Meet with them again to review what you've done, and check to see if there is anything else you can do to make the situation better.

7. If you are working with a neighborhood or other body of people, have periodic meetings with the entire group. That way, you let everyone know you are concerned about their issues and are trying to address them.

Active listening is one of the most important skills a leader/manager can have. If you are not well versed in it, I recommend that you take a class in which there is plenty of skill practice, so you can hone your skills. I have taught this for many years, and one of the pitfalls I witness is that people interview rather than listen, and they parrot rather than rephrase. As I said, parroting validates that you heard the words, but did you understand what the person was trying to convey?

In conflict situations, one of the most important things that must happen is that each party to the conflict be able to clearly state the other party's position, especially what they are feeling. The facts of their position are much less important than their emotional reaction. This leads to another SOP. Always deal with the elements of a conflict in this sequence:

FEELINGS > FACTS > SOLUTIONS

Many left-brained problem-solvers go directly for solutions. I point out to them that the other person's feelings represent data to consider in solving the problem. If you haven't dealt with those properly, you will find that the problem comes back to bite you.

DON'T HOPE IT WILL GO AWAY

If you happen to be one of those individuals who is conflict-averse, your response may be to hope if you just ignore it, the conflict will go away. It isn't going to happen!

Be proactive in managing conflict. There is a saying in psychology, called "saving up brown stamps." It refers to the days when people collected green stamps when they purchased something, and when they filled a book with those stamps, they could cash it in for a premium of their choice. That was a positive approach.

Brown stamps, however, are purely psychological, and not so positive. If those physical books of green stamps represent attaboys, then brown stamps are the opposite, little annoyances and grievances. Just like with green stamps, when you accumulate a certain number of brown stamps, you cash them in. And cashing them in means all that pent-up anger comes out in a torrent, and you often say things you later regret.

My advice: Don't save up brown stamps. It is far less unpleasant to deal with them one stamp at a time than it is to deal with the entire book.

IN SUMMARY

Managing stakeholders properly can make or break a project. It is so important that PMI introduced it as a new process group. Good human relations skills are essential to be good at dealing with controversial or conflictual issues in projects and should be a priority in your professional development plans.

CHAPTER 19

Applying Alan Mulally's Principles to Project Management

met Alan when he was president of Boeing Commercial Airplanes. I had seen the PBS series *21st Century Jet*, which documented the journey to develop the Boeing 777, and I was impressed by the management of this huge program. Because I teach project management, I wrote Alan and asked if I might be able to interview him to learn more of the inside details of how projects were managed at Boeing. Alan had originally been the engineer in charge of the program and was promoted to president midway through.

His reply was doubtful, but he kept the door open, and when I later had a teaching job in Seattle, he invited me to visit him. During that visit, he told me that he had 11 principles that he followed in managing. He gave me permission to use them, and I later published a book titled *Working Together* (Lewis, 2001) with his assistance. He even contributed a foreword to the book.

Working Together was released a few days after the 9/11 attacks on the World Trade Center. Following that attack, Boeing lost

418   PROJECT PLANNING, SCHEDULING & CONTROL

half of its sales within days. Through the application of his principles, Alan was able to save Boeing from going bankrupt. That is a story that would take a book to cover, so I will defer that to another time. However, my point is that his actions saved the company and later were responsible for his being chosen to save Ford from bankruptcy in 2006.

Ford was hemorrhaging money at the rate of $16 billion annually in 2006 (that's $46 million *per day*) when Mulally was tapped to be its CEO. He promised to have the company profitable again within three years, without taking government bailout money—a goal he achieved.

Mulally remained at the helm of Ford until 2014, proving it was no fluke. Three years after he retired, his replacement was terminated for failing to maintain the performance that Alan had achieved.

I have been a student of leadership for most of my adult life, and both my master's thesis and my doctoral dissertation were on field studies of leadership. Having worked for seven years in a small company and another eight years in a company with 1,200 employees, part of a global corporation, I was not convinced that the CEO had that much impact on the performance of the business. That opinion was changed by Mulally; the chief executive could indeed change the performance of a behemoth—and it was largely through *leadership*.

When Mulally was named CEO, the head of Human Resources at Ford called to alert me that it was about to happen, and to tell me that my book about Alan's principles would be mentioned. It was one of the deciding factors in hiring him, the head of HR said, and he told me that the media would most likely begin calling.

Boy was he right. Within a half-hour of the announcement, my phone began to ring. The big question I was asked was, "Do you think he's right for Ford? He isn't a car guy."

I responded that he didn't have to be a car guy. "Ford knows how to build cars," I said. "It's about leadership, not how to build cars."

I stand confirmed in that conviction. If you want to read the full story, read *American Icon*, by Bryce Hoffman (2012). It's an interesting read on a journey taken by a man who is my gold standard for an executive who is a true leader. Even *Forbes* ranked Alan the third best leader in 2012. I'm probably prejudiced, but I would have ranked him number one.

MULALLY'S WORKING TOGETHER PRINCIPLES

As I mentioned at the beginning, these principles were developed by Alan over the years that he was an engineer, manager, and eventually CEO at Boeing Commercial Airplanes. They are covered in depth in *Working Together*, so I will just briefly comment on them here. I strongly encourage you to adopt them in your projects, teams, and organization.

EXPECTED BEHAVIORS AND CULTURE

- People first
- Everyone is included
- Compelling vision, comprehensive strategy, and relentless implementation plan
- Clear performance goals
- One plan
- Facts and data . . . we can't manage a secret . . . the data sets us free
- Everyone knows plan, status, and areas that need special attention
- Propose a plan, positive "find-a-way" attitude
- Respect, listen, help, and appreciate each other
- Emotional resilience . . . trust the process
- Have fun . . . enjoy the journey and each other

People First

People are more important than profits, things, or positions. As I pointed out in an earlier chapter, I consider this to be a central premise for optimizing organizational performance—recognizing that *Projects are People*®, as is the organization itself. Without people, you can't have a business, even if you assume that robots are so advanced that they can run the business. You still need people to design and build the robots in the first place, and even if robots could be programmed to diagnose and repair each other, people cannot yet be left out of the equation.

If you take care of your people, ensuring that their needs are met through performance of their work, they will be more likely to be committed to the organization itself and also more likely to do better work. The key is to recognize interdependence. Jan Carlzon, former CEO of Scandinavian Airlines, turned the normal pyramid that represents the organizational hierarchy upside down, so that he was at the bottom, indicating that he was there to enable the performance of all his people. We sometimes hear this called *servant leadership*.

Everyone Is Included

Over the years, I have known managers who kept everything to themselves, in the belief that knowledge is power, and they wanted to have power over their people. This is very unenlightened, to say the least. Not only is it condescending to others, but it limits their ability to make informed decisions in their daily work.

This does not mean that you share all information with all employees if doing so could jeopardize a business deal that is not yet complete. However, it does mean that you share information relevant to an employee's job, and you treat them as partners in the job rather than subordinates.

If you are familiar with the movement that introduced self-directed work teams, these were an attempt to fully practice this principle, but they failed in many cases because they were not understood by senior managers and were therefore misapplied. It is outside the scope of this book to go into detail about this program; for more, read *Leading Self-Directed Work Teams*, by Kimbell Fisher (1999).

Compelling Vision

Along with these principles, Alan later added that you need a comprehensive strategy and relentless implementation plan to execute the vision. (These are discussed in detail in *Relentless Implementation*, by Alan Mulally and Adam Witty from 2021.)

Vision itself, however, is vital to the success of an organization of any kind. The Founding Fathers of the United States had a vision for the country, stated in the Constitution. In the 235 years since the first draft was written, the country has changed dramatically, but the core values expressed represent that vision, and most Americans still subscribe to it.

A vision tells people what the company stands for and what it intends to do for its clients or customers, and it provides guidance for every action taken and every decision made. The mission of the company is to perform in accordance with the vision. This means every individual and every unit of the company should align with that vision in their practices as well.

One Plan

It is common for businesses to have plans for every department that intend to maximize the advantages desired by each department but which do not necessarily serve the needs of the organization itself. Some, in fact, can be diametrically opposed to the company vision. It is the job of executive leaders to ensure that all plans support the overall company vision and mission.

Clear Performance Goals

You can't have clear performance goals if you don't have a clear vision, comprehensive strategy, and relentless implementation plan. As a consequence of lacking these, you will find people focused on goals that may be detrimental to the company's success. You will have silos, turf wars, and other dysfunctional artifacts of people putting their personal aims above that of the organization.

Facts and Data

Alan revised his principles slightly from those he had at Boeing. He originally said, "The data sets us free" and "You can't manage a secret." Both are true: Data is important to avoid falling into the trap of using opinions rather than facts to make important decisions. And when people avoid revealing problems out of fear of retribution, those problems sit smoldering until they eventually erupt into a crisis. Having a "shoot the messenger" culture encourages people to hide problems.

Everyone Knows

In keeping with the principle of not being able to manage a secret: no matter what the problem, when everyone knows about it, they can contribute. There have been numerous stories of problems being solved by people who normally would have been seen as incapable of such solutions. I found in my engineering career that technicians sometimes could see solutions that the engineers could not discover.

Propose a Plan

In his Boeing days, Alan said, "Whining is okay"—occasionally, and this was followed by, "Propose a plan, find a way." Anyone who is committed to their work may feel down when they find themselves faced with what appears to be an insurmountable problem, but having an attitude that you will find a way out is important. I used to tell my people they weren't being paid to tell me why something couldn't be done, but just the opposite. I had a boss who would ask, "If you had unlimited resources, could you make it happen?" If you said yes, he would say that you weren't getting unlimited resources, but you should make it happen anyway.

Respect, Listen, and Help

We expect a collaborative approach to our jobs. You may find that there are individuals you have difficulty working with, but they are there to perform certain tasks just as you are, and when they need help, you should be willing to give it if you are able.

Emotional Resilience

"Emotional resilience" goes along with "Propose a plan." If you let problems launch you into a tailspin, you won't be able to propose a plan. Life is going to throw you a curveball occasionally, but you must be able to handle it. Seldom will it represent the end of the world.

Have Fun, Enjoy the Journey and Each Other

Someone once said to me, "Work isn't supposed to be fun. That's why it's called work." Then quit calling it work and rename all activities fun. See it as a game to be played, with winning defined as delivering value to customers, which also conveniently results in a return on investment that meets the requirements of stockholders. In the early days of my engineering career, I absolutely loved my job. I was getting paid to do what I had done for fun since age 16 as a ham radio enthusiast.

In 1981, when I began teaching seminars full time, I loved teaching, and I never considered it to be work in the negative sense of the word. This is the best life has to offer. We should all be engaged in something that makes a contribution to the world, and we should enjoy doing so.

 IN SUMMARY

Practicing Mulally's principles is the essence of good leadership. We really could say that this is another model of leadership, comparable to Situational Leadership, the Grid®, and others. I have a YouTube video that provides a more business focus than this, which you can find here: https://youtu.be/hFwRyW4BRCk.

CHAPTER 20

Complexities and Pitfalls in International Projects

N
ew dimensions are added to the management of international projects that don't exist in domestic ones. These are time zone issues, language difficulties, and cultural differences.

TIME DIFFERENCES

The simplest of these is the time zone issue. Even the difference between the United States and western Europe is five or six hours. Your workday is effectively reduced from eight to four hours. If you live in a place like New York City, it may only be three hours. If Americans begin work at 8 a.m., it is already 1 p.m. in England and 2 p.m. in Germany, France, Spain, Italy, and Scandinavia. By noon our time, it is 5 p.m. in the European countries and people are leaving work. Of course, this represents the eastern United States; for California, at 8 a.m. the Europeans are already going home.

I work with a company in Chandigarh, India. They maintain my learning management system and develop custom applications for me. At 8 a.m. EST here it is 5:30 p.m. in India. I often go to my home office at 2 a.m. so that there are several hours in which I can communicate with them in real time.

I work with another company in Australia, and at present they are 15 hours ahead of me. It is 11 p.m. tomorrow "down there" when I begin my official workday. If I encounter a problem of some kind, it will be tomorrow or late this evening my time before they will be able to address it.

I have an administrative assistant in the Philippines. It is 12 hours ahead there, so my assistant works what might be called a second shift so that he is available to me from 5 a.m. to around 1 p.m. (my time). The benefit I get from working with the company in India and the assistant in the Philippines, like so many others who have globalized their sourcing, is that the labor rates are significantly lower than those here in the United States. The work product is first rate, and the inconvenience of time differences is minimal for me. (Most meeting management programs will automatically present the meeting time corrected for your time zone.)

Mix-Ups and Misunderstandings

There is one factor that often causes confusion internationally, and that is what day the week begins on. In Europe it is Monday, but in the United States it is Sunday. I was talking to one of my British friends on a Sunday and said, "I'll see you later this week." He said, "No, you'll be here next week."

He was winding me up, as the Brits say, because to him, we were at the end of his week and I would not arrive until day one of the following week, which would begin for him on Monday.

For a moment I almost panicked, because I had booked flights and thought I was on the wrong week. It is not a trivial issue.

LANGUAGE ISSUES

While India is the second-largest English-speaking country in terms of population (the United States is number one), this ranking is deceptive. There are two issues. First, in India they speak a version of British (as opposed to American) English. Second, the degree of fluency ranges from survival level to native (meaning equivalent to a native speaker of a language). Formal education levels can impact fluency, with many well-educated speakers at or near native fluency, and those with a lower level of formal education sometimes operating closer to survival level.

The company that does app development for me has assigned a fellow as project manager, and here is one of the questions he asked me about a feature of the app:

"Can we display the proper data as per suggested words like which idea has been linked to the particular suggested word?"

As you can see, the structure of the sentence is approximately equivalent to nineteenth-century British English, which is no longer spoken in the United Kingdom or United States but which is still being taught in Indian universities. However, I have no idea what he means by *proper data*. I do understand *suggested word* and *idea linked to that suggested word*, but I don't know what he is asking me. So, we must go back and forth several times for me to understand him; otherwise, I will get a solution that does not deliver the result I want.

Fortunately, I am communicating with them in writing. I was in India for two weeks about 20 years ago, and they speak so fast that it becomes a blur to my ears. They understand each other perfectly, but I must ask them to slow down so I can understand.

Two of my best friends are British. We have absolutely no difficulty communicating, other than that some words sound the same but have different meanings. A salad to us can be chicken, egg, or potato. It can also be greens and vegetables. To Brits it will be something else. Bill Bryson, an American author, wrote the wonderfully funny *Notes from a Small Island*, in which he pointed out some of the many words and expressions that totally confused him when he arrived in England at age 18 and checked into a bed-and-breakfast intending to just get his bearings. I read it on a plane returning to the United States and laughed so much that the lady beside me had to ask what I was reading.

The other huge problem that can affect working relationships is accents. Even in England, I once had a fellow in a class I was teaching whose accent was too strong for me to understand. He would ask me a question and other members of the class would have to "translate" for me. I found that the Scottish accent can be just as indecipherable to some people from the south of England as it is to some Americans.

We have the problem here in the United States with different regional accents. For example, I was teaching a computer class in Philadelphia once and referred to pointing with the cursor. However, being from the south (North Carolina), I pronounced "pointing" with a very soft emphasis on the "t," and he couldn't hear it. It took several minutes to figure out what he couldn't understand. I now say poin-Ting to make it clear to my students.

CULTURAL DIFFERENCES

It would require several volumes to treat the many differences that exist between cultures around the world. As a simple example, the British refer to the first floor in a building as the one Americans would call the second floor. To them, the American first floor is their ground floor.

In Germany, Austria, and other European countries, employees do not call their immediate supervisor by their given name; it will be Mr. Brown or Ms. Brown. Americans immediately call everyone by their first name, and this can be insulting. German, among other languages, also differentiates between the pronoun "you" in personal or formal relationships. The parents of a young woman told me that she had a boyfriend once who began using the personal "you" with them very soon after he had begun dating their daughter. This conveyed a much more serious relationship with the young woman than they felt he had the right to assume so early.

Deal-Breakers

In 2002 an associate arranged for me to visit China for two weeks to introduce project management and deliver training programs throughout the country. I mentioned this trip in an earlier chapter. In one major city I spoke at a university that was interested in having me teach so they could include this topic in their MBA program. It was a very friendly occasion, and the woman in charge of the program was very enthusiastic about offering PM there.

A week or so after I returned home, I got a very nice snail mail letter from her stressing how excited she was about working with me and expressing her desire to get started right away. I replied with equal enthusiasm, and indicated that my associate, who was native Chinese and lived in Beijing, was going to work very closely with her to make all the arrangements.

I never heard from her again. Nor did my associate. I didn't realize until later that I insulted her by "passing off" to my associate the relationship she had with me. In many cultures, and especially Asian cultures, there are strict rules about status levels and relationships. I was head of my company, and she was head of the MBA program. Even though my associate had made the arrangements, she still expected to deal one-on-one with me, not him.

In another situation, a project manager from the United States was sent to Japan to close a deal with a telecom company. The papers were signed, and the American said to the Japanese president, "This is great. How soon will the system go live?"

The president replied, "It will be in time to meet your requirements."

The American pressed him for a date. Again, the Japanese man replied that it would be ready in time to meet the American's requirements. The fellow was clueless enough to ask again, and the president walked out and tore up the contract.

I had a longtime associate in Singapore, who provided training throughout Southeast Asia. I sent one of my instructors over to deliver a program on risk management, and a couple of days after the program I received a call from my associate. He was furious. He explained that the president of the company where they delivered the program was in the class, and my instructor never once acknowledged him or talked with him about what they were going to use the program for.

My associate had made a point of introducing my instructor to the president, but following that, the instructor just started teaching without further acknowledgment. It almost cost me my relationship with my associate—he was that angry.

These are just a few examples of the sensitivity of some issues in other countries and show how easy it is to lose a job because of misunderstanding or ignorance of the issue.

Insults and Embarrassment

When cultural differences exist, a violation of one culture by another can lead to embarrassment or insult to the person. Americans are very sensitive to queuing up to check into a hotel or board an airplane, but in some cultures such is not the practice. It is a first-come, first-served approach, which they all understand, so no one is offended if someone else jumps into the line ahead of them. When this happens to Americans, however, they are offended. I have personally had to remind myself of that old saying, "When in Rome do as the Romans do," and have had to behave as the local people do, pressing my way through the crowd. It always feels uncomfortable to me to do so, as I am violating my own cultural rule, but if I don't, I may never get to the front of the line.

Another example of ways that differences can cause insults is gender issues. Please understand that I am not criticizing the culture of any country or group. I am simply pointing out what happens when differences exist.

A friend of mine, let's call her Mary, told me that she and a delegation of account managers were sent to Japan to coordinate various business arrangements with them and the British parent company. Her counterpart was a Japanese man, and during the visit, he refused to talk with her. When she returned to England, she wrote him and told him she was his contact. He replied that his assistant, a woman, was her contact. He was not going to deal with a woman.

While she was in the plant in Japan, Mary got to know some of the workers. A young Japanese man asked her, "Don't you think it's unfortunate that I have to report to a woman?" Mary was so caught off guard that she had no idea what to say.

When I was in Singapore, a fellow told me that an American friend who lived in Singapore came home one day and his gardener told him that a visitor had stopped by. The American tried to figure out who it was, but the gardener had forgotten his name. Finally, he said, "He fat, like your wife." In Asia, being fat is considered a sign of affluence, and to be described as fat is not considered an insult, although it is to many Americans.

Once, on a trip overseas, I was in the Frankfurt, Germany, airport. I had to use the men's room, and while standing at a urinal, realized that a custodian had come in and was sweeping the floor. I looked over my shoulder and saw that the custodian was a woman. My first reaction was embarrassment, but I quickly thought, I'm never going to see her again.

 IN SUMMARY

I could go on, but you get the idea. When you work on international projects or teams, you can expect language barriers and cultural differences to present challenges. I found *Kiss, Bow, or Shake Hands?* by Terri Morrison and Wayne A. Conaway (both the original and the revised and updated 2015 edition) very useful.

I suggest you try to educate yourself as much as possible on important issues in the countries you interact with. If you sense that there is friction between yourself and someone from another country, have a one-on-one with them and ask what might be bothering them. This way you can work to resolve any issues that may exist before they become a problem.

CHAPTER 21

Remote Teams

The COVID-19 pandemic mandated that much of what is done in teams be conducted with members in remote locations. To call these distributed groups a team is inconsistent with what most of us think of as a team, yet it is a coordinated effort and fits the definition of a team.

Interestingly, Yael Zofi (2012) wrote a book titled *A Manager's Guide to Virtual Teams* long before the pandemic began, because with globalization of business, distributed teams were becoming more commonplace. But how do you define a team?

A team is a group of individuals who work together to produce a result and enjoy doing so.

I personally don't see dyads as a team, but the general definition does not exclude them. Then there are mega-teams, which are teams made up of teams. An example of a mega-team is a big airplane development program, such as the program that created the 777, which involved 97,000 people in several countries scattered around the globe, all working together to produce a marvel of an airplane.

Generally speaking, there is nothing special about a distributed or a local team. However, there is a greater need for communication with a distributed team, because studies have found that when two people are separated by more than 30 feet, communication between them diminishes dramatically. Hewlett Packard once discovered that when they had distributed teams with people in Singapore, California, New York, and London, it was very important to ensure that individuals on the critical path in a project talk as often as possible to prevent problems.

Because it is more difficult to think of your distributed group as a team, it is important to stress this frequently, and to do things to clarify roles and responsibilities, keep everyone informed, and work on processes more than you might as a local team. As I tell my students in my Leading Project Teams class, teams don't just happen, they must be built (Sampietro & Villa, 2014; Lewis, 2004).

My experience with project teams has been that most project managers don't spend any time on team building. The work itself is what takes priority, and since many project teams are matrix form, there doesn't seem to be much point to team building. These project managers believe team building is reserved for groups that reside in one location and report to a single team leader.

I suggest that a team is a team, regardless of location or the fact that individual members may report to someone other than the team leader. This creates problems of mixed loyalties and must be overcome by gaining commitment to the project team itself.

As I mentioned in Chapter 20, I have been working with distributed teams since 2006. I work with a company in Chandigarh, India, that develops software products for me. I have an administrative assistant in the Philippines. And I have associates in Singapore, Sweden, Malaysia, and throughout the United States.

JUST A FEW SUGGESTIONS

Here are some of the ideas I have learned from others during my career and during the COVID-19 pandemic.

Meeting Management

There are a few rules for holding meetings that apply equally to online or in-person meetings. You should have a timed agenda; that means that each item on the agenda should have a fixed amount of time allocated to it. The agenda should be published ahead of time so everyone can come prepared.

To ensure that you stick to the time for each item, you should assign the role of timekeeper to someone; don't do it yourself. You facilitate, and that takes all your attention. The timekeeper should alert you when you are out of time. You always have the option to run over on one section, but not on the meeting itself. People may have booked other engagements following your meeting, and you must respect their time.

You should also assign the role of notetaker to someone. The notetaker should record ideas, solutions, and other things that take place during the meeting, and then send copies of those notes to everyone following the meeting.

Most importantly, if someone announces a problem in a general meeting, do not try to solve it in the meeting. Send the related team members to a special problem-solving meeting following this one. Never shoot the messenger who shares a problem; you can't solve problems you know nothing about.

The Five-Minute Rule

The key to successful online meetings is to keep everyone occupied (and this goes for in-person meetings too). Attention spans are about five or six minutes. This means that you need to give participants in the meeting something to do about every five minutes. With Zoom, you can assign small groups to breakout rooms and have them complete assignments together. These can be discussions, problem-solving, planning, or creating something, but keep them busy doing something of value.

Then have each group report to the entire group what they have produced. You can also use polls to keep their attention. You can pre-assign research tasks for them to do, and have them report these when the meeting gets going. Again, you need to specify that reports be no more than five minutes.

Another practice that is useful, whether for Zoom meetings or in-person classroom sessions, is to engage the audience with stories. Instead of making points with direct narration, couch it in an interesting story. The telling of stories not only captures attention but also tends to be remembered for far longer—sometimes for life—than straight narration of facts and figures.

Finally, recognize that our population is highly visual and will pay more attention to visual data that supports whatever you're telling them. If you can make them laugh occasionally, you will help energize them and keep them from drifting off. While some of them may not like this approach, you can quiz them periodically. If you make it fun by awarding points for correct answers, you can make the meeting productive and fun at the same time.

Lights, Camera, Action

I do think that you must insist that people turn on their cameras when you are conducting meetings online. We rely heavily on seeing the faces of people when we talk with them. Studies have found that as much as 97 percent of the meaning of a communication is carried by the nonverbal "channel," which would be intonation, gestures, facial expressions, eye-accessing cues, and pacing. Having only the audio channel limits the nonverbal information severely.

Another reason for having cameras on is, quite frankly, to ensure that team members are actually paying attention. One of my instructors noticed that a woman in an online class was watching a TV program rather than paying attention to what he was doing. In line with this, you need to ban cell phones; they are being paid to be in your meeting, and out of respect for the other members of the group, they should give full attention to the proceedings. If they don't like that rule, they have other options for employment.

Getting Balanced Participation

Another thing you may find is that those individuals who tend to be reticent in colocated teams may become even more reticent in an online meeting. I have always tried to draw out those individuals because they often have valuable contributions to make, but you will lose them if you don't deliberately ask them to contribute.

One way to do this is to go one by one through the group and ask for their suggestions or ideas. You can also state the rule that they can pass occasionally, but they may not pass all the time. Otherwise, there is little reason to have them in the meeting.

There is another reason for reticence besides personality—implied status differences. Technicians, for example, feel that engineers outrank them, and they may be reluctant to express ideas. You need to validate that ideas are welcome from all members of the group. It may take some time for this to become a norm, but when it does, it can be a powerful source of solutions to problems.

I would also like to suggest that you reread Chapter 19 on the principles that Alan Mulally promotes for leading teams and organizations. You should read them to your team as well. Tell them that these seem reasonable, and you expect everyone to abide by them. In addition, read the book by Zofi about virtual teams. You will find some useful ideas there.

IN SUMMARY

I don't think online team meetings and activities are that much different from in-person ones. The real difference is that it is harder to coordinate physical things with each other, and it is a little more difficult to read all the nonverbal communication channels. Many of the standard rules for meetings and group activities still apply, however, and if anything good came from the COVID-19 pandemic, it is that more people are now used to online activities than they were 10 years ago when the fifth edition of this book was published.

Schedule Computations

O nce a suitable network has been drawn, with durations assigned to all activities, it is necessary to perform computations to determine the longest path through the project. If start and finish dates for the project have already been dictated, these calculations will tell whether the required dates can be met. On the other hand, if a start date is given, the computations will provide the earliest completion date for the project.

The simplest computation that can be made for a network will determine the total working time on the longest path through the project and will reveal whether any latitude exists on paths parallel to the longest path. The longest path is called the *critical path*, since a slip on this path will cause a corresponding slip in the completion of the project. This computation specifies how many weeks (or days or hours, depending on the time units being used) it will take to complete the project if no holidays or vacation periods exist. Naturally, holidays and/or vacations will intervene during certain parts of the year so that the actual *calendar time* for the project is likely to exceed the *working time*.

It is also important to note that the conventional way to compute project working times is to ignore resources initially. In other words, activities are treated as though they have *fixed durations*, based on the assumption that certain levels of resources will be available when the work begins.

Furthermore, these durations are estimated from historical data and are based on the assumption that a person who possesses the skill level to do the required work is available. As was pointed out in previous chapters, if these conditions are not met, the actual working times will deviate from estimated times, sometimes considerably.

NETWORK RULES

In order to compute project working times, two *universal* rules apply to defining how networks function. (The software you use may impose additional rules, which will be presented in the user manual.) These universal rules are as follows:

Rule I: Before a task can begin, all tasks preceding it must be completed.

Rule 2: Arrows denote logical precedence. Neither the length of the arrow nor its angular direction have any significance. (It is not a vector but a scalar.)

BASIC SCHEDULING COMPUTATIONS

Although no one is likely to do manual network computations in this day of abundant scheduling software, it is important to understand how the computer makes these computations. Otherwise, it is easy to fall into the *garbage-in, garbage-out* problem. Furthermore, the computer output is not easily understandable unless the computation method is understood. What does float really mean, for example?

The following material will explain how the basic computations are performed, with no concern for resource limitations. That is, these computations all are based on the assumption that the required resources will indeed be available when the time comes to do the work. This is equivalent to saying that the organization has an *unlimited* pool of people, which of course is never the case. For this reason, a schedule that assumes unlimited resources is considered to be the *ideal* or *best-case* situation, and provides a starting point for resource-constrained project scheduling. Chapter 9 deals with the allocation of resources to yield a realistic working schedule.

We will use the example given in Chapter 8 of preparing a meal to illustrate scheduling computations. That network is shown in Figure A.1, using activity-on-node (AON) notation. A solution using activity-on-arrow (AOA) notation will be presented later. The numbers in the duration (DU) cells are working durations in minutes. Each activity contains cells in which we can enter the *earliest start* and *earliest finish* as well as the *latest start* and *latest finish* for the activity. Other notation schemes are used in other books and with various software packages, but this one seems to me to be very simple to understand.

In order to locate the critical path and compute the earliest and latest start and finish times for noncritical project activities, two sets of computations are necessary. These are called *forward-pass* and *backward-pass* calculations.

FIGURE A.1 AON Network for Preparing a Meal

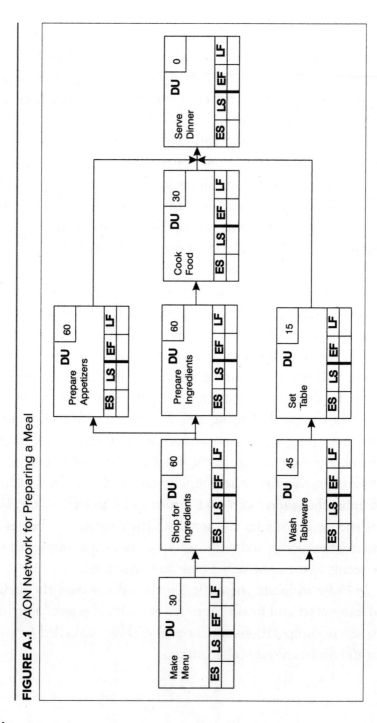

Forward-Pass Computations

A forward pass is made through the network to calculate the earliest achievement times for each activity in the network. If we remember that each activity has a start and a finish, then we can talk about early start and early finish times, as mentioned previously. This really amounts to having start and finish *events* for each activity, but they are not usually shown in activity-on-node diagrams. As was stated previously, the durations for the activities in Figure A.1 are *working minutes*. The project is shown as starting at time $T = 0$. For schedules spanning several days or weeks, once activity start and finish times are determined, they can be converted to calendar dates, but that step will be omitted in this appendix. For our simple project, we will compute the total project time in minutes and then convert that to hours.

Figure A.2 shows the first steps in the forward-pass computation. "Make Menu" starts at $T = 0$. It takes 30 minutes. That means it has an early finish 30 minutes after it starts, or at $T = 30$. As soon as "Make Menu" is finished, two activities can start—"Shop for Ingredients" and "Wash Tableware." This means that the early finish for "Make Menu" becomes the early start for these two succeeding tasks.

It takes 60 minutes to do the shopping, so the early finish for that task is 90 minutes. You simply add its duration to its early start time to get its early finish. The same is done for "Wash Tableware." Again, the early finish for each task becomes the early start for succeeding ones. We continue this process until we get to "Serve Dinner."

At this point, "Prepare Appetizers" has an early finish of 150 minutes, "Cook Meal" has an early finish of 180 minutes, and "Set Table" has 90 minutes for its early finish. Which one becomes the early start for "Serve Dinner"? Remember, Rule 1

FIGURE A.2   First Step: Forward-Pass Computation

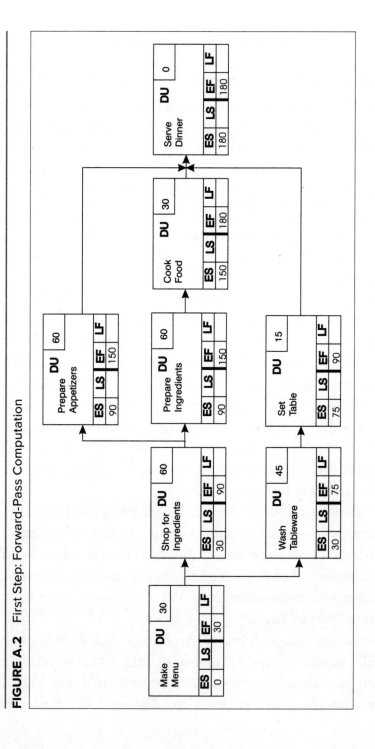

presented earlier says that you can't start a task until all tasks preceding it have been completed. Since "Cook Meal" ends the latest (has the largest early finish time), its early finish becomes the early start for the serving task.

Given the activity durations shown and the sequences detailed by the network, the project has a completion 180 minutes after it begins. Because we are usually trying to meet an imposed completion time for most projects, this working time can now be compared to the target to see if that target can be met, given an anticipated start date or time. If it cannot, then either the project must start earlier, the end date must slip out, or the network must be changed to compress (shorten) the critical path.

For our example, suppose we had planned to come home from work at 5 p.m. and have dinner prepared to serve at 7 p.m. Since we have found that it will take three hours to prepare the meal, this won't work. We will have to either shorten the time of some tasks, start the process at 4 p.m., or revise the network in some way. Naturally, we could shave 30 minutes off the project by preparing the menu the day before. For many projects, however, such a solution would not be an option, so we will say for now that this option is not available and see what our other approaches are.

In that case, the question is, how will the network have to change in order to finish in two hours? The answer to this question is never obvious in a complicated network (although it is fairly obvious in this one). As a general rule, in order to see what else in the network might have to change, more information is needed. Specifically, we need to know the *latest* times by which each activity can be achieved and still meet the 180-minute completion.

You might ask, "Why not use the 120-minute completion, since that is what is required?" The answer is that a *best-case* computation is made first, so that we can see which paths have latitude and which one(s) is critical. The best case is considered to be that 180 minutes is acceptable. A shorter time is a worse case because you will have to squeeze time out of something. A longer time is also a worse case, as you are stretching the project out unnecessarily.

For that reason, we assign a 180-minute late finish to "Serve Dinner," which means that it has the same early finish and late finish times and zero duration, making it actually an *event.* This is an example of the only kind of event that is actually shown in activity-on-node networks, and it is called a *milestone.*

Now that the late finish time has been set for "Serve Dinner," we do a backward-pass computation to determine the latest event times on all activities that will permit achievement of the 180-minute completion.

Backward-Pass Computations

Beginning with "Serve Dinner," and assigning a late finish time of 180 to it, we subtract its duration of zero from that time to get its late start (see Figure A.3). Naturally, that gives a late start of 180. This late start time must be the late finish for all the predecessors to "Serve Dinner," so that time is entered into the cells for each activity. In the case of "Prepare Appetizers," we subtract its duration of 60 minutes from its late finish of 180, to get 120 minutes. This number becomes its late start time. For "Cook Meal," we do the same and get a late start of 150. In turn, we use 150 as the late finish for "Prepare Ingredients," subtract its duration, and get 90 minutes for its late start.

Notice the junction at the beginning of "Prepare Appetizers" and "Prepare Ingredients." The late start for "Prepare Appetizers"

FIGURE A.3 Backward Pass to Determine Latest Times

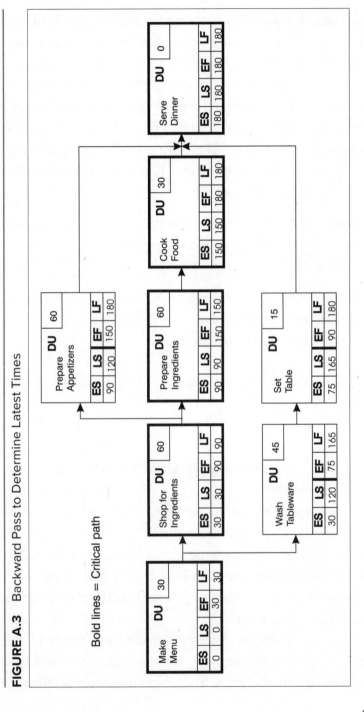

Bold lines = Critical path

Make Menu	**DU**	30			Shop for Ingredients	**DU**	60			Prepare Appetizers	**DU**	60			Prepare Ingredients	**DU**	60			Cook Food	**DU**	30			Serve Dinner	**DU**	0	

Make Menu: ES 0, LS 0, EF 30, LF 30

Shop for Ingredients: ES 30, LS 30, EF 90, LF 90

Prepare Appetizers: ES 90, LS 120, EF 150, LF 180

Prepare Ingredients: ES 90, LS 90, EF 150, LF 150

Cook Food: ES 150, LS 150, EF 180, LF 180

Serve Dinner: ES 180, LS 180, EF 180, LF 180

Wash Tableware: **DU** 45, ES 30, LS 120, EF 75, LF 165

Set Table: **DU** 15, ES 75, LS 165, EF 90, LF 180

is 120 minutes, and that for "Prepare Ingredients" is 90 minutes. Which one of these should we use for the late finish of the predecessor, "Shop for Ingredients"? If we allowed shopping to finish as late as 120 minutes, "Prepare Ingredients" could not start until that time, and if you work forward from there to the end of the project, you will see that this will push the end time out to 210 minutes instead of 180. We can now offer the following rules for assigning early and late times to activities that have multiple predecessors or successors.

> **Rule:** When two or more activities follow a predecessor, the latest finish for the predecessor will be the earliest *late start* for the successors.

> **Rule:** When two or more activities precede another, the earliest start for the successor will be the *latest* of the late finish times for the predecessors.

Continuing in this way, you arrive at the late activity times shown in Figure A.3.

Activity Maximum Float

Now examine "Prepare Appetizers." Note that its early start is 90 and its late start is 120. The difference of 30 minutes is called the *activity float*. This float represents latitude for the activity. So long as this activity starts no later than 120 minutes and takes no longer than its duration of 60 minutes, the project can be finished within 180 minutes.

Note the activities that run through the center of the diagram. They all have the same early and late start and the same early and late finish times. These activities have no float and are

called *critical*. The path containing those
activities is, in turn, called the *critical path*.
What we have done is apply the *critical path*
method to locate that path. By making the
final activity late finish the same as its early

> An activity is a
> critical activity
> any time it has
> no float.

finish, we have forced one path to have no float. As you can see,
it is the longest path.

The term *float* derives from the fact that "Prepare Appetizers"
can start as early as 90 minutes and as late as 120 minutes, so we
say that it can float around for the difference of 30 minutes. Note
that float is always calculated by taking the latest start minus
the earliest start, or the latest finish minus the earliest finish. In
equation form:

$$\text{Max. float} = LF - EF$$

or

$$\text{Max. float} = LS - ES$$

where LS means late start, LF means late finish, ES means early
start, and EF means early finish.

The Value of Float

It is tempting to think that float is undesirable. The first suggestion that people sometimes make is to finish a task that has float
as early as possible and move resources onto the critical path to
shorten it, so that you wind up with no float anywhere. To see
why this is not a good idea, we must remember that the durations
for all tasks are *estimates*, that they have 50–50 likelihoods if
averages have been used, and that we often have made those estimates using poor history, so they are suspect to begin with. Given

those facts, it is highly advisable to have float on all but the critical path to compensate for unforeseen problems, estimating errors, and so on.

What about the critical path itself? That series of activities must be managed in such a way that all tasks are completed on time, or the project will be delayed (unless lost time on one activity can be recovered on a later one). It is very risky to allow a critical path task to slip under the assumption that you will recover the time later. Murphy's Law invariably prevails when you do this. In fact, the best working rule I know is, do whatever is necessary to stay on schedule.

> The best practice in managing projects is to do whatever is necessary to stay on schedule.

CALCULATIONS FOR AN AOA NETWORK

The calculations for AOA networks are done in exactly the same way as those for AON networks. The only real problem is with notation. Figure A.4 is the same diagram for preparing a meal in AOA format. In the first edition of this book, I learned that people were confused by the notation, as I had split each node in half and placed an early time on the left side and a late time on the right. However, as was pointed out earlier, each node contains at least two events, and if several activities enter or leave, there will be several events contained. I have looked at a number of systems of notation, and no single one is unambiguous. For that reason, I have placed the early and late times on each end of all arrows. On the left end will always be the early start and late start, and on the right end will always be the early finish and late finish. Each node is numbered for easy reference. See Figure A.4.

FIGURE A.4 AOA Diagram for Preparing a Meal

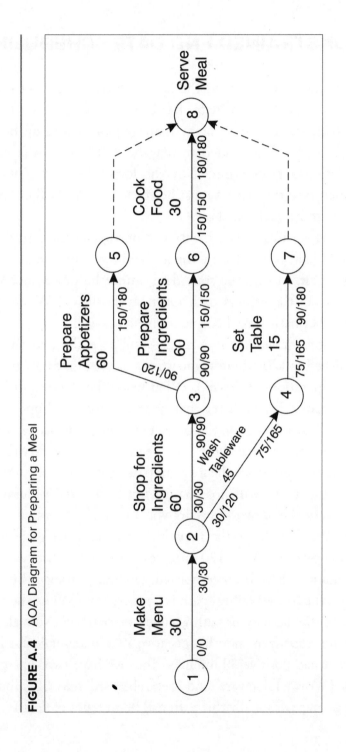

CONSTRAINED END DATE SCHEDULING

As was mentioned earlier, the usual situation for most projects is that an end time (or date) has been imposed, either by contract with the customer or by management, based on business considerations. This end date may be earlier than the earliest completion date determined by the forward-pass computation, in which case the project must be started earlier or the schedule must be shortened somehow.

In many cases, as was mentioned previously, the start date for a project is also dictated by the availability of resources or some other factor, so that the start date cannot be moved up. When this is true, the critical path must be shortened. When this is done, other paths may become problems as well.

For the network just analyzed, suppose the end time was established as 120 minutes (you want to serve dinner at 7 p.m. and start preparations at 5 p.m.). What would be the overall impact on the project? To answer that question, we will impose a late finish of 120 minutes on the project and do a new backward-pass calculation. Note that there is no need to do a new forward-pass computation yet, since the forward pass determines only the early times, and these will not change until an activity duration is changed or the network is redrawn.

Figure A.5 shows the network with the latest project completion constrained to 120 minutes. When the backward-pass computations have been completed, we find a strange thing. The float on the former critical path is now *negative!* When the float is negative, the activity or path is called *supercritical.* Note also that "Prepare Appetizers" now has negative 30 minutes of float, whereas before it had positive 30 minutes. Thus we have two supercritical paths. ("Wash Tableware" and "Set Table" still have 30 minutes of float, because originally this path had 90 minutes of float.)

FIGURE A.5 End Date Constrained

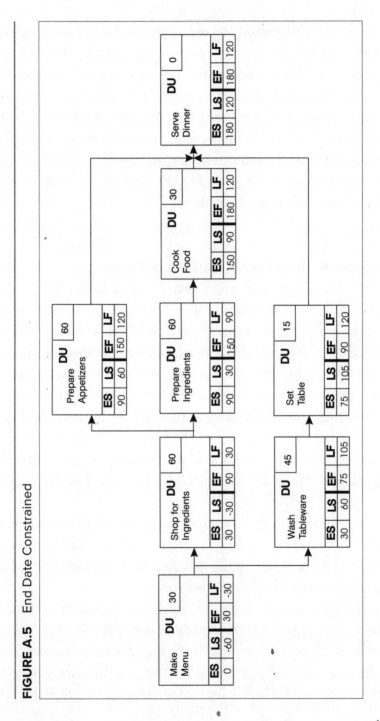

It is also interesting to examine the late times on "Make Menu" and "Shop." These times are now negative. In the case of "Make Menu," this is telling us that the activity needs to start 60 minutes before it is planned to start, which we already knew.

If we cannot start the project early, we will have to shorten the critical path by at least 60 minutes to meet our deadline. Let's suppose we can do this by taking 30 minutes off the time of "Prepare Ingredients" and another 15 minutes each out of "Make Menu" and "Shop for Ingredients." We might get time out of "Prepare Ingredients" by buying frozen vegetables rather than fresh, so that they don't have to be chopped. If these adjustments are made, we have the result shown in Figure A.6.

We now have a situation that is not desirable as a general rule. We have two critical paths. "Prepare Appetizers" is critical, as are "Prepare Ingredients" and "Cook Food." For this particular project, we might not be concerned about having two critical paths, but most of the time this would be very undesirable. The reason is that when you have no float, anything that goes wrong with the task and increases its duration will cause your overall project finish time to slip by the amount of the increased duration (unless you can reduce the times taken by subsequent tasks). The presence of two critical paths increases the risk.

For this reason, you should try to get rid of all but *one* critical path. This can be done only by changing the duration of one or more activities, allowing the end date to be extended or redrawing the network into a new configuration.

The issue is how to decide which critical path to eliminate. There is no single answer to this problem. Float is only one kind of risk involved in a project. There are also risks from technical problems, poor estimates, weather and other uncontrollable factors, and so on. Table A.1 lists some of the factors that should be

FIGURE A.6 Network with Times Reduced

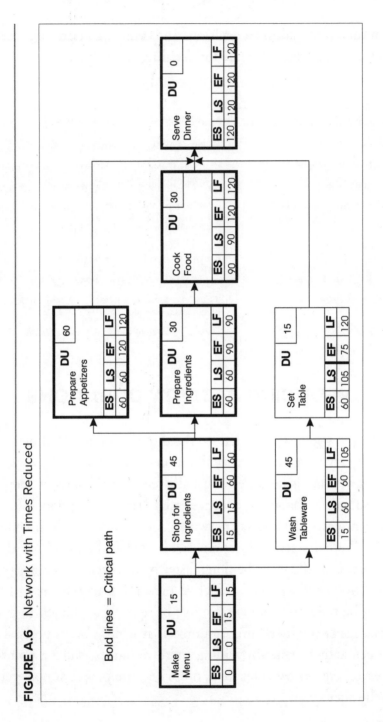

Bold lines = Critical path

considered in making a decision. The comments that follow each factor explain the rationale for deciding what to do.

TABLE A.1   Factors to Consider in Eliminating a Dual Critical Path

Number of activities	Path with most activities might be most risky.
Skill level of people	Path with least-skilled people could be most risky.
Technical risk	Path with greatest technical risk should have float.
Weather/uncontrollable factors	Give float to activities with uncontrollable factors.
Cost	Give float to activities that cost most to do.
Historical data	Activities with least historical data—give float; activities that were historically a problem—ditto.
Available backup plan	Give float to activities with no obvious backup.
Business cycle	If business tends to get hectic at certain times, give float to activities affected.
Difficulty	Give float to activities that are most difficult.

REDUCING ACTIVITY DURATIONS

When it is necessary to reduce the duration of a critical path, we usually try to reduce activity durations rather than redrawing the network. That is because we usually feel that the logic is more or less sound, so changing sequences might not be an option. When it is, techniques like lead-lag networks, for example, can be used first.

Whether activity durations can be reduced depends on three factors. Can the work be done faster by increasing *efficiency* (perhaps by using a more productive person)? Can the *scope* of the work be reduced? Can extra effort be applied to the job to get it done faster (by increasing resources)? It is not always possible to reduce activity time by adding more resources, since a point of *diminishing returns* is reached, often because people simply get in each other's way.

There are, of course, two ways to increase human resources applied to a project. One is by adding bodies. The other is by working the same number of people more hours per day, which we call working *overtime*. In both cases, you tend to get diminishing returns very quickly. I know of one company that measured the impact on productivity of working overtime. It measured productivity for a normal 40-hour week and then again at the end of three weeks in which people worked 50 hours per week. Productivity after working overtime was back down to the normal 40-hours-per-week level, and errors had increased.

When productivity declines without errors increasing, it is often because people are pacing themselves. They think like a marathon runner who knows that if she runs too fast at the beginning and uses up her energy, she will be unable to finish the race. On the other hand, when error rates increase, it is usually because people are truly fatigued.

We also find that people doing knowledge work suffer the same kind of problems. One study found that when people put in 12 hours of overtime on knowledge work, you probably get an increase in output from them equivalent to what you would expect in 2 normal working hours!

CONVERTING ARROW DIAGRAMS TO BAR CHARTS

While an arrow diagram is essential to do a proper analysis of the relationships between the activities in a project, determine activity float, and identify the critical path, the best tool for the people who are actually doing the project work is the bar chart. People find it much easier to see when they are supposed to start and finish their jobs if they are given a bar chart. The schedule shown as an arrow diagram in Figure A.4 has been portrayed as a bar chart in Figure A.7, making use of what we've learned about the schedule from the network analysis.

In this figure, critical path activities are shown as solid bars, while those with float are shown as hollow bars with dots trailing to indicate the amount of float allowed each activity. Note that each activity is shown starting at its earliest possible time, so that float is reserved to be used only if absolutely necessary. This is the conventional method of displaying bar charts.

Note that both "Wash Tableware" and "Set Table" have 90 minutes of float. Naturally, it is the same float, and initially, before the project begins, there are 90 minutes of float available for either activity. However, if all of the float is used up on "Wash Tableware," there will be none left for "Set Table," and it would therefore be critical.

> **PARKINSON'S LAW**
> Work always expands to take the time allowed.
>
> **LEWIS'S LAW FOR FLOAT**
> If you give it to them, they'll take it!

This illustrates a real pitfall of bar charts. Assume that different individuals are doing two sequential activities that share a common amount of float. Since the chart does not show the interrelationships of activities, it is hard for the people performing the work to tell that the float is shared. They look at the chart and think that they each have the designated float. Then, if each tries to make use of the float, the project is in trouble.

In fact, Parkinson's Law can be applied to project float. Parkinson's Law says that work always expands to fit the time allowed. When applied to float, this means that *when you allow float, people will use it!* For this reason, some software can be set up so that float is not displayed. The implication of such a schedule is simply that the work should be done as shown.

FIGURE A.7 Bar Chart for Project to Prepare a Meal

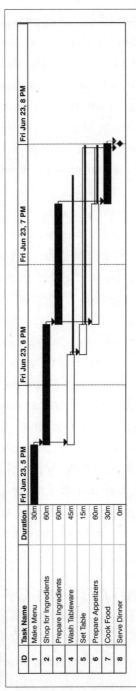

ID	Task Name	Duration	Fri Jun 23, 5 PM	Fri Jun 23, 6 PM	Fri Jun 23, 7 PM	Fri Jun 23, 8 PM
1	Make Menu	30m				
2	Shop for Ingredients	60m				
3	Prepare Ingredients	60m				
4	Wash Tableware	45m				
5	Set Table	15m				
6	Prepare Appetizers	60m				
7	Cook Food	30m				
8	Serve Dinner	0m				

I personally do not like this approach. I prefer to explain to team members that float is shared, and I encourage them to keep float in reserve, to be used only if necessary. Indeed, it is always a good idea to keep float in reserve, to be used if an estimate turns out to be wrong or if an unforeseen problem causes the work to be delayed. As someone told me recently, every project should be planned as if there will be at least some percentage of the total time when the entire city will have a power blackout and nothing will get done.

McGregor formulated a management model some years ago stating that some managers see workers as undependable, wanting only a paycheck from the job, and so on. He called this a *Theory-X* outlook, and he postulated that a manager with such an outlook would tend to get the expected results.

The opposite outlook, which is more positive, he called a *Theory-Y* view. This would naturally be the more desired view, as a manager would tend to get the more positive result. It is easy to see Parkinson's Law and Lewis's Law for Float as Theory-X outlooks. However, I don't see them that way. In today's downsized, right-sized, understaffed organization, people simply have to do their work in priority order, and this leads to putting things off until they absolutely have to be done. Thus, if people have float, they tend to take it, but unfortunately they may take it at the beginning of an assignment; if they encounter a problem with the work later on, no float is left to help get the work done on time.

LIMITATIONS OF THE CRITICAL PATH METHOD

It is important to remember that conventional critical path analysis, which has been used for this network, assumes that unlimited resources exist in the organization, so that all activities can be done as planned. As the bar chart shows, however, there are a number of points at which activities are running in parallel. If those activities require the same resources, then there may not be enough to get the job done as shown, and the schedule cannot be met. This subject is addressed in Chapter 9.

Multiple Calendars

One final subject must be considered in doing basic network computations. It is possible that not all project activities will follow the same working schedule. Does everyone work Monday through Friday? Do some people work only weekends?

Some projects may include activities that require actual working days to complete; others do not. Pouring concrete must be done during the workweek. However, that concrete may cure over a weekend. For this reason, it is important that multiple calendars be considered in scheduling.

For example, a situation in which one group works a conventional Monday–Friday schedule and another group works only weekends is shown in Figure A.8.

Now, suppose the two groups are scheduled to do two sequential tasks, with Group 1 working exactly one week (M–F), followed by the people in Group 2, who are supposed to finish their work over the weekend. However, Group 1 gets behind on their work by one day. How much is the schedule affected? As Figure A.9 shows, the work will slip an entire week because Group 1 gets behind only one day!

FIGURE A.8 Multiple-Calendar Network

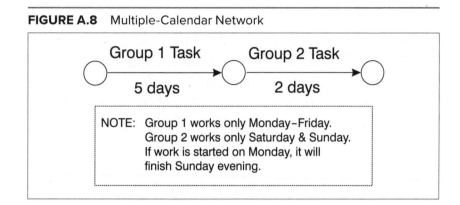

FIGURE A.9 A One-Week Slip

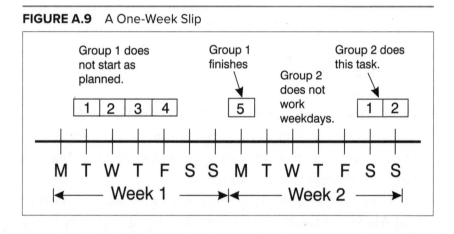

This kind of problem highlights the occasional need for multiple calendars in scheduling. They are called calendars because holiday and overtime dates differ for the two groups. If the software being used does not permit the use of multiple calendars, it may still be possible to "fake it" and force the schedule to reflect correct working dates, but this may be difficult to do. For this reason, software should be selected with this potential requirement in mind.

GLOSSARY

Activity The work or effort needed to achieve a result. It consumes time and usually consumes resources.

Activity Description A statement specifying what must be done to achieve a desired result.

Activity-on-Arrow A network diagram showing sequence of activities, in which each activity is represented by an arrow, with a circle representing a node or event at each end.

Activity-on-Node A network diagram showing sequence of activities, in which each activity is represented by a box or circle (that is, a *node*) and these are interconnected with arrows to show precedence of work.

Authority The legitimate power given to a person in an organization to use resources to reach an objective and to exercise discipline.

Backward-Pass Calculation Calculations made working backward through a network from the latest event to the beginning event to calculate event late times. A forward-pass calculation determines early times.

Calendars The arrangement of normal working days, together with nonworking days, such as holidays and vacations, as well as special work days (overtime periods) used to determine dates on which project work will be completed.

Change Order A document that authorizes a change in some aspect of a project.

Control   The practice of monitoring progress against a plan so that corrective steps can be taken when a deviation from plan occurs.

CPM   An acronym for critical path method. A network diagramming method that shows the longest series of activities in a project, thereby determining the earliest completion for the project.

Crashing   An attempt to reduce activity or total project duration, usually by adding resources.

Critical Path   The longest sequential path of activities that are absolutely essential for completion of the project.

Dependency   The next task or group of tasks cannot begin until preceding work has been completed, thus the word *dependent* or dependency.

Deviation   Any variation from planned performance. The deviation can be in terms of schedule, cost, performance, or scope of work. Deviation analysis is the heart of exercising project control.

Dummy Activity   A zero-duration element in a network showing a logic linkage. A dummy does not consume time or resources but simply indicates precedence.

Duration   The time it takes to complete an activity.

Earliest Finish   The earliest time that an activity can be completed.

Earliest Start   The earliest time that an activity can be started.

Estimate   A forecast or guess about how long an activity will take, how many resources might be required, or how much it will cost.

Event   A point in time. An event is binary. It is either achieved or not, whereas an activity can be partially complete. An event can be the start or finish of an activity.

Feedback   Information derived from observation of project activities that is used to analyze the status of the job and take corrective action if necessary.

Float   A measure of how much an activity can be delayed before it begins to impact the project finish date.

Forward-Pass Method   The method used to calculate the earliest start time for each activity in a network diagram.

Free Float   The amount of time that an activity can be delayed without affecting succeeding activities.

Gantt Chart   A bar chart that indicates the time required to complete each activity in a project. It is named for Henry L. Gantt, who first developed a complete notational system for displaying progress with bar charts.

Hammock Activity   A single activity that actually represents a group of activities. It "hangs" between two events and is used to report progress on the composite it represents.

Histogram   A vertical bar chart showing (usually) resource allocation levels over time in a project.

i-j Notation   A system of numbering nodes in an activity-on-arrow network. The i-node is always the beginning of an activity, while the j-node is always the finish.

Inexcusable Delays   Project delays that are attributable to negligence on the part of the contractor, which lead in many cases to penalty payments.

Latest Finish   The latest time that an activity can be finished without extending the end date for a project.

Latest Start   The latest time that an activity can start without extending the end date for a project.

Learning Curve   The time it takes humans to learn an activity well enough to achieve optimum performance can be displayed by curves, which must be factored into estimates of activity durations in order to achieve planned completion dates.

Leveling   An attempt to smooth the use of resources, whether people, materials, or equipment, to avoid large peaks and valleys in their usage.

Life Cycle   The phases that a project goes through from concept through completion. The nature of the project changes during each phase.

Matrix Organization   A method of drawing people from functional departments within an organization for assignment to a project team, but without removing them from their physical location. The project manager in such a structure is said to have *dotted-line* authority over team members.

Milestone   An event of special importance, usually representing the completion of a major phase of project work. Reviews are often scheduled at milestones.

Most Likely Time   The most realistic time estimate for completing an activity under normal conditions.

Negative Float or Slack   A condition in a network in which the *earliest time* for an event is actually later than its *latest time.* This happens when the project has a constrained end date that is earlier than can be achieved, or when an activity uses up its float and is still delayed.

Node   A point in a network connected to other points by one or more arrows. In activity-on-arrow notation, the node contains at least one event. In activity-on-node notation, the node represents an activity, and the arrows show the sequence in which they must be performed.

PERT   An acronym for program evaluation and review technique. PERT makes use of network diagrams as does CPM, but in addition applies statistics to activities to try to estimate the probabilities of completion of project work.

Pessimistic Time   Roughly speaking, this is the *worst-case* time to complete an activity. The term has a more precise meaning that is defined in the PERT literature.

Phase   A major component or segment of a project.

Precedence Diagram   An activity-on-node diagram.

Queue   Waiting time.

Resource Allocation   The assignment of people, equipment, facilities, or materials to a project. Unless adequate resources are provided, project work cannot be completed on schedule, and resource allocation is a significant component of project scheduling.

Resource Pool   A group of people who can generally do the same work so that they can be chosen randomly for assignment to a project.

Risk   The possibility that something can go wrong and interfere with the completion of project work.

Scope   The magnitude of work that must be done to complete a project.

Statement of Work   A description of work to be performed.

Subproject   A small project within a larger one.

Time Now   The current calendar date from which a network analysis, report, or update is being made.

Time Standard   The time allowed for the completion of a task.

Variance   Any deviation of project work from what was planned. Variance can affect costs, time, performance, or project scope.

Work Breakdown Structure   A method of subdividing work into smaller and smaller increments to permit accurate estimates of durations, resource requirements, and costs.

REFERENCES AND READING LIST

Ackoff, Russell. *Ackoff's Fables: Irreverent Reflections on Business and Bureaucracy.* New York: Wiley, 1991.

Ackoff, Russell. Systems *Thinking for Curious Managers.* Devon, UK: Triarcity Press, 2010

Ackoff, Russell. *The Art of Problem Solving.* New York: Wiley, 1978.

Adams, James L. *Conceptual Blockbusting: A Guide to Better Ideas,* 2d ed. New York: W. W. Norton, 1979.

Adams, John D. (ed.). *Transforming Leadership: From Vision to Results.* Alexandria, Va.: Miles River Press, 1986.

Ailes, Roger. *You Are the Message: Secrets of the Master Communicators.* Homewood, Ill.: Dow Jones-Irwin, 1988.

Albrecht, Karl. *The Northbound Train.* New York: AMACOM, 1994.

Archibald, R. D., and R. L. Villoria. *Network-Based Management Systems (PERT/CPM).* New York: Wiley, 1967.

Argyris, Chris. *Overcoming Organizational Defenses: Facilitating Organizational Learning.* Boston: Allyn and Bacon, 1990.

Avruch, Kevin, *Culture and Conflict Resolution.* Washington, DC: United States Institute of Peace, 1998.

Axelrod, Robert. *The Evolution of Cooperation.* New York: Basic Books, 1984.

Barker, Joel A. *Future Edge.* New York: William Morrow, 1992.

Barker, Joel A. *Wealth, Innovation & Diversity.* Videotape. Carlsbad, Calif.: CRM Learning, 2000.

Barnhart, Robert K. *The Barnhart Concise Dictionary of Etymology: The Origins of American English Words.* New York: HarperCollins, 1995.

Bedi, Hari. *Understanding the Asian Manager.* Singapore: Heinemann Asia, 1992.

Beer, Stafford. *Brain of the Firm,* 2d ed. New York: Wiley, 1981.

Bennis, Warren G. *Managing the Dream: Reflections on Leadership and Change.* Cambridge, Mass.: Perseus, 2000.

Bennis, Warren G., and Burt Nanus. *Leaders: The Strategies for Taking Charge.* New York: Harper & Row, 1985.

Benveniste, Guy. *Mastering the Politics of Planning.* San Francisco: Jossey-Bass, 1989.

Blanchard, Benjamin S. *Engineering Organization and Management.* Englewood Cliffs, N.J.: Prentice-Hall, 1976.

Block, Peter. *The Empowered Manager,* 2d ed. San Francisco: Jossey-Bass, 2000.

Bossity, Larry, and Ram Charan. *Execution: The Discipline of Getting Things Done.* New York: Crown, 2009.

Brooks, F. P. *The Mythical Man-Month: Essays on Software Engineering.* Reading, Mass.: Addison-Wesley, 1975.

Bryson, Bill. *Notes from a Small Island.* William Morrow, 2015.

Bunker, Barbara Benedict, and Billie T. Alban. *Large Group Interventions: Engaging the Whole System for Rapid Change.* San Francisco: Jossey-Bass, 1997.

Burns, James McGregor. *Leadership.* New York: Harper & Row, 1978.

Buzan, Tony. *The Mind Map Book.* New York: NAL/Dutton, 1996.

Campbell, Clark A. and Mick Campbell. *The New One-Page Project Manager: Communicate and Manage Any Project with a Single Sheet of Paper.* Hoboken, N.J.: Wiley, 2012.

Carlzon, Jan. *Moments of Truth.* New York: Perennial, 1987.

Chen, Yanping, and Francis N. Arko. *Principles of Contracting for Project Management.* Arlington, Va.: UMT Press, 2003.

Cialdini, Robert B. *Influence: The Power of Persuasion,* New Expanded Edition. New York: Harper Business, 2021.

Cooper, Robert G. *Winning at New Products.* New York: Basic Books, 2001.

Covey, Stephen. *The 7 Habits of Highly Effective People.* New York: Fireside Books, 1989.

Covey, Stephen R. *The 8th Habit: From Effectiveness to Greatness.* New York: Free Press, 2004.

Crosby, Philip. *Quality Is Free.* East Rutherford, N.J.: Signet, 1980.

de Bono, Edward. *Serious Creativity.* New York: Vermilion, 2015.

de Bono, Edward. *Six Thinking Hats.* Boston: Little, Brown & Co., 1985.

DeCarlo, Douglas. *eXtreme Project Management.* San Francisco: Jossey-Bass, 2004.

Deming, W. Edwards. *Out of the Crisis.* Cambridge, Mass.: Massachusetts Institute of Technology, 1986.

Dimancescu, Dan. *The Seamless Enterprise. Making Cross-Functional Management Work.* New York: Harper, 1992.

Downs, Alan. *Corporate Executions: The Ugly Truth about Layoffs—How Corporate Greed Is Shattering Lives, Companies, and Communities.* New York: AMACOM, 1995.

Drucker, Peter F. *Management: Tasks, Responsibilities, Practices.* New York: Harper & Row, 1974.

Dyer, Wayne. *You'll See It When You Believe It.* New York: Avon Books, 1989.

Eisenstein, Paul A. "How Toyota's Kentucky Operations Mix People, Processes to Be Best." *Investor's Business Daily,* December 4, 2000.

Englund, Randall L., and Robert J. Graham. *Creating an Environment for Successful Projects,* 3d ed. San Francisco: Berrett Koehler, 2019.

Englund, Randall L., and Alfonso Bucero. *The Complete Project Manager: Integrating People, Organizational and Technical Skills,* 2d ed. San Francisco: Berrett-Koehler, 2019.

Fisher, Roger, and William Ury. *Getting to Yes.* New York: Penguin, 1991.

Fleming, Q. W. *Cost/Schedule Control Systems Criteria.* Chicago: Probus, 1988.

Fleming, Quentin W., and Joel M. Koppelman. *Earned Value Project Management.* Upper Darbey, Pa.: Project Management Institute, 1996.

Fortune, Joyce, and Geoff Peters. *Learning from Failure: The Systems Approach.* Chichester, UK: Wiley, 1998.

Frame, J. Davidson. *Managing Projects in Organizations.* San Francisco: Jossey-Bass, 1995.

Frame, J. Davidson. *The New Project Management,* 2d ed. San Francisco: Jossey-Bass, 2002.

Frame, J. Davidson. *Project Finance: Tools and Techniques.* Arlington, Va.: UMT Press, 2003.

Frankl, Viktor. *Man's Search for Meaning,* 3d ed. New York: Touchstone, 1984.

Freiberg, Kevin, and Jackie Freiberg. *Nuts! Southwest Airlines' Crazy Recipe for Business and Personal Success.* New York: Broadway Books, 1996.

Gardner, Howard. *Frames of Mind: The Theory of Multiple Intelligences.* New York: Basic Books, 1993.

Garten, Jeffrey E. *The Mind of the C. E. O.* New York: Basic Books, 2001.

Gause, Donald, and Gerald Weinberg. *Exploring Requirements: Quality before Design.* New York: Dorset House Publishing, 1989.

Gehring, Dean R. *Applying Traits Theory of Leadership to Project Management.* Project Management Institute, Vol. 38, No. 1, 44–54, 2007.

George, Michael. *Lean Six Sigma: Combining Six Sigma Quality with Lean Production Speed.* New York: McGraw-Hill, 2002.

George, Michael. *Lean Six Sigma for Service.* New York: McGraw-Hill, 2003.

Ghantt, Thomas. *The Lost Art of Project Status Reporting.* Denver: Plumbline Publishing Group, 2012.

Gleick, James. *Chaos: Making a New Science.* New York: Penguin, 2008.

Godin, Seth. *Linchpin: Are You Indispensable?* New York: Portfolio Hardcover, 2010.

Goldratt, Eliyahu M. *Critical Chain.* Great Barrington, Mass.: North River Press, 1997.

Goldsmith, Marshall. *What Got You Here Won't Get You There.* New York: Hyperion, 2007.

Graham, Robert J., and Randall L. Englund. *Creating an Environment for Successful Projects.* San Francisco: Jossey-Bass, 1997.

Grantt, Adam. *Think Again: The Power of Knowing What You Don't Know.* New York: Viking, 2021.

Hammer, Michael, and James Champy. *Reengineering the Corporation.* New York: Harper Business, 1993.

Hampden-Turner, Charles, and Fons Trompenaars. *Building Cross-Cultural Competence.* New Haven, Conn.: Yale University Press, 2000.

Hancock, Graham. *Fingerprints of the Gods.* New York: Crown, 1995.

Hargrove, Robert. *Mastering the Art of Creative Collaboration.* New York: McGraw-Hill, 1998.

Harnish, Verne. *Mastering the Rockefeller Habits: What You Must Do to Increase the Value of Your Growing Firm.* New York: Select Books, 2002.

Harry, Mikel, and Richard Schroeder. *Six Sigma: The Breakthrough Management Strategy Revolutionizing the World's Top Corporations.* New York: Currency, 2000.

Harvey, Jerry B. *The Abilene Paradox: And Other Meditations on Management.* San Diego: University Associates, 1988.

Heller, Robert. *Achieving Excellence.* New York: DK Publishing, 1999.

Heller, Robert, and Tim Hindle. *Essential Manager's Manual.* New York: DK Publishing, 1998.

Herrmann, Ned. *The Creative Brain.* Lake Lure, N.C.: Brain Books, 1995.

Herrmann, Ned, and Ann Herrmann-Nedhi. *The Whole Brain Business Book,* 2d ed. New York: McGraw-Hill, 2015.

Hersey, Paul, and Kenneth Blanchard. *Management of Organizational Behavior: Utilizing Human Resources,* 4th ed. Englewood Cliffs, N.J.: Prentice-Hall, 1981.

Highsmith, James A., III. *Adaptive Software Development.* New York: Dorset House, 2000.

Hoffman, Bryce. *American Icon: Alan Mulally and the Fight to Save Ford Motor Company.* New York: Crown, 2012.

Ittner, Christopher D., and David F. Larckner. "A Bigger Yardstick for Company Performance." London: *Financial Times,* October 16, 2000.

Janis, Irving, and Leon Mann. *Decision Making.* New York: Free Press, 1977.

Jones, Russel A. *Self-Fulfilling Prophecies.* Hillsdale, N.J.: Lawrence Erlbaum, 1977.

Kaplan, Robert, and David Norton. *The Balanced Scorecard: Translating Strategy into Action.* Boston: Harvard Business School Press, 1996.

Kayser, Tom. *Mining Group Gold.* New York: McGraw-Hill, 1995.

Keane. *Productivity Management: Keane's Project Management Approach for Systems Development,* 2d ed. Boston: Keane Associates, 1995.

Keirsey, David. *Please Understand Me II.* Del Mar, Calif.: Prometheus Nemesis Book Company, 1998.

Kepner, Charles H., and Benjamin B. Tregoe. *The Rational Manager.* Princeton, N.J.: Kepner-Tregoe, Inc., 1965.

Kerzner, Harold. *In Search of Excellence in Project Management.* New York: Van Nostrand, 1998.

Kerzner, Harold. *Project Management: A Systems Approach to Planning, Scheduling, and Controlling,* 5th ed. New York: Van Nostrand, 1995.

Kiemele, Mark J., and Stephen R. Schmidt. *Basic Statistics: Tools for Continuous Improvement,* 3d ed. Colorado Springs, Colo.: Air Academy Press, 1993.

Knight, James A. *Value Based Management: Developing a Systematic Approach to Creating Shareholder Value.* New York: McGraw-Hill, 1998.

Koch, Richard. *The 80/20 Principle.* New York: Doubleday, 1998.

Kohn, Alfie. *Punished by Rewards.* Boston: Houghton Mifflin, 1999.

Kouzes, James M., and Barry Z. Posner. *The Leadership Challenge: How to Get Extraordinary Things Done in Organizations.* San Francisco: Jossey-Bass, 1987.

Kuhn, Thomas. *The Structure of Scientific Revolutions.* Chicago: University of Chicago Press, 1970.

Leider, Richard J. *Life Skills: Taking Charge of Your Personal and Professional Growth.* Paramus, N.J.: Prentice Hall, 1994.

Leider, Richard J. *The Power of Purpose: Creating Meaning in Your Life and Work.* San Francisco: Berrett-Koehler, 1997.

Lerner, Michael. *The Politics of Meaning.* Reading, Mass.: Addison-Wesley, 1996.

Lewis, James. *Fundamentals of Project Management,* 2d ed. New York: AMACOM, 2001.

Lewis, James. *Mastering Project Management.* New York: McGraw-Hill, 1998.

Lewis, James. *Project Leadership.* New York: McGraw-Hill, 2002.

Lewis, James. *The Project Manager's Desk Reference,* 2d ed. New York: McGraw-Hill, 2000.

Lewis, James. *The Project Manager's Pocket Survival Guide.* New York: McGraw-Hill, 2003.

Lewis, James. *Team-Based Project Management.* Baltimore, MD.: Beard Books, 2004.

Lewis, James. *Working Together.* Baltimore, MD: Beard Books, 2005.

Lewis, James, and Robert E. Dudley. *The McGraw-Hill Guide to the PMP Exam.* New York: McGraw-Hill, 2005.

Lewis, James, and Louis Wong. *Accelerated Project Management.* New York: McGraw-Hill, 2004.

Lipton, Bruce. *The Biology of Belief.* Carlsbad, Calif.: Hay House, 2008.

Lipton, Bruce, and Steve Bhaerman. *Spontaneous Evolution: Our Positive Future.* Carlsbad, Calif.: Hay House, 2009.

Maidique, Modesto, and Billie Jo Zirger. *The New Product Learning Cycle.* Research Policy. (Cited in Peters, 1987.)

Maier, Norman R. F. *Psychology in Industry.* Boston: Houghton Mifflin, 1955.

Maloney, Lawrence D. "For the Love of Flying." *Design News*, Vol. 51, Number 5, March 4, 1996.

March, James, and Herbert Simon. *Organizations*. New York: Wiley, 1966.

Maslow, Abraham. *Motivation and Personality*, 2d ed. New York: Harper & Row, 1970.

McCartney, Scott. "Out of the Blue: How Two Pacific Nations Became Oceanic Aces of Air-Traffic Control." *Wall Street Journal*, December 29, 2000.

McClelland, David. *Power: The Inner Experience*. New York: Halsted Press, 1975.

McGraw, Phillip. *Life Strategies: Doing What Works, Doing What Matters*. New York, Hyperion, 1999.

McKersie, Bryan. *Research Projects Are Different, Volume 1*. Kindle Direct, 2019.

McKersie, Bryan. *Research Projects Are Different, Volume 2*. Kindle Direct, 2020.

Michalko, Michael. *Thinkertoys*. Berkeley, Calif.: Ten Speed Press, 1995.

Miller, William C. *The Creative Edge: Fostering Innovation Where You Work*. Reading, Mass.: Addison-Wesley, 1986.

Mintzberg, Henry. *Mintzberg on Management*. New York: Free Press, 1989.

Moder, Joseph J., Cecil R. Phillips, and Edward W. Davis. *Project Management with CPM, PERT, and Precedence Diagraming*, 3d ed. New York: Van Nostrand, 1983.

Morrison, Terri, and Wayne A. Conaway. *Kiss, Bow or Shake Hands*, 2d ed. Holbrook, Mass.: Adams Media Corporation, 2015.

Mouzelis, N. P. "Bureaucracy," *The New Encyclopaedia Britannica*, 15th ed. Macropaedia 3 (1974).

Mulally, Alan, and Adam Witty. *Relentless Implementation: Creating Clarity, Alignment, and a Working Together Operating System to Maximize Your Business Performance.* Charleston, SC: ForbesBooks, 2020.

Nadler, Gerald, and Shozo Hibino. *Breakthrough Thinking.* Rocklin, Calif.: Prima Publishing, 1990.

NASA. *100 Rules for Project Managers.* (No publication info. Do a Google search for the online PDF.)

Nellore, Rajesh. "R&D Structures to Keep the Focus on Products." London: *Financial Times*, December 11, 2000.

Packard, Vance. *The Pyramid Climbers.* New York: McGraw-Hill, 1962.

Page, Rick. *Hope Is Not a Strategy.* New York: McGraw-Hill, 2003.

Pasmore, William. *Designing Effective Organizations: The Sociotechnical Systems Perspective.* New York: Wiley, 1988.

Pattakos, Alex, and Elaine Dundon. *Prisoners of Our Thoughts.* Oakland, CA: Berrett-Koehler, 2017.

Patterson, Kerry, Joseph Grenny, David Maxfield, Ron McMillan, and Al Switzler. *Influencer: The Power to Change Anything.* New York: McGraw-Hill, 2008.

Patterson, Kerry, Joseph Grenny, Ron McMillan, and Al Switzler. *Crucial Confrontations: Tools for Resolving Broken Promises, Violated Expectations, and Bad Behavior.* New York: McGraw-Hill, 2005.

Patterson, Kerry, Joseph Grenny, Ron McMillan, and Al Switzler. *Crucial Conversations: Tools for Talking when Stakes Are High.* New York: McGraw-Hill, 2002.

Patterson, Marvin. *Accelerating Innovation: Improving the Processes of Product Development.* New York: Van Nostrand Reinhold, 1993.

Peter, Lawrence J. *The Peter Principle.* New York: William Morrow & Co., 1969.

Peters, Tom. *Liberation Management.* New York: Knopf, 1992.

Peters, Tom. *Thriving on Chaos.* New York: Knopf, 1987.

Peters, Tom. "The WOW Project." *Fast Company,* May 1999.

Peters, Tom, and Bob Waterman. *In Search of Excellence.* New York: Warner Books, 1988.

Pink, Daniel H. *Drive: The Surprising Truth about What Motivates Us.* New York: Riverhead Books, 2009.

Pinto, Jeffrey K. *Power and Politics in Project Management.* Upper Darbey, Pa.: Project Management Institute, 1996.

Pinto, Jeffrey K. (ed.). *The Project Management Institute Project Management Handbook.* San Francisco: Jossey-Bass, 1998.

Ray, M., and R. Myers. *Creativity in Business.* Garden City, N.Y.: Doubleday, 1986.

Rickards, Tudor. *Problem Solving through Creative Analysis.* Epping, Essex, England: Gower Press, 1975.

Rosen, Robert H. *Leading People: The 8 Proven Principles for Success in Business.* New York: Penguin Books, 1996.

Rosenthal, R., and L. Jacobson. *Pygmalion in the Classroom.* New York: Holt, Rinehart, and Winston, 1968.

Saaty, Thomas L. *Decision Making for Leaders.* Pittsburgh: RWS Publications, 1995.

Sabbagh, Karl. *Twenty-First Century Jet.* New York: Scribner, 1996.

Safko, Ron, and David K. Brake. *The Social Media Bible: Tactics, Tools, and Strategies for Business Success.* Hoboken, N.J.: Wiley, 2009.

Sampietro, Marco, and Tiziano Villa. *Empowering Project Teams.* New York: CRC Press, 2014.

Schmidt, Terry. *Strategic Project Management Made Simple.* New York: Wiley, 2009.

Schuster, John P., Jill Carpenter, and Patricia Kane. *The Power of Open-Book Management.* New York: Wiley, 1996.

Senge, Peter. *The Fifth Discipline.* New York: Doubleday, 1990.

Senge, Peter. Interview in *Fast Company*, May 1999.

Smith, Hyrum W. *The 10 Natural Laws of Successful Time and Life Management.* New York: Warner Books, 1994.

Smith, Preston G., and Donald G. Reinertsen. *Developing Products in Half the Time.* New York: Van Nostrand, 1995.

Stacey, Ralph D. *Complexity and Creativity in Organizations.* San Francisco: Berrett-Koehler, 1996.

Steiner, Claude. *Scripts People Live By*, 2d ed. New York: Grove Weidenfeld, 1990.

Stone, Douglas, Bruce Patton, and Sheila Heen. *Difficult Conversations.* New York: Penguin, 2000.

Sugimoto, T. "Estimation on the Project Management Workload." In *Proceedings of the International Conference on Project Management*, Singapore, July 31 to August 2, 2002.

Sykes, Charles. *Dumbing Down Our Kids.* New York: St. Martin's Press, 1995.

Sykes, Charles. *A Nation of Victims: The Decay of the American Character.* New York: St. Martin's Press, 1992.

Tracy, Brian. *The Psychology of Achievement* (Compact Disks). Nightingale-Conant, 2010.

Treacy, Michael, and Fred Wiersema. *The Discipline of Market Leaders.* Reading, Mass.: Addison-Wesley, 1995.

Tulgan, Bruce. *The 27 Challenges Managers Face.* San Francisco: Jossey-Bass, 2014.

von Oech, Roger. *A Kick in the Seat of the Pants.* New York: Warner, 1986.

von Oech, Roger. *A Whack on the Side of the Head.* New York: Warner, 1983.

Vroom, Victor, and Arthur Jago. *The New Leadership.* Englewood Cliffs, N.J.: Prentice Hall, 1988.

Vroom, Victor, and Phillip Yetton. *Leadership and Decision Making.* Pittsburgh: University of Pittsburgh Press, 1973.

Walpole, Ronald E. *Introduction to Statistics*, 2d ed. New York: Macmillan, 1974.

Watzlawick, Paul, John Weakland, and Richard Fisch. *Change: Principles of Problem Formulation and Problem Resolution.* New York: Norton, 1974.

Weisbord, Marvin. *Productive Workplaces.* San Francisco: Jossey-Bass, 1987.

Weisbord, Marvin (ed.). *Discovering Common Ground: How Future Search Conferences Bring People Together to Achieve Breakthrough Innovation, Empowerment, Shared Vision, and Collaborative Action.* San Francisco: Berrett-Koehler, 1992.

Weisbord, Marvin, and Sandra Janoff. *Future Search: An Action Guide to Finding Common Ground in Organizations and Communities.* San Francisco: Berrett-Koehler, 1995.

Wheatley, Margaret. *Leadership and New Science.* San Francisco: Berrett-Koehler, 1992.

Wheelright, Stephen C., and Kim B. Clark. *Revolutionizing Product Development.* Free Press, 1992.

Whitaker, Ken. *Managing Software Maniacs.* New York: Wiley, 1994.

White, Gregory L. "In Order to Grow, GM Finds that the Order of the Day Is Cutbacks." *Wall Street Journal,* December 18, 2000.

Wilson, Larry. *Changing the Game.* New York: Fireside, 1988.

Wing, R. L. *The Tao of Power.* New York: Doubleday, 1986.

Wood, Michael. *The Helix Factor: The Key to Streamlining Your Business Processes.* Marmora, N.J.: Natural Intelligence Press, 1998.

Wysocki, Robert K. *Adaptive Project Framework: Managing Complexity in the Face of Uncertainty.* Boston: Addison-Wesley, 2010.

Wysocki, Robert K. *Effective Project Management,* 2d ed. New York: Wiley, 2000.

Wysocki, Robert K., and James P. Lewis. *The World-Class Project Manager.* Boston: Perseus Books, 2000.

Young, S. David, and Stephen F. O'Byrne. *EVA® and Value-Based Management.* New York: McGraw-Hill, 2001.

Zander, Rosamund Stone, and Benjamin Zander. *The Art of Possibility.* Boston: Harvard Business School Press, 2000.

Zofi, Yael. *The Manager's Guide to Virtual Teams.* New York: AMACOM, 2012.

INDEX

ABOUT THE AUTHOR

James P. Lewis, PhD, is an experienced project manager who has taught seminars on the subject throughout the United States, England, and the Far East since 1981. His solid, no-nonsense approach is largely the result of the 15 years he spent in industry, working as an electrical engineer engaged in the design and development of communication equipment. He held various positions, including project manager, product engineering manager, and chief engineer, for Aerotron, Inc., and ITT Telecommunications, both of Raleigh, North Carolina. He also was a quality manager for ITT Telecom, managing a department of 63 quality engineers, line inspectors, and test technicians.

While he was an engineering manager, he began working on a doctorate in organizational psychology, because of his conviction that a manager can succeed only by developing good interpersonal skills.

Since 1981, Dr. Lewis has trained more than 60,000 supervisors and managers in Argentina, Canada, England, Germany, India, Indonesia, Malaysia, Mexico, Singapore, Sweden, Thailand, and the United States. He has written articles for *Training and Development Journal*, *Apparel Industry Magazine*, and *Transportation and Distribution Magazine*, and is the author of *Mastering Project Management*, Second Edition; *The Project Manager's Desk Reference*, Third Edition; *Working Together: The 12 Principles Employed by Boeing Commercial Aircraft to Manage*

Projects, Teams, and the Organization; Project Leadership; and *The Project Manager's Survival Guide;* coauthor with Louis Wong of *Accelerated Project Management,* published by McGraw-Hill; and author of *Fundamentals of Project Management: How to Build and Manage a Winning Project Team,* Second Edition, and *Team-Based Project Management,* published by the American Management Association. He is coauthor, with Bob Wysocki, of *The World-Class Project Manager,* published by Perseus in 2001. Several of his books have been published in Chinese, and *Project Leadership* has been translated into Spanish and Russian.

He has a BS in electrical engineering and a PhD in psychology, both from NC State University in Raleigh. He is a member of the Institute of Noetic Sciences. He is also a certified Herrmann Brain Dominance Instrument practitioner and Certified Integral Coach® through New Ventures West of San Francisco.

He is president of The Lewis Institute, Inc., a training and consulting company specializing in project management, which he founded in 1981.